STONE VOICES

STONE VOICES

THE SEARCH FOR
SCOTLAND

NEAL ASCHERSON

HILL AND WANG
A DIVISION OF FARRAR, STRAUS AND GIROUX
NEW YORK

To E.M.A.

Hill and Wang
A division of Farrar, Straus and Giroux
19 Union Square West, New York, 10003

Copyright © 2002 by Neal Ascherson
All rights reserved
Printed in the United States of America
Originally published in 2002 by Granta Books, Great Britain
Published in the United States by Hill and Wang
First American edition, 2003

Owing to limitations of space, all acknowledgements for permission to
reprint previously published material can be found on page 327.

Library of Congress Cataloging-in-Publication Data
Ascherson, Neal.
　　Stone voices : the search for Scotland / Neal Ascherson.— 1st American ed.
　　　　p.　　cm.
　　Originally published: London : Granta Books, 2002.
　　Includes bibliographical references and index.
　　ISBN 0-8090-8491-0 (hc)
　　1. Scotland—Civilization. 2. National characteristics, Scottish.　　I. Title.

DA.772.A83 2003
941.1—dc21

2002191945

www.fsgbooks.com

1　3　5　7　9　10　8　6　4　2

Preface

Some countries are tidy with their past. Until recently, English historiography resembled the work of a landscape gardener at a stately home: vistas of Saxon lawn and Norman shrubbery led up past Tudor and Hanoverian flowerbeds to the terrace of the present, where the proprietor sat contentedly surveying his estate. Other countries are restless, grubbing up old interpretations in each generation. Russia, where the past is said to be unpredictable, offers a history scene of churned-up mud and broken-down cement-mixers, loud with disputing gardeners. Twentieth-century France evolved two largely incompatible narratives, a Red republican version and a White or clerical-conservative one, whose respective visitors hardly glanced at each other across the fence.

But there are also countries which have left the past in its original condition: a huge, reeking tip of unsorted rubbish across which scavengers wander, pulling up interesting fragments which might fetch a price or come in handy. Scotland has been one of these. This is nothing to be ashamed of. The lack of any commanding 'story' which dictates how the past should be understood allows space for imagination and originality. It is true that in the last ten or fifteen years Scottish historians have set to work and produced a series of ambitious and comprehensive narratives, from prehistory to the return of a Scottish Parliament in 1999. But this revolution has not yet reached the schools, where Scottish history is still neglected – perhaps, in fact, taught less (and less coherently) than it was fifty years ago.

To many Scots, although they are proud of their history, the past remains a pile of dramatic, often gory tableaux. One shows Bruce breaking his good axe on an English helmet; another shows Columba stepping from his boat on to the Iona sands. Prince Charles Edward offers his soft hand to Cameron of Locheil, and Mary offers her neck to the executioner. John Maclean speaks to a sea of working men in Glasgow, and James Watt stares at a kettle. But which came first, and what are the connections between them?

This book is not a history of Scotland. There are plenty of good ones now. Instead, I have tried to make a virtue of this fragmented awareness of Scotland's past, and to examine the way in which many of those tableaux have set up their own independent myths. In doing so, paradoxically, a set of continuities appeared.

One is the enduring importance of small groups bound by loyalty, usually based on kinship ties or on local origins or both. A second is what I have called the 'St Andrew's Fault'. This is the traumatic chasm dividing the confident minority from the mistrustful majority, which seems to date from the wholesale uprooting of traditional society between about 1760 and 1860. A third is the persistence of an idea of 'freedom', usually collective rather than individual. And the fourth continuity is what I mean by 'stone voices': the way in which human experience in this difficult northern place has been built so intimately into the geology and the post-glacial ecology of Scotland that a people and its stones form a single cultural landscape.

I want to thank several authors on whose work and research I have drawn for particular sections of this book. Above all, my gratitude to James Hunter, the historian of Gaeldom and the crofters; to Professor Tom Devine (especially for his monumental *The Scottish Nation: 1700–2000*, with its revelations about the 'Lowland Clearances'; to Thorbjörn Campbell's dazzling book about the Covenanters' memorials, *Standing Witnesses*; to the political analyses of Lindsay Paterson and David McCrone; to the archaeological writings of Ewan Campbell and Christopher Tolan-Smith; to Nicholas Canny's *Making Ireland British: 1580–1650* and to Michael Fry's truculent masterpiece, *The Scottish Empire*.

I will never forget the friendship and enthusiasm of Will Storrar, of the Centre for Theology and Public Issues, Edinburgh. He made possible our 'bus party' referendum campaign in 1997, and sponsored a Visiting Fellowship at New College, University of Edinburgh, which allowed me to study the 'e-democracy' operations of the Scottish Parliament. From my old colleagues at the *Scotsman* in the 1970s, whose remarks and sometimes outbursts are quoted here, I ask forgiveness. I am proud to have worked with them, and I owe most of what I learned in that decade to the sagacity and courage of the paper's then editor, Eric Mackay.

Not for the first time, I had the luck to be managed by two masterly editors who are also friends, Neil Belton at Granta and Elisabeth Sifton at Farrar Straus & Giroux. Finally, my love and thanks to Isabel Hilton, my wife, who patiently made space for the absences and preoccupation involved in writing this book.

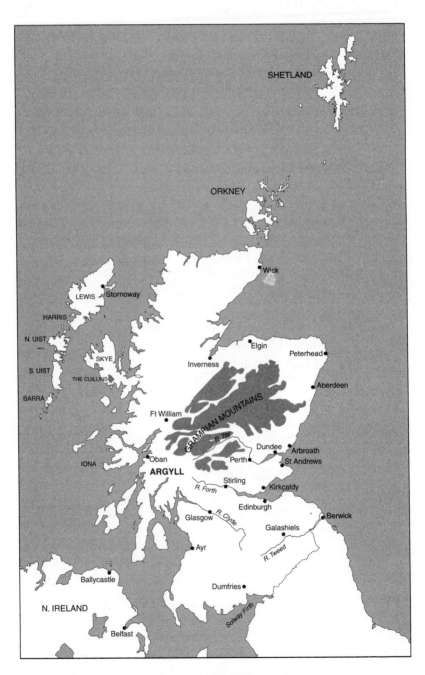

SCOTLAND

1

The inward gates of a bird are always open.
It does not know how to shut them.
That is the secret of its song,
But whether any man's are ajar is doubtful.
I look at these stones and know little about them,
But I know their gates are open too,
Always open, far longer open, than any bird's can be . . .

Hugh MacDiarmid, 'On a Raised Beach'

Every day, I would drive to the hospital in Oban, taking just under an hour each way. That year there was an unexpected gift of a summer, with the big rains staying away from May until September. Enough fell in the mornings or at night to wet the land, from the season of rhododendrons glaring into the ruins of the big house through to the September rowans, gathered in heavy red swags outside the small house to which its owner would never return. In the afternoons, it was fine, sometimes very hot, and the grass in the fields was cut early and easily for silage.

On the way, I passed a great many stones, some of them raised up as monuments or gathered together into funeral cairns which had once stood taller than houses. I had known these stones all my life, and for most of that life I had assumed that they were unchanging. As a small child, in fact, the difference between natural stone formations – 'living rock' – and old masonry had not been at all obvious to me. Masses of stone like the foundation blocks of the Dean Bridge in Edinburgh might equally well, as far as I was concerned, have been put there by men or abandoned there by glaciers or extruded from the magma by a volcano. They seemed to me no more or less intentional than the equally black and angular basalt crags rising out of Princes Street Gardens to support the Castle. I liked the style and the feel of these dramatic stones; that was the point, and explanations about what was artefact and what was 'nature' seemed beside that point. In the dark, Cyclopean cities of sandstone and granite left by the Victorians, a good many Scottish children grew up with the same impression.

In his poem 'On a Raised Beach' MacDiarmid wrote:

> . . . *We are so easily baffled by appearances*
> *And do not realise that these stones are one with the stars.*
> *It makes no difference to them whether they are high or low,*
> *Mountain peak or ocean floor, palace, or pigsty.*
> *There are plenty of ruined buildings in the world but no ruined*
>   *stones.*

It is not the stone which can be ruined, but the stone artefact created by human sculpting or building or even by the transforming power of human imagination alone. Five thousand years ago, slabs of Dalriadic schist weighing many tons were prised off the face of a cliff, slithered downhill to the level ground, levered and lugged upright in foundation pits and then commanded to change their substance – to become ritual spires of condensed fear and memory. The slabs which cracked apart on their journey or as they were raised upright merely turned into two slabs. But a standing stone which falls becomes a ruin.

One standing stone which broke in recorded times is close to the Oban road. A long gorge runs from Loch Awe down towards Kilmartin, dug by a vanished glacial river, and where the gorge widens out, near the farm called Creagenterivebeg or Creagantairbh Beag, at a place called Tigh-a-Char, the wreck of the thing sits up against the wall of the road to Ford.

This was the tallest stone in the district. The stump still protrudes six feet out of the earth, and the broken slab lying beside it shows that the stone originally stood some fifteen feet high. The Royal Commission on the Ancient and Historic Monuments of Scotland states that 'it was blown down in 1879'. The local historian Alan Begg agrees, but is cautious about which of that year's storms did the damage. He writes with awe of the 'huge Druid-like stone which broke and fell . . . My grandfather who worked in Ederline and Craigenterive Mor used to say the great stone fell "the night of the Tay Bridge Disaster". Thinking back it seems to me now, according to the old of the time, that "all sorts of things that took place happened on the night of the Tay Bridge Disaster".'

Further along the main road to Oban, there is the stone at Kintraw. Today you would never know it had ever fallen down, and yet everyone in the district remembers that it collapsed in the winter of 1978 for reasons not clear: a bull stropping his itchy flank, or a Dutch camper backing his Dormobile without looking in the rear mirror, or perhaps Keats's unimaginable touch of time.

But in contrast to the monoliths of Ballymeanoch or Creagantairbh, this fall was unacceptable. Kintraw, or the terrace bearing the stone and the cairn beside it, is one of the most spectacular and celebrated outlooks in the West Highlands. The A816, after crossing a high plateau of 'frowning crags' and 'horrid desolation', suddenly plunges down a defile and bursts out onto a vast view: the head of Loch Craignish three hundred feet below, the sea stretching away towards the mountains of Jura and the horizon which is the rim of Ireland, the yacht masts in the anchorage at Ardfern glimmering across the water.

Artfully positioned in the middle of this view, on a grassy platform beside the road, are the stone and the cairn. The image of a tomb with its mourning pillar-stone, silhouetted against the prospect of nature like a romantic contemplative in a Caspar David Friedrich painting, is irresistible. In fact, there are two cairns here, and archaeological investigation has not clearly associated the stone with either of them. But nobody is bothered about that. The place is a resource; it has Outstanding Natural Beauty; it is Heritage, which requires heritage management. So this stone, unlike the others, was put back.

First there was an archaeological rummage around the socket, which turned up nothing much. A photograph taken in 1979 shows the stone lying prone on the grass beside the square excavation pit. It resembles a pulled tooth, its lower shaft an unpleasant greenish-white where it had been grasped in the earth's gum. Then the stone was reinserted, this time with its base in a concrete plinth. In the process, the workers set it at a different angle, no longer aligned to its original axis, which enraged all those who fancied that it had been carefully positioned to mark astral and seasonal events.

The repair squad also took the opportunity to correct a slight tilt which had apparently developed over the millennia. The big bird which used to perch on the Kintraw Stone to digest its kills ('the Buzzard Stone') has resumed its place. All expectations have been generously satisfied. As the Swedish archaeologist said when his Crown Prince reopened the famous Bronze Age cairn at Kivik in south Sweden, restored with a new entrance passage and specially wrought bronze doors: 'It looks older than ever before.'

But the first stones which came into view on my way to Oban were the huge uprights at Ballymeanoch. There are the remains of a henge monument here, and a later circular cairn, and six standing stones arranged along what may have been the two flanks of a broad ceremonial avenue. It brings to mind the 'cursus' monuments of the same age which are found all over Britain, the two parallel banks which can run for many miles uphill and downhill across the landscape. Unearthly beings, invisible or impersonated by robed shamans, may have been invited to pass along these avenues, between earth banks or files of standing stones, and perhaps the living people lining the route hid their eyes as they passed.

In my lifetime, one of the stones fell. It was an outlier, not in the main alignments, famous because there was a hole through it. Deep cup-marks have been ground into the faces of almost all the stones; it could have been Neolithic patriarchs or Victorian cattle-boys who persisted with the grinding until one pit penetrated to the other side. It became a peephole. Engaged couples met one another's eyes through it; papers scrawled with wishes were threaded from one side to the other. Then, at some moment in the last century, it fell or rather broke off halfway down. Nobody knew what to do with it. The stump was eventually uprooted, and archaeologists found cremated bone in the foundation pit. The top section, with the hole, lay around in the grass and got in the way of farming. A few years ago, it was dumped into a field-drain some yards away. Today it lies on the edge of the drain among other dislocated pieces of schist.

The new hospital where my mother was, the Lorn and Islands, is built on the southern fringe of Oban. Beyond its roof you can see the big Hebridean ferries entering and leaving the bay. The ambulances arriving from Lochgilphead, Tarbert or Campbeltown come over the southern hill and then swing off the main road directly into the hospital reception bay.

One day they brought an old friend of ours, Marion Campbell of Kilberry. She lay in the same ward under an oxygen mask, eyes closed, silver hair scattered on the pillow. Marion was an historian, novelist and poet; she was a patriot antiquary, a sailor in war and a farmer in peace; she was the mother of scientific archaeology and of community museums in Mid-Argyll. Only two days before, I had telephoned her, and found her cursing and joking at the onset of what she said was a nasty cold. I told her how much I was enjoying her biography of Alexander III, published at last after many years. This cheered her. 'Purr, purr!' she responded.

It wasn't a cold that had brought the ambulance so suddenly out to Kilberry, on its windy headland over the Sound of Jura. Going out into the corridor, I waylayed a doctor and asked her what was wrong with Marion. She answered, after a slight pause, that she was not a well lady at all, and watched me to see what I made of that.

Later in the ward, I was talking to my mother about the Ballymeanoch stones, and the one that fell, and saying that nobody seemed sure when it had fallen. A muffled voice came from behind me. 'Well, I know!' said Marion, suddenly awake. 'It was in 1943, and a Shetland pony was sheltering up against it from the storm when it broke off. Must have terrified the poor beast.' She paused, and then said: 'Nobody would believe now that I remember the stone when it was up, and how I used to look through the hole.' She slept again, and later that afternoon they came to put screens around her bed. They tried to drain her lung, but it was too late. She must have known how ill she was.

Marion died on the third evening after they brought her into hospital, unconscious in a little side room across the corridor. At the moment of her death, I had left the ward and was downstairs in the hospital cafeteria, drinking coffee to bring myself awake for the drive home. The news came to me at Kilmartin next morning.

After Marion's death, my mother talked about their first meeting. There had been a dance some years before the war at Stonefield on Loch Fyne – another big Campbell house, now a hotel. She thought now that Marion's family, probably matchmaking, must have pushed her to come. Anyway, there in the Stonefield drawing room was this small, pretty girl in a blue dress, standing by herself and looking quite bewildered. Her goldy-brown hair had a natural curl. Although my mother was more than sixteen years older, they made friends immediately.

At her funeral, after the service, we all drove behind the hearse to Kilberry where the family burial ground is next to the castle. It was pouring as we formed up to walk down the track through the dim green wood. First went the piper, then the coffin on men's shoulders, then a small girl walking by herself, her long fair hair dripping and lank. We followed, best shoes slipping in the mud, a procession under umbrellas. But as we passed the front of the castle, the sun broke out; the sky turned blue, and the rain glittered as it rushed into the unkempt trees.

On the night of Marion's funeral, as I was making my way to Glasgow to take a train south, my mother suddenly weakened; one after another, the systems of her body gently slowed down and stopped, and she died early the next morning, long before dawn. I had reached London, and was making myself coffee when the telephone rang.

She was ninety-six years old. Marion was eighty. When my mother was a little girl, most people in the district spoke Argyll Gaelic, made their own clothes, grew oats and went fishing after cuddy (saithe and lythe) in oval rowing boats they had often built with their own hands. They lit their houses and byres with paraffin, and they walked miles daily to work or to school. Christmas, a pagan or Papist institution, was observed scarcely or not at all, and they kept the Sabbath – after going to the kirk – in heavy silence at home. In spite of this Christian piety, a boat pushing out into the sea would always be turned sun-wise towards its course; a body taken from the kirk to a grave would be carried sun-wise around the building.

When Marion was small, there were still many travelling families in the landscape, encamped in woods or at the end of little side lanes, or moving along the roads with their horses and caravans in search of tinker work. Duncan Williamson, who was born on the shore and who through his mother belongs to the famous traveller-clan of the Townsleys, says that they would camp near the standing stones at Ballymeanoch or Nether Largie when they came by Kilmartin. Near, but not too near. His father told him that the stones protected the travelling people who lit fires and bedded down by them, but they did not like to be touched. As a child, Duncan once climbed one of them, but his father was shocked and pulled him off angrily. Afterwards Duncan fell very ill.

The stones, and especially the ruined stones, illustrate the new ways in which archaeologists discuss the past. They avoid the word 'authentic' when they are talking about objects. They parry it by asking: 'Authentic to whom, and when?' This thing may be a stone tool or a timber post which was 'provably' manufactured five millennia ago. But the 'authenticity' is not in the thing itself, like some trace element with a diminishing half-life. It is in the beliefs about the thing which have been held by human beings through all those years – changing beliefs, sometimes credulous, sometimes inexplicable. The polished stone axe may originally have been made to be treasured rather than used, something to be gifted and amassed but never intended to cut down a tree or butcher a dead stag. Much later, until a few hundred years ago, its finders thought it was a 'thunder-stone' cast down from the sky. Later still, early archaeologists assumed that it was a practical implement, bound it into a haft and timed the minutes required to cut through an oak log with it. All these beliefs about use or origin are authentic. That cairn at Kivik in Sweden is largely reconstruction or even innovation, but it left the Crown Prince who 'opened' it with an authentic sense of pride and achievement. The last word about the authenticity of anything from a bronze rapier to a new nation remains a proverb: 'This is my grandfather's axe. My father gave it a new handle, and I gave it a new head.'

Instead of authenticity, stones have biographies. Some of the biography is incised or chipped or rubbed into them. Some of it – the different uses, mythical or practical, to which they were put by humans – can be read in a written document or inferred from other material evidence (like the cremated bone in the socket at Ballymeanoch). Much of it remains unreadable. But a surprising amount of an object's biography is simply lying around, waiting to be noticed. It has remained unstudied because historians and archaeologists have been so exclusively obsessed with an artefact's birth – and have almost ignored its life.

Nobody made this point more sharply than Francis Haskell, apostle of the study of taste in art history:

> Art historians generally concern themselves with the processes of creation. Who painted such and such a picture? When was it painted? What does it represent? What does its style tell about the influences on the artist? Sometimes they venture into wider fields. How important for the painter were the political, the social or the religious circumstances of the time? What about the patron who commissioned the picture? . . . But once the picture is completed, the historian usually loses interest. What it may have meant to the man who ordered and paid for it, or to the artist's contemporaries and successors, to the critics and historians of the time or later – all this tends to be neglected . . .

What is true about the study of paintings is also true about the study of material culture. Only now, in our own time, are archaeologists forcing themselves to look beyond the 'processes of creation' to the long life of successive meanings which followed creation. Some monuments are so prominent and have such an accretion of semiotic biography that it is impossible to ignore it. Stonehenge is the best example; English antiquaries in the seventeenth and eighteenth centuries conjectured that it was an 'Ancient British Druids' Temple'; New Age enthusiasts in our own time have understood it as a vast stellar observatory or as the landing place of visitors from another galaxy; the archaeologist David Clarke has interpreted its many rebuildings and rearrangements in prehistory as evidence of power struggles between competing elites. Maes Howe in Orkney is an enormous funerary mound built five thousand years ago,

but the runic graffiti inside its chamber show that to Norse settlers and 'Jerusalem-farer' Crusaders it signified a treasure
mine, a weather shelter or a private place for illicit sex
('Ingibjörg the fair widow: many a woman lowered herself to
come in here').

And nations? They are artefacts too, but they have two sorts
of biography. One is the narrative 'story' of the territorial community which, in this case, goes under the title of Scotland: the
battles and famines and kings and coal mines. But the other
biography is that of an abstraction, of a supposedly changeless
artefact named Scotland, and that biography in turn becomes
a rumination about origins and processes of creation. This
second sort of Scotland is 'ancient'; it began long ago, time out
of mind. There has always been acute interest in the truth or
falsehood of the narrative, in its 'how we began' versions and
its 'where we came from' versions. But not enough attention is
paid to how these versions played to their audience down the
centuries. Take the Covenanters (the popular term for the
extreme Presbyterians who rejected Crown authority in the
seventeenth century and fought a rural guerrilla war for their
principles). Their fight and martyrdom are indissolubly part of
the Scotland narrative, of 'Scotland's Story'. But, as a matter of
fact, we know almost nothing about how they regarded their
nation, or what paradigm of an unchanging Scotland they carried in their heads. As literate small farmers, they must have
been raised on the heroic stories of Bruce and Wallace,
Scotland's liberators in the medieval wars of independence
against England, and they may have understood Scotland as a
place where power had always been contractual, where no
honest man surrendered freedom of conscience 'but with his
life'. There are signs that they considered moral austerity and
respect for eternity (their own ideals) as 'Scottish'. For example, one of their gravestones condemns a brutal government
soldier who played football with a Covenanter's head as 'by
birth a Tyger rather than a Scot'. But nothing is known with

any certainty, because so few historians have gone to look for the answer.

One particular stone brought all these arguments to a head in Scotland. On St Andrew's Day 1996, I stood outside the gates of Holyrood House, at the foot of the Canongate, and watched as the 'Stone of Destiny' began its uphill journey along the Royal Mile to its new resting place in Edinburgh Castle.

It was borne on the back of a polished military Land Rover, a dirty great hunk of yellowish rock nestling on an expensive blue velvet pall and shielded – like a pope – by a perspex lid. Driven at walking pace, which only increased the illusion of a state funeral, the Stone slowly advanced between the fixed bayonets of soldiers and sailors lining the street. Each squad presented arms as the cortège approached. And behind the Land Rover, in a convoy of black limousines, crept the high-heid yins, the heraldic class in its robes. A few were familiar, like the law lords and the Moderator of the Church of Scotland, but the rest – the Hereditary Flag-Bearers, Captains-General, Gold Sticks, Lord High Constables, Kings at Arms and Commissioners of Regalia – are now ignored by the Scottish media and thus totally unknown to the population.

The onlookers on the pavements were sparse, and did not applaud. They seemed uncertain about what reaction was expected of them; whatever it was, they refrained from it. Their view, when reporters dared them to express one, was that the Stone belonged to the nation, which meant to everyone in Scotland. They found this mournful pageant a bit alienating, and in a way it was meant to be. For the Queen, the Stone still remains her personal property; she had sent her son the Duke of York to escort it to Edinburgh Castle where it would be deposited 'on loan' between coronations, visible to her subjects for £5.50 a peep.

Only up at St Giles, where the street passes the old Parliament house and widens out, was there some commotion.

Here a substantial crowd had collected, spilling across the roadway. When the Land Rover appeared with its load, they cheered quietly. When the Royal Marines band played 'God Save the Queen', they booed quietly. A few banners were pushed up: 'Scotland Asked for a Parliament and Got a Stone'. But whatever the emotion in the crowd was – a strong but unreadable one – it was not anger. 'It's a first step,' said a woman who had travelled from Greenock, hoping for a moment of history to tell to her grandchildren. 'A first stepping-stone to freedom,' added someone nearby. He sounded unconvinced.

This was the strangest day in this Stone's biography since it had been kidnapped by the invader Edward I of England in 1296, exactly 700 years before. Upon this Stone, kept at Scone Abbey near Perth, the Scottish kings had been seated during the ceremony of their inauguration, a ritual in which pagan Gaelic, Christian and feudal elements were combined. Many myths of its origin and antiquity – some oral traditions, some written accounts apparently invented for political ends – have survived. The most extravagant claimed that it had been the stone which Jacob used for a pillow in the desert towards Haran, when he dreamed about the ladder to Heaven and the angels ascending and descending.

Edward seized it, as he had seized the Crown of Arthur from Llywellyn ap Gruffydd in Wales a few years before, in order to symbolize the end of national identity and continuity. But perhaps he also wanted to dream and to hear the Lord speak from the top of the ladder: 'The land whereon thou liest, to thee will I give it, and to thy seed; And thy seed shall be as the dust of the earth, and thou shalt spread abroad to the west, and to the east, and to the north, and to the south . . .'

The Stone was taken to England and lodged with the Abbots of Westminster. Later, a wooden throne was made with a cavity for the Stone underneath the seat, so that English monarchs who sat on this 'St Edward's Chair' in Westminster Abbey for their coronation demonstrated their supposed ascendancy over the Scottish kingdom, although Scotland in fact remained unconquered and independent. Later still, as the English rite of coronation came to be defined as a 'sacrament', associated with supernatural changes in the nature of the crowned one, the presence of the Stone was assumed to be one of the indispensable ingredients which made the magic possible. This dogma passed down the centuries and into the Union between England and Scotland, and – among courtiers and in the ancient apartments behind Westminster Abbey – it was still substantially intact in 1996.

Edward had hoped that the removal of the Stone would sever the legitimacy and authority of Scottish kings. This proved to be quite wrong. Indeed, it was an English thought. Scotland, a poor and still precariously united country, did not have the sort of layered, obedient society which responds at once to the manipulation of symbols. But the theft of the Stone remained a Scottish grievance against England down the centuries, predictably revived in the nineteenth century with its climate of historicizing, heraldic but initially non-political nationalism.

On Christmas Day 1950, four Scottish students who had hidden in Westminster Abbey managed to wrench open the chair and pull out the Stone. Laying it on a coat, they dragged it across the floor and out to a waiting car and, after many adventures, brought it back to Scotland. There it migrated from one hiding place to another until, more than a year later, it was left in the ruins of Arbroath Abbey and the authorities were invited to collect it. There may have been negotiations and a deal – none of the students was ever prosecuted. But that is one of many facets of the story which are still unknown. What was more significant, as it turned out, was the pang of exultation which so many Scots – often to their own astonishment – felt when they heard the news that Christmas morning. Long after their interest in the rights and wrongs of the break-in had flagged, people remembered their own feelings and sought to interpret them. Somewhere in the old house, they had heard a door opening.

Scotland was a very different place by 1996. In the previous twenty years, the prospect of independence or self-government had come to dominate Scottish politics. More people supported devolution (a Scottish parliament running Scotland's internal affairs within the United Kingdom) than supported 'Independence in Europe', the new slogan of the Scottish National Party. But at election after election for seventeen years, the Scots had been voting in growing majorities for the Labour Party only to find themselves governed by the Conservatives under Margaret Thatcher and then John Major. Slowly but alarmingly, the political temperature was beginning to rise. By 1996, an unofficial Constitutional Convention of opposition parties, trade unions, churches and many other bodies had been sitting for seven years and had drawn up detailed plans for a modern parliament elected by proportional representation. But Mrs Thatcher had always flatly refused even to discuss the idea of an elected legislature in Scotland, and John Major had carried her refusal on into the 1990s. His instincts had told him that 'Celtic' nationalism was mostly a media scare, absurdly exaggerated. Back in 1991, a few months after he succeeded Mrs Thatcher, I had a brief conversation with him about Scotland and about devolution, which he dismissed as 'loopy'. The problem, he said amiably, was much simpler. 'The Scots just feel left out of things up there, and I have a good deal of sympathy with that. I ought to go there much more often and so should the rest of the Cabinet. If they see us around more, they'll feel a lot less cut off.'

Journalists, professors and politicians had expected the Scottish Tories to be slaughtered almost to extinction at the 1992 elections. Nobody was more amazed than the Tories when their vote actually rose by 1.6 per cent. But the far-sighted among them saw that this was just a stay of execution; the tide of outraged national feeling was still rising, and the only hope of survival was to swim with the patriotic mood. Michael Forsyth, who became Secretary of State for Scotland in 1995, set out on a policy of tartan gesture-politics. This reached its climax on 3 July, 1996, when an incredulous House of Commons heard John Major announce that the 'Stone of Destiny' would be returned to Scotland. 'The Stone remains the property of the Crown,' the Prime Minister said. 'I wish to inform the House that, on the advice of Her Majesty's Ministers, the Queen has agreed that the Stone should be returned to Scotland. The Stone will, of course, be taken to Westminster Abbey to play its traditional role in the coronation ceremonies of future sovereigns of the United Kingdom.'

These three sentences, respectively reeking of royal absolutism, constitutional fairy tale and transformative magic (by the use of a tutelary fetish inserted under royal buttocks), were entirely correct usage in the English grammar of power. This was the language which any prime minister was obliged to use when mentioning royal property, the Crown in Parliament and the nature of coronations. How else can one talk about undead institutions? But the substance – the decision to recognize nationalism as a genuine 'problem' in Scotland and to appease it – had been much harder for John Major to accept.

The Stone had been brought back into Scotland, across the Tweed bridge at Coldstream, two weeks before it was paraded through Edinburgh. It had spent the intervening days in a laboratory at Historic Scotland's conservation centre, where scientists were able to construct a very imperfect physical biography.

As one of the experts said, the Stone is 'unprepossessing'. It is a rough, quarried block of yellowish sandstone, weighing about 150 kilograms. Undecorated, it has been much chiselled and battered about. Somebody competent with stone-tools set out to engrave a rectangle into one of the flat sides, and somebody incompetent finished the job. Other people cut recesses into each end, inserting iron staples connected to carrying-rings by crude figure-of-eight loops. The Stone also bears two erratically cut crosses and some other scoring. Its corners have been knocked off, on the underside. The material is Lower Old Red Sandstone, of exactly the type which is found around Scone itself.

And this Stone, too, is broken. Iain Hamilton, QC, one of the students who repossessed it in 1950, said that it had fallen into two parts as they pulled it out from the coronation chair. Almost certainly, it had already been broken at some unknown past moment, and older photographs are said to exist showing a crack. But this fracture upset the students, although they found that it was easier to conceal and transport the Stone in two pieces, and in Scotland they had it bonded together again with two inserted metal pins and a layer of cement. The pins came to light when the Historic Scotland craftsmen carried out a much less visible repair in 1996. With the pins was a triangular scrap of paper inscribed 'SCO'. So far, nobody has explained this or admitted to putting it there. Possibly it was a spell. It must have been lurking underneath the young Queen Elizabeth when she sat on St Edward's Chair, freshly mended and reunited with the Stone, for her coronation in 1953.

Was this the 'authentic Stone of Destiny' or 'Stone of Scone'? In 1996, historians and petrologists looked very closely at the evidence, material and documentary, and they concluded that this was beyond any doubt the object removed from Westminster Abbey in 1950. With slightly less assurance, they agreed that it was almost certainly the same Stone which Edward I had removed from Scone in 1296. They had answered the questions put to them. But beyond those questions lay a whole series of different narratives about authenticity, all converging on the Stone.

First come the old stories of origin. In the best-known version, a Scythian prince – sometimes called Gadelus – passes through Egypt and marries Scota, the daughter of Pharaoh.

When he sets out again on his westward journey, Scota brings with her the Stone; they reach Spain, rule there for a time, then sail on to Ireland and set up the Stone on the hill of Tara. Finally, they make the voyage from Ireland to Scotland, founding the Dalriada kingdom which will come to rule all the lands which are eventually known as Scotland. The identification of the Stone as 'Jacob's Pillow' seems to have been added quite late, just possibly after Edward had taken it to London.

The Stone, however, is not Egyptian, Spanish or Irish, or even a slice of 'Dalriadic schist' from Argyll. It is just a lump of local Scone rock. It may have been used to inaugurate Pictish kings, before Kenneth mac Alpin unified the Pictish and Dalriadic kingdoms in about 845 and moved the capital of his new combined realm – named 'Alba', not yet 'Scotland' – to Scone in Pictland. The purpose of the tales becomes clear: the Stone is to authenticate the lineage of Dalriada and the Scottish dynasty by tracing it back to the Bible story and the seed of Abraham.

The next clutch of narratives tells how the Stone has been used to deliver two more recent forms of political authenticity. One was Scottish. John of Fordun wrote in the fourteenth century that 'no king was ever wont to rule in Scotland unless he had first, on receiving the name of king, sat upon this stone at Scone'. The Stone was taken out of the Abbey for the occasion, and the king was lifted onto it in the course of the ceremonies. Stones used as royal inauguration chairs exist elsewhere in Europe, especially in Ireland, and it may be that the seating on a stone was a symbolic union between the ruler and the earth itself, a king mounting the hard ground of his dominion. The seating seems always to have been a part of the proceedings, but the other rituals of an inauguration could be changed around between one reign and the next. This informality was important, because it meant that inauguration in Scotland was never a single indivisible act. So although it hurt the Scots very badly to lose the Stone, a king could become a king without it.

In England, the Stone came to be read differently. At first, it sat in Westminster Abbey as a mere trophy of conquest. But the English kings had long since abandoned inauguration for the ceremony of coronation, a change which sought to revive half-forgotten or quite imaginary Roman or Merovingian practices including the ritual of anointing with holy oil. By the time of Henry IV's coronation in 1399, the business had been promoted to a full-blown 'sacrament' in which the monarch received not just political and social legitimacy but divine authority as well.

A sacrament, to the faithful, is a form of miracle. It is a supernatural event made possible by correct ritual in which God intervenes to change the 'natural' order. Wine becomes blood; a mortal prince becomes God's Anointed One. If any element is left out of the spell, it may not be potent and, within a few centuries, the presence of the Stone under the English coronation chair had become one of those indispensable catalysts which made the miracle happen.

· Here there was already a wide gap between English and Scottish ideas of how the Stone could authenticate a monarch. And over the following centuries, the gap grew wider. Edward I had claimed that the mumbo-jumbo on the grass at Scone could not possibly validate a genuine king with a claim to sovereign independence. This was propaganda, but it threatened to undermine Scotland's international status, and sheer self-preservation was among the motives which now induced the Scots to follow the fashion and adopt 'continental' coronation for monarchs. And yet the new rite never quite took root. The Scottish nobility never felt easy with the idea of a king who owed his power to God and not to his peers, and in the 1320 Declaration of Arbroath (the astonishing Latin letter to the Pope which is Europe's earliest nationalist manifesto), they warned that even their beloved King Robert I, 'The Bruce', was subject to contract. 'If he should turn aside from the task that he has begun and yield Scotland or us to the English king and people, we should cast [him] out as the enemy of us all . . . and should choose another king to defend our freedom.'

The ensuing centuries, even after the 1707 Treaty of Union, did not close the gap between interpretations. But the gap only became manifest in the twentieth century, above all in the two episodes of the 1950 recovery and the 1996 return of the Stone. Those episodes were about authenticity too, but in new, quite unexpected forms.

The Christmas break-in at the Abbey electrified people in Scotland, because it was cheeky and patriotic and put right an old wrong – but also because the Stone had prompted an authentically Scottish act. No grave committee in Edinburgh had recommended this, no body composed by the Kirk and the Faculty of Advocates and the other institutions preserved by the Union. A bunch of twenty-year-old nobodies, shabby law students and a young woman in a tweed skirt, had asked nobody's leave. They had asserted, in effect, that the Union's articles did not stand at the end of every road. Beyond it, above it, there survived some residual Scottish right to change an aspect of the relationship between Scotland and England.

The students became heroes of a sort. Nobody, in contrast, became a hero in 1996. The popular reaction to the official return of the Stone of Destiny, by leave of the Queen and at the initiative of the Prime Minister and the Secretary of State for Scotland, was comically different.

In spite of all that carefully staged parading and heraldry, the sheer lack of popular enthusiasm was impressive. Those small Canongate and High Street crowds were not incurious, and not immune to emotion, but they were grudging. Historians were at once reminded that the Scots had long ceased to imagine that the Stone had supernatural properties (if they ever did). Scotland, the men and women on the pavements seemed to feel, remained exactly the same country that it had been the day before the military cortège had crossed the bridge at Coldstream separating England from Scotland. It was good to have our Stone back, but it was not transforming. This contrasted sharply with the protests of the then Dean of Westminster and his Chapter, when informed of the plan to return the Stone to Scotland. Their view was that the Stone was a sacred, even a sacramental object. The implication seemed to be that the effectiveness of the coronation sacrament might be compromised, even though the Stone was to be returned to London for coronations. It was a fair conclusion that it was now the English, rather than the Scots, who attributed magical powers of authentication to the Stone.

Does this imply that the Scots took a calm and rational approach to the return of the Stone? They affected to do so, but they did not. Especially on the Left, exasperated voices wanted to know why London thought the Scots so dumb that they could be bought for an 'auld cludgie cover', or (as Ian Bell translated the thought in his *Scotsman* column) an 'old cesspit lid'.

Nobody should have been fooled by this surly line of talk. The Stone itself does matter; it did and it does signify a great many things to Scots. What was being said here was that the context mattered more than the object. And the context was England's illegitimate possession of the great cludgie cover and the ways in which that possession represented Scottish perceptions of their relationship to England.

The Dean of Westminster had warmed Scottish hearts by his intense reluctance to let go of the Stone. That was England as historically minded Scots preferred to see her: imperial, miserly and indifferent to the cultures of smaller nations. But they were deprived of that satisfaction in another very similar drama of theft, counter-theft and repatriation which was going on at the same time.

This was the strange, almost unnoticed affair of the 'Holyrood Bird'. Unlike the Maltese Falcon, the Bird was made of brass, not gold. It is a lectern in the form of an eagle, made in

Renaissance Italy in 1498 and gifted by the Pope to the Bishop of Dunkeld. From Dunkeld it was moved to Holyrood Abbey in Edinburgh, now a beautiful ruin next to the royal palace of Holyrood House. There it remained until 1544, when an English army led by the Earl of Hertford attacked Edinburgh during the 'Rough Wooing' – the attempt by Henry VIII of England to force Scottish acceptance of the marriage of his son Edward to the ten-year-old Mary, Queen of Scots. Hertford, later Duke of Somerset, sacked the Abbey and brought the Bird back to England with him as loot. His chief siege engineer, Richard Lee, was rewarded with the rectorship of St Stephen's in the city of St Albans and presented the Bird to the parish church.

Beginning in the eighteenth century, there were regular requests for the lectern's return. But it's fair to say that – in contrast to the Stone – few Scots were aware of its loss. In 1982, however, the Bird reappeared in Edinburgh as an item in an exhibition of medieval Scottish craftsmanship called 'Angels, Nobles and Unicorns', with an account of its own biography. There were angry articles and readers' letters in the Scottish papers. The Bird went back to St Albans, but three years later, on St Andrew's Night 1985, it disappeared from the church. Later, a group describing themselves as 'Siol nan Gaidheal' (Seed of the Gael), who may or may not have been the youth group of the Scottish National Party which uses that name, contacted the media and stated that the Bird was now safely concealed on Scottish soil, 'somewhere in the West Highlands'.

The Hertfordshire police pursued their inquiries, without provocative zeal. Communication with those who had taken the lectern was established, but there were no arrests. In the 1990s, the parish authorities at St Stephen's said that they would support the repatriation of the Bird to Scotland if it were first returned to them. Nothing happened, however, until April 1999, on the eve of the first elections to the restored Scottish Parliament, when the lectern was 'delivered anonymously' to the Netherbow Arts Centre in Edinburgh. It is now in the care of the new Museum of Scotland, while the parish of St Stephen's goes through the final formalities of relinquishing ownership.

In short, English common sense had skilfully denied the Bird the status of a Scottish national grievance. Perhaps it was a display of what the 1968 radicals used to call 'repressive tolerance'. At all events, no such solution was possible for the Stone of Destiny. It was too famous, too sacred to England, too precious to the Scottish sense of injustice. But now, as the prospect of the Stone's repatriation appeared, the Scots began to react in an unexpected way.

No sooner had the intention to return the Stone been announced in the House of Commons by John Major than a chorus of Scottish voices arose insisting that it was not the real thing. There was a voluble revival of older suggestions, first heard in the nineteenth century, that this was not in fact the original Stone of Destiny on which the kings of Scotland had been inaugurated. Some argued that the 'real' Stone had never left Scotland at all in 1296, but that Edward I had been fobbed off with a fake. The original (this version went on) had been hidden in one of a catalogue of rumoured places; there were perhaps half a dozen of them. A second choir of deniers claimed that although the real Stone had indeed been taken by Edward and lodged at Westminster, this was not the object trundled across the River Tweed at Coldstream and up the High Street. The true Stone had been recovered by the patriot students in 1950 – but not returned. The English had been fooled by (or, in one version, had tacitly agreed to accept) a mere replica deposited for them to find in the Abbey of Arbroath. Again, the original Stone was alleged to lie still buried or hidden somewhere within Scotland.

The scientific evidence from the examination in 1996 leaves no room for the second of these theories. This is, beyond reasonable doubt, the object which the English king took from

Scone 700 years ago. And the proposal that he was deceived into removing the wrong piece of rock has no evidence to support it. Had it been true, why did the Scots subsequently ask the English to return it? And, in the words of the historian and archaeologist David Breeze, 'If the Stone had been secreted in Scotland, why was it not produced for the inauguration of Robert the Bruce in 1306 when he strove so hard for legitimacy?' But literal truth is not exactly the point here.

Normally, people inclined to faith rather than to reason tend to affirm the authenticity of a relic, not to deny it. In Scotland, it was the opposite. It had become important and alluring to many people to believe, in the teeth of all probability, that the Stone placed in Edinburgh Castle was a fake.

Why was this? And what was the connection between the unexpected coolness displayed by the Edinburgh crowds and these compulsive denials? It was the fact that over time the Stone's importance had become essentially that of the grievance it evoked. What mattered about the Stone was precisely its absence: the fact that it had been carted off by an English king in an act of plunder which was also intended to be a symbolic act of conquest. Not the Stone, but the presence of the Stone at Westminster served to define one of the underlying realities of the English–Scottish relationship, and it continued to do so even after the 1707 Treaty of Union fused the two kingdoms into one 'Great Britain'.

The Stone slowly ceased to be Scottish lost property. Instead, its significance to Scots became that of wrongfully acquired English/British property. 'The Stone-in-London' became, in the modern period, an indispensable foundation stone for the reconstruction of a Scottish national – and eventually political – identity.

That puts a new slant on the outburst of scepticism in 1996. It was an outburst of anxiety. Edward had gambled that Scotland would not be Scotland without the Stone at Scone. Seven centuries later, the sceptics feared that Scotland might not be recognizably Scotland without the Stone squatting reproachfully in its wooden cell at Westminster. For the older generation, still tormented by inner self-doubt, it was unfair that Scotland should be deprived of a grievance in return for a Stone. But for the young and sanguine, those who would stand singing in the restored Scottish Parliament only three years later, it was a good bargain.

2

There are few things more interesting in geological science than those snatches of human history, or those peculiarities of human condition, which we find associated, necessarily often, but usually very unexpectedly, with certain formations and groups of rocks ... I have been told by the late Dr Malcolmson of Madras – a man who stood high both in medical and geologic science – that he found the diseases of India vary according to the formation of the country. I attempted showing on a former occasion, that a large proportion of the world's wars of independence have been prosecuted in its primary and its trap [igneous rock] districts. And we now see how in Scotland even, a subterranean life, spent amid the Coal Measures, separated in destiny and standing one portion of the people as widely from all the others as the Russian serf is separated at the present time from the free-born Englishman.

Hugh Miller, *Edinburgh & Its Neighbourhood, Historical and Geological*

The biography of the Stone is about the enigma of its origins and the petrological facts of its composition. It is about its wanderings in a royal cart, in a patriot's old Ford Anglia and in a military Land Rover. It is about the indecipherable sequence of battering, gouging, smoothing, cracking and boring to which this slab has been subjected for a thousand years or so. But what matters most to the biography is the Stone's own life, the mass of imputed human meanings encrusted about it so thickly that the distinction between what is alive and what is inanimate grows shadowy.

There are many kinds of revelation. But the most powerful is the vision which transcends the mental boundary between life and non-life, and Scotland is a place where this sort of revelation often approaches. Staring into a Scottish landscape, I have often asked myself why – in spite of all appearances – bracken, rocks, man and sea are at some level one. Sometimes this secret seems about to open, like a light moving briefly behind a closed door. In writing about birds and stones whose 'inward gates' are open, MacDiarmid came as near as one can to finding the answer.

Why Scotland? The best explanation I know is an air photograph. It is one of the masterpieces of Patricia MacDonald, who spends fine days cruising above her country in a small aircraft (she uses the camera; her husband Angus does the flying and writes the text). This particular plate shows Croy Hill, near Kilsyth, in the Central Belt which runs east and west between Edinburgh and Glasgow. It is a bare, even bleak stretch of moorland. But it is not blank. Across the picture runs an oblique line or rampart: the Antonine Wall, built by the Romans as a military work connecting the Forth and Clyde estuaries. There is a disused mine-dump (called a 'bing' in Scotland), left by a colliery or an oil-shale pit. There are a few withered, wind-crippled trees, a string of cold lochans or pools, a stone quarry. And across the whole expanse, like a drift of white hairs, lie hundreds upon hundreds of fibre-fine human tracks and sheep tracks.

It is utterly a scene of Scotland. But it is also a portrait of the special way in which the tribes who presently dwell there feel about their country. People abroad who long for their homeland see an image of landscape or 'nature'; for Slovaks it may be a green mountain, for Canadians a silent lake in the forest, for Russians the special way a summer path turns among small birch trees. But most Scots cannot call up a vision of their landscape which does not bear the mark of man.

There are two reasons for this, and the first is the dominance of geology over Scottish patterns of living. Human settlement and activity are no more than a form of lichen which can take hold in the less exposed crevices and surfaces of the land. The glaciers drove their U-shaped valleys down to the sea and onwards to form sea-loch fjords. Vanished rivers or flows of meltwater dumped fans of sediment where the glens opened out, some of them barren deposits of boulders or gravel, others terraces of fine debris which decayed into fertile soil. Where the coal measures approached the surface, men opened mines and built mining villages. Where the sea was shallow and enclosed, people settled around salt-pans. Volcanoes erupted, died and were worn away to basalt plugs over tens of millions of years, and on those red or black knobs fortresses were built. In Scotland, most communities are improvisations in strait circumstances.

A second reason, deriving mostly from that geology, is poverty. Much of Scotland's soil is shallow and acid. The rock pokes through the worn sleeve of the turf; erosion gullies fan downwards from the ridges; the deciduous trees have short trunks and low, crouching canopies. This has been a hard country to live in, as in many ways it still is. Scottish earth is in most places – even in the more fertile south and east – a skin over bone, and like any taut face it never loses a line once acquired. Seen from the air, every trench dug over the millennia and every dyke raised, every hut footing and post hole, fort bank and cattle path, tractor mark and chariot rut seems to have inscribed its trace.

Would it be possible to imagine an empty Scotland, a land whose forests had not yet been felled and where only a few hunter-gatherer bands of humans went warily to the river-crossing for fear of bears and wolves? Given the right weather, there is a place where I have experienced this illusion. This is the view across the Firth of Forth, looking across from St Monans or Pittenweem towards the southern shore of the great estuary.

You ought to see, straight across the water, the capital city of Edinburgh itself, the port of Leith and the coastal towns of East Lothian. But in certain lights a shadow effaces them all, and an almost uninhabited country is revealed over there.

The black double cone of Arthur's Seat can clearly be seen, but there is no city at its feet. The shore below North Berwick Law is empty. Far inland, the snowy sierras of this desolate land rise up. And a single thread of smoke rises into the sky, apparently from some invisible hut.

Perhaps there are hunters there. Or perhaps the fire has been lit by the Iron Age people who will in time become the Votadini, a Celtic tribal confederation which will eventually raise some kind of citadel on the future Castle rock of Edinburgh and bury a hoard of Roman silver on the summit of Traprain Law. The Votadini will enjoy, rather than endure, a few centuries of Roman occupation, acquiring luxuries and learning skills like the use of window-glass. For generations after the Romans leave they will remain until – after defeat by Anglian invaders in about AD 600, at the battle of Catraeth – they are driven out and migrate as refugees to another Celtic country which is now called Wales.

The poet Aneirin wrote his epic *Gododdin* about this tragedy (the word is a later form of 'Votadini'):

> *Three hundred men hastened forth,*
> *wearing gold torques, defending the land,*
> *and there was slaughter.*
> *Though they were slain, they slew,*
> *and they shall be honoured till the end of the world.*

They had feasted for a year in the king's hall at Dun Eidyn (Edinburgh), drinking from golden vessels, before marching to Catraeth. But Aneirin also mentions the smoking hearth in the royal hall, 'the well-fed fire, the pine-logs blazing from dusk to dusk'.

It is that thread of smoke in the empty view across the Firth which matters most. This is the land which was not called 'Scotland' until centuries after the Votadini had left, but in which the human race and its work have become compounded with the landscape. Is there a difference in quality between the trace of what a glacier did to this landscape half a million years ago, and the trace of what a coal mine did to it a hundred years ago? And, coming back to my bewilderment as a child, is there really such a category difference between the interlocking stone rings of Edinburgh's Moray Place, glimpsed from Patricia MacDonald's Cessna, and the curving sea-cliffs of Tantallon along the coast? Or between the spire of the Bass Rock, rising from the sea off North Berwick, and the huge stone spike of St Mary's Cathedral in the West End of Edinburgh?

The Bass Rock and the cliffs are supposed to belong to 'the natural creation'. The New Town mansions of Edinburgh and the cathedral are presented as the antithesis of nature: sandstone and granite which have not just been tamed and domesticated, as they are quarried and then sawn up by masons into ashlar blocks, but transcended altogether. But that view of human action as the opposite of natural process is out of date. It was the conventional, 'Faustian' view of the relationship between man and world. It was the triumphalist notion of Homo Sapiens as a self-realizing subject crowned with fire, a notion which was common to Hegelians, to Marxists and to all adherents of the religion of Progress. But the savageries of the twentieth century and the sick planet we are rolling into the twenty-first have left little of that faith behind.

Scotland's landscapes, offering a new way to understand humanity's integral place in creation, can help to replace that Faustian, dualist world-view. This is a good place in which to understand the secret of the unity of 'artificial' and 'natural', of the planned and the accidental. Perhaps this is why Scotland in the Enlightenment and the Victorian age produced such a majestic dynasty of geologists and pioneering thinkers about the origins of life and landscape: James Hutton, James Hall and his adversary Robert Jameson, Roderick Murchison, Charles Lyell, Hugh Miller and the great publisher of popular science Robert Chambers, who wrote the Victorian best-seller *Vestiges of Creation*.

At the end of most streets in Edinburgh's Old Town rises the crimson wall of Salisbury Craigs, a lesson in the unimaginable forces and lapses of time which have gone to shape the world. The Craigs are a basalt intrusion, a fossil tide of volcanic rock which surged through the foundations of a dead volcano some 200 million years ago. Geology and palaeontology, with their revelations of deep time and alien life-forms, towered up wherever nineteenth-century Scots turned their eyes. The 'testimony of the rocks' threatened their moral universe, its narrative incompatible with a creation myth or even with a creator, let alone with assumptions about man made in God's image. And yet these savants never turned away from the evidence they deciphered from geology, even though some of them – Hugh Miller, especially – struggled to reinvent a Genesis story which might include the fossil record and somehow hold the cosmos together. James Hutton, who was born and went to school in the shadow of the Craigs, had already begun to understand their lesson in the 1780s. In his *Theory of the Earth*, first published in 1788 to the terror of his more pious readers, he wrote: 'The result, therefore, of our present enquiry is that we find no vestige of a beginning – no prospect of an end.'

Old Edinburgh is shaped like a gigantic lecture theatre, with the end wall covered by a chart of the earth's origins. If geology, human origins and their impact on the moral law preoccupied the city's Victorian intellectuals, it is not surprising that geology was also a favourite topic in the town's leading daily newspaper, the *Scotsman*. Other newspapers at other times have secured mighty scoops: the secret sins of a leader, the invasion of a distant country. But Edinburgh's paper, founded in 1817, achieved the exclusive revelation of the biggest story on earth. On 7 October 1840, the *Scotsman* scooped the Ice Age.

On Blackford Hill, on the southern limits of Edinburgh and only a short walk from the refined terraces of Morningside, there is a shallow grotto known as the Agassiz Rock. Here, in 1840, the Swiss naturalist and geologist Louis Agassiz arrived in the company of Charles Maclaren, the *Scotsman*'s first real editor. Maclaren wanted his guest's opinion on certain curious marks on the rock's surface.

In 1840, Jean Louis Rodolphe Agassiz was the young genius of European palaeontology. He was thirty-three, and had been a professor since the age of twenty-five. His book on Brazilian fishes had been warmly praised by Cuvier; his research on fossil fish species had brought him into correspondence with Hugh Miller. Meanwhile he was embarking on a study of the age and development of Alpine glaciers which had already led him to speculate that ice might once have been widespread over northern Europe. He had come to Scotland to address a meeting of the British Association for the Advancement of Science, to be held in Glasgow in September. But Agassiz was impatient to escape from the cities and head for the hills. In the mountains of the Highlands, far older than the Alps and far less obscured by trees, he could seek evidence for his theory that there had been a 'universal glaciation'.

Maclaren described what happened when he brought his Swiss friend to Blackford Hill. 'The surface of the clinkstone, for the space of ten or twelve inches in length, is smoothed and marked by striae or scratches in a direction approximate to horizontal . . . Agassiz instantly exclaimed: "It is the work of The Ice!" '

Many scholars admired what Agassiz had written about pre-historic fish. But his glaciation theory was another matter, and many of the formidable Scottish and English scientists who listened to his paper in Glasgow were sceptical. They were well aware that something had been scratching and gouging rocks in antiquity, and that stones carried by a moving force – just possibly ice masses – could be responsible. But they preferred explanations like the Mud Flow Theory or the Floating Iceberg Hypothesis. They could understand why an excitable young Swiss professor longed to extend his own Alpine glaciers over the whole northern hemisphere, but the evidence for this wild vision was simply lacking.

The editor thought otherwise, especially after the visit to Blackford Hill. Charles Maclaren was a deeply serious man of passionate opinions (in 1829, he had fought a duel with the editor of the rival *Caledonian Mercury* – pistols at only twelve paces – but both missed). He was typical of those omniscient, self-educated sages who dominated Edinburgh at the time, and he sat fascinated in the audience in Glasgow as Agassiz, supported by his new book, *Etudes sur les Glaciers*, unfolded his ideas.

As soon as the meeting was over, Agassiz set off by stagecoach into the Highlands. The revelations began almost instantly. At every stop – starting at Inveraray, when his coach bumped over a terminal moraine as he went to call on the Duke of Argyll – he saw plain evidence that this was a post-glacial landscape. But his final proof was found in Glen Roy, in Lochaber, where he identified the mystifying terraces known as 'the parallel roads' as the shores of vanished glacial lakes. (Charles Darwin, a few years earlier, had wrongly suggested that the 'roads' had been created by the action of the sea.)

At each stop, Agassiz scribbled down his impressions in letters which he sent to Robert Jameson in Edinburgh. The plan had been that they should appear in the *Edinburgh New Philosophical Journal*, but the first letter from Agassiz missed the journal's deadline. Jameson was vexed, but then remembered his friend Maclaren, editor and amateur geologist. He passed the letter on to the *Scotsman*. 'As it is of great importance from a geological point of view, I send it for insertion in your journal. It proves the former existence of glaciers in Scotland.'

It was nineteen years before *The Origin of Species*. The doomed battle to save the scriptural account of a divine creation and reconcile it with the true antiquity of the planet was still being fought, and had not yet been lost. It was a battle which cost not only reputations, faiths and friendships, but sanities and even lives. Its intensity is summed up in the life of the Cromarty stonemason Hugh Miller, a radical Presbyterian who had educated himself into a world authority on fossil fish and who was to become one of Scotland's great radical journalists.

Miller had been warmly welcomed at the Glasgow conference, and Agassiz had named an extinct fish-species for him – *Pterichthys Milleri*. But some years later, in 1844, Miller was appalled by the publication in Edinburgh of *Vestiges of Creation*, in which the anonymous author (Robert Chambers) cleverly anticipated some of Darwin's concepts of evolution. Struggling to rescue the idea of a divine agency, Miller grew desperate enough to propose that the 'seven days of Creation' specified in Genesis did correspond to seven distinct periods of life-forms identifiable in the geological record – but only if the 'days' were measured in millions of years rather than in hours. But by the time that this thesis appeared, in *Testimony of the Rocks* in 1859, Miller was already dead. After frantic months of self-loathing in which despair about the eviction of a creator from the universe led to paranoid delusions of guilt, he shot himself through the heart in December 1856.

In 1840, by contrast, the defences of the Book of Genesis were bruised but not yet breached. *Scotsman* readers were happy enough to study illustrations of prehistoric animals after tea. But they still assumed that they lived in a land whose dramatic and beloved outlines were drawn by the hand of God. In delivering the Ice Age to those large, quiet families in Morningside or North Berwick, Maclaren was taking a risk.

Prefaced with an essay by Maclaren, and with letters by Jameson and Agassiz himself, the first article appeared at enormous length in the *Scotsman* of 7 October 1840. Maclaren had in fact written it himself, a learned but highly readable summary of Agassiz's views illustrated with simple and striking graphics. Headlined 'The Glacial Theory – First Paper', it began as follows: 'Professor Agassiz of Neufchatel has recently been studying the glaciers of the Alps with great care, and has been led by his investigations to certain bold, novel and highly interesting conclusions . . .'

They certainly were. The 'First Paper' was followed by no fewer than eight others, carrying the series on to the end of January 1841. All appear to have been written by Maclaren. It is not clear whether Agassiz was able to check or correct them after his return from the Highlands. Probably not, because the last article in the series was marred by a grave error on Maclaren's part. Agassiz had noticed the five hundred or so dolerite boulders lying around in Queen's Park (the open expanse out of which Salisbury Craigs and Arthur's Seat rise), and had declared that they had been brought there by the ice. But Maclaren denied this; for all his faith in his Swiss friend, he could not believe that a glacier was powerful enough to carry huge blocks of stone hundreds of feet uphill almost to the crest of Arthur's Seat. Louis Agassiz, familiar with his own living glaciers at home, knew better.

From the *Scotsman*, the entire British public learned for the first time that there had been an Ice Age in their own land and throughout the northern hemisphere. Conventional religion was faced with proof that much of the world had been overrun, buried and reshaped by an ice-cap and glaciers hundreds of feet thick – and at a relatively recent period. Here was a cataclysm which the Book did not even mention.

Charles Maclaren himself continued to write about geology and prehistory. His last article, published in 1861, discussed the flint tools uncovered at Saint Acheul in France by Boucher de Perthes and insisted – to the distress of the many fundamental Creationists who still hung on as readers of the *Scotsman* – that they had been made by early human beings living at the end of the glacial period. But this was stale news to more sophisticated subscribers; discussions about 'primitive' men and about a 'Stone Age' were already common currency when Boucher de Perthes made his discoveries in the 1850s. The hand-axes of Saint Acheul could not have the impact of the Ice Age story, which had proved so devastating in its suddenness and in its subversion of all thinking about landscape. The monumental scoop of 1840 remained the pinnacle of Maclaren's – and his paper's – achievement.

3

Navel stone of Caledon
marker of millennium
eye of seer, druid's tongue,
word of carlin – stand upon
this footprint made for everyone.

A step for Scotland carved in stone
a parliament without a throne
a country each of us can own
a wisdom, knowing as we are known,
a going forth and coming home.

Who among us now will work
for light that penetrates the dark
for freedom climbing like the lark
for the democratic spark –
whose the tread that fits this mark?

Tessa Ransford, 'Incantation 2000'

In 1985, Professor Gwyn Alf Williams published a book called *When Was Wales?* There's no more astute title for a work of national history.

In one sense, it mocks the one-dimensional flatness of the nationalist vision: the glowing mosaic, the stained-glass window, which is the eternal fatherland. Gwyn Williams knew that Wales and Welshness were living and constantly changing things. But even he, at the end of his life, came to fear that Wales might not have a future. 'Wales is an artefact which the Welsh produce. If they want to.' Perhaps they no longer wanted to. What was certain was that if they continued to lose their sense of history, then no more artefacts would be produced. 'Some kind of human society, though God knows what kind, will no doubt go on occupying these two western peninsulas of Britain, but that people, who are my people and no mean people, who have for a millennium and a half lived in them as a Welsh people, are now nothing but a naked people under an acid rain.'

So he wrote this book, whose sub-title is 'A History of the Welsh', in a last attempt to open up quarries in the past which could serve to build a future. And it was only half in mockery that he offered his question, 'When Was Wales?' He showed that there were many moments from which to choose. No serious historian – and Gwyn Williams was fiercely serious – thinks that there exists an 'essential' nation, most truly itself within particular borders, or in a particular fashion of poetry, or at a particular season in the past. But the best of the serious historians understand that a people focuses upon its national history in just that way, always with a touch of melancholy at the thought of how 'we' have declined since some defining scene. And yet the choice of that scene – identifying the time when 'we were really ourselves' – alters as the centuries and the rulers and the *Zeitgeist* alter. That is the fascination of it. It is the contrast between the fairy tale of a reinvented past and the reality of present feelings which can be decoded from that past.

There is an almost universal tendency to slip backwards in time as emotions mount. 'When was France?', once answered by 'the reign of the *Roi Soleil*' or 'the Frankish time', became 'the Gaulish/Celtic millennia before the Romans'. Germany, in a hurry to find an imperial destiny before it was too late, looked beyond Goethe in Weimar, and recognized Hermann in the forest as he waited to ambush Roman legions. In the nineteenth century, the 'Oxford School' of historians laid down that England's 'when' was in the Anglo-Saxon period (although the

English people have obstinately continued to think that the Welsh-rooted Tudor dynasty and Good Queen Bess brought England to its true self).

As for 'When was Britain?', that question is painfully relevant in the first years of the twenty-first century. As lately as the 1950s, the answer might have been placed in the very recent past, reflecting self-confidence: 'Britain was when we stood up to Hitler alone in 1940' or even, 'Britain was when we set up the National Health Service'. But little of that self-assurance remains. Britain, as anything more than a state issuing passports, is losing definition and conviction. The last fifty years have produced no convincing trophy of 'British' achievement to add to past glories, and the 'when' – the Empire, the War – has begun to sound distant and nostalgic.

Scotland's 'when' has receded too. And, as with France or Germany a hundred years ago, the move is away from 'civilized', cosmopolitan achievements of human taste or spirit towards cloudier, hairier times. This change of focus, manifesting itself only in the last ten years or so, took Scottish intellectuals by surprise and saddened many of them. In the quarter-century of argument and agitation for self-government which preceded 1999, Mel Gibson's *Braveheart* was never what they had meant. On the contrary, they had looked forward to a small but outward-looking nation which would take its place in the European Union, distancing itself firmly from what they perceived as the dull-witted insularity of England.

In the 1980s, among the earnest, highly educated patriots who kept up the pressure for self-government, there had been a proud consensus about 'when was Scotland'. The quintessential Scotland, it was agreed, had existed during the Scottish Enlightenment.

Inevitably, there is no accepted version of when the Scottish Enlightenment began or ended. Some would begin it with the publication of Francis Hutcheson's *Inquiry into the Originals of our Ideas of Beauty and Virtue* in 1724. Most scholars and critics still set the whole episode within the 'short eighteenth century' which finished with the outbreak of the Napoleonic Wars. But even that curtailed period contained the flourishing in Edinburgh (and to a lesser extent Glasgow and other Scottish cities) of philosophers, economists, political thinkers, natural and applied scientists, anatomists, mathematicians, geologists, architects, painters and poets. Their minds, universal and optimistic in cast, changed the understanding of the natural world and the self-understanding of the human race.

The argument about when the Scottish Enlightenment ended is much more interesting than the definitions of when it began. The 'short' version contains many great names, from David Hume and Adam Smith to James Hutton or Robert Burns. But why should the Golden Age close in about 1800? Teachers adore dividing culture into compartments. But in reality, and especially in Scotland, the Enlightenment and the 'Romantic Age' were continuous; apart from the sceptic David Hume, the eighteenth-century *lumières* of Edinburgh were mostly God-fearing, if not God-terrified, while life in the classical streets of Edinburgh's New Town in the 1820s remained 'Augustan with attitude'.

It is absurd to suggest that the world-view of Walter Scott, Francis Jeffrey, James Hogg or Lord Cockburn, great figures of Scottish culture after 1815, had nothing to do with the Enlightenment. The broad interpretations of human nature and the cosmos which had developed in eighteenth-century Edinburgh or Glasgow were simply carried forward by the new generation of natural scientists and geologists, by botanists and physicians, by the 'Common Sense' philosophers and theologians, through most of the Victorian age. Even in the twentieth century, the polymath, multidisciplinary approach of Patrick Geddes (1854–1932), pioneer of modern urban planning, showed a clear line of descent from the earliest Scottish thinkers about social structure – although his own personal life, dedicated to self-renewal and experiment, was a flight into Romantic chaos.

But this answer to 'When was Scotland?' – the Enlightenment, short or long – had a weakness. It was not the 'people's' answer. Most Scots knew little about David Hume or Adam Ferguson. Instead, they looked back for inspiration to a bewildering variety of other icons and episodes. One was the 'Scotland of inventors': the familiar recitation which proclaims that Scottish genius devised everything from steam locomotion through television to penicillin. A second was the imaginary rural Scotland devised by the Burns industry, a lusty, kindly world of farmhouse patriarchs and upwardly mobile 'lads o' pairts'. A third, now scarcely surviving, was the tradition of the Covenanters, the ultra-Calvinist small farmers who took up arms in the seventeenth century to fight for a theocratic Scotland governed by Christ the King and his elect; their lonely 'martyrs' graves' are scattered across the Lowland hills. And a fourth theatre of national identity, much the oldest, was the enduring memory of the late-medieval Wars of Independence against England, with their heroes William Wallace and King Robert I, 'the Bruce'.

Nationalism has an incurable obsession with 'origins'. In Scotland, symptoms of this obsession began to be noticeable in the 1980s. Politically, it was a bleak time. The surge towards Home Rule or independence in the 1970s had ebbed away when the 1979 referendum on the Labour government's devolution plan failed to gain the required 'Yes' majority in Scotland. There followed eighteen years of Conservative government under Mrs Thatcher and John Major, who both flatly rejected all proposals for devolution. Under the surface, however, a new strain of cultural and sometimes 'ethnic' nationalism began to flourish. The writers and pop musicians who were prominent in this movement were entirely disillusioned by party politics (the vote for the Scottish National Party, which had fallen from a peak of popularity in 1977, remained stagnant through most of the 1980s). But all that they sang and published was driven by grief for their country, and by a resentment which often showed an anti-English edge. By 1990, was it harder to be a child with an English accent in a Scottish schoolyard than it had been ten years before? The evidence is only anecdotal, but many Scots would say that it was.

Politics stood still, but Scotland was moving. Soon there were signs that 'essential Scotland' was also migrating, but upstream against the current of time. These signs could be tiny, such as the prominence given in 1985 to the 1,300th anniversary of the battle of Nechtansmere (Dunnichen) where in 685 a Pictish army had decisively defeated an Anglian invasion. They could be semi-satirical, like the fad for 'Pictish' identity expressed in car-stickers and leaflets. They could be registered in sport: the new custom of booing 'God Save the Queen' at football matches, or the quiet, almost unnoticed spread of the game of shinty, the Gaelic field game whose nearest relation is the Irish sport of hurling. Or they could be astonishing. Nobody was prepared for the impact of *Braveheart* in 1995, a wildly crude Hollywood distortion of the Wallace story which knocked Scotland over. Even in distant Argyll, a young woman I knew married a bare-legged man in a kilt whose face was painted blue and white. 'Freedom!' It wasn't a word which Scotland's sophisticated politicians cared to shout, not even the Nationalists. But Mel Gibson as William Wallace shouted it, and to the dismay of many wise and patient men and women, the young seemed to know what he meant.

It was in this period that the long-obstructed plans for a new Museum of Scotland were finally put in motion. Those who planned it and created its exhibition strategy had not the slightest intention of contributing to any 'nationalist' mood. Indeed its display chief, the celebrated English archaeologist David Clarke, aimed to make a progressive museum which was 'object-led' and not chronological in the old familiar way, in order that nobody could use it to illustrate some fraudulent national narrative or 'Scotland's Story'. No more 'Romans'. No more 'Celts' or 'Picts', as if they were solid ethnic identities. Instead, each showcase would cut across time; one case might show 'objects of authority' (royal or chieftainly gear from the Bronze Age to the late Viking period), while another would be devoted to 'transport' – bridle ornaments from 1000 BC, a Roman cart tyre, fragments from an early-medieval boat and so on.

This austere strategy did not entirely work out. Clarke got his way with the 'Early Peoples' gallery, but other display areas, starting with the 'Kingdom of the Scots' section, slipped into a more traditional and patriotic relationship to visitors' expectations. And by November 1998, when the new Museum was finally opened in Edinburgh by the Queen, the political landscape had completely changed. Labour was in power in London, and devolution was back on the agenda. Scotland had been promised its parliament, and in this new atmosphere of cheerful national self-assertion, people asked why the Museum did not tell 'Scotland's Story' in the plain way they expected. They were puzzled by the answers. Soon there was a row when it was noticed that the Museum contained nothing about the life or deeds of William Wallace. The correct answer would have been that this was a museum of artefacts, not a gallery of heroes. Instead the Museum unwisely replied that no authentic Wallace relics existed. This was a crass error. The complainers – that implacable corps of know-alls who take exercise each morning in the letter columns of the *Scotsman* and the *Herald* – pounced with cries of delight. What about the famous 1297 letter from Wallace to the Hanseatic merchants of Lübeck, still kept in that city, reassuring them that 'the kingdom of Scotland, God be thanked, has been recovered by war from the power of the English'?

But the Museum's concentration on objects has had a more unexpected consequence. At one level, it was a huge success. By concentrating scattered or little-known collections in one place, and adding a mass of entirely unknown treasures rescued from other museum storerooms, it confronted the Scots for the first time with the true magnificence of their own material culture. A small nation not noted for modesty was for once overawed by itself. 'We had no idea . . .' said the visitors. Few curators in the world have had the luck to stage a popular revelation on that scale.

Objects . . . but which objects? Floor by floor, the Museum shows artefacts from every period, from prehistory to the arrival of cyber industry in 'Silicon Glen'. But in the competition for attention, it is the early material which wins effortlessly.

This is a paradox, a warning about how bigger and newer do not always add up to better. Human success in tiny centres of settlement can be spectacular, even when the rest of a territory is harsh and unrewarding. The land eventually named Scotland was always in some sense a poor country, in that geology and climate put tight limits on the size of the population and its standard of living. But in the few areas able to support complex communities, most of them coastal strips or islands, the early inhabitants often produced cultural work of a standard equal to anything in the rest of Europe. This was true of the early Bronze Age, and especially true of the post-classical and early medieval centuries, the misnamed 'Dark Ages' which began to close as Norse influence weakened and a Kingdom of Scotland began to establish itself.

Up to about the twelfth century AD, the peoples who inhabited this land could produce work in stone, metal, ivory or manuscript illumination whose quality still astounds the world. But after that, the material culture grows scanty and thin. In the west, the revival of a Gaelic principality as the 'Lordship of the Isles' (c.1150 to 1493) produced some 'Celtic' masterpieces in the old tradition. But the best that mainland Scotland could make in the Middle Ages was seldom up to Italian, French or German standards of ecclesiastical, royal or lordly craftsmanship. The Kingdom of Scotland had to fight against starvation as well as invasion, and its artefacts were mostly things of the mind and memory: the words of the Declaration of Arbroath, the prayers and curses of the Reformation, the poetry from Dunbar to MacDiarmid, the songs. How does a Museum of Objects commemorate the Covenanters, except with a tattered flag, a gallows leaflet or a Bible? How can a shelf of books, however world-shaking their contents, do justice to the power of the Scottish Enlightenment? The Lübeck Senate supplied the Museum with a facsimile of that letter from William Wallace, but how can a parchment sheet evoke the passionate myth of 'the Guardian' whose name was given to wells and trees and stones all over the country?

Against the pre-mediaeval show in the new Museum, the rest of Scottish history stands no chance. In the early galleries are arrayed the Pictish symbol-stones, reproduced pages from the *Book of Kells* written and illuminated on the isle of Iona, the ponderous silver chains found in Lowland hills, the Hunterston Brooch, the Dupplin Cross, the Deskford carnyx (a boar-headed Celtic trumpet), the eighth-century 'Breccbennach' (the 'speckled peaked thing', the little jewelled Monymusk Reliquary once believed to hold St Columba's bones, which was carried with the Scottish army into the battle of Bannockburn in 1314), the man-eating lioness from Roman Cramond, the black necklace of jet beads laid in a tomb in Argyll more than three and a half millennia ago. Visually, there is no contest. And by rights, the Stone of Destiny should be in the Museum of Scotland too, a symbol of power whose pagan mass would glower at the tiny, equally powerful symbol of the 'Breccbennach' Reliquary.

In short, the Museum helped to drive 'when was Scotland' at least a thousand years back into the past. That was absolutely not intended. But it was the consequence of basing a national history display on objects rather than narrative. When it opened, a Museum official observed – a touch defensively – that 'This is not a hands-on museum. It's a brains-on museum.'

But it is neither. This is above all an eyes-on museum.

In the silence, the objects from before 1200 steal the show. Imagination flies straight to them, and stays there with the 'barbaric' jewellery, the undeciphered rock inscriptions, the stone faces with their narrow noses and bulging lentoid eyes, the vivid and yet utterly lost language of Pictish carved symbols. And yet this new rush into ancient identities cannot even claim to give Scotland a new 'when'. For almost all of them relate to times before Scotland had been invented.

The hill of Dunadd stands by itself. It rises abruptly from the Moine Mhor, the Great Moss, the levels of peat-bog and heather which stretch away to the west towards Crinan. From the summit, you catch a gleam of sea from the Sound of Jura. In summer, the wind from the Atlantic carries up to you the scent of bog-myrtle, the lowing of cattle in the rich pastures near Kilmartin, the noise of a busy tractor. The narrow river Add curls around the foot of Dunadd, the traces of its old meanders and oxbows still written on the plain. To the north are the hills of Lorn.

Just below the summit of Dunadd there is a small outcrop of bare rock. Along it, more or less in line, runs a sequence of carvings: a deep-cut basin, a faint footprint, a majestic ridge-backed boar in the 'Pictish' style and then another, much sharper outline of a shod foot. Beside the second footprint are the almost-effaced marks of an inscription in the branching 'ogham' script, once thought illegible but now in part read to show the Old Irish word FINNMANACH – Finn the monk or monastery tenant. There may well have been more carvings. Marion Campbell of Kilberry, who identified the first footprint, thought that she could make out another complex design behind the boar. That is hard to confirm, for some joker early in the last century scratched in just this space the figure of a man smoking a pipe, with the name 'King Fergus'.

It is a royal place. It is, for most Scots, the place where

Scotland began. To this hill, in the early sixth century, came Fergus mor mac Erc with his three sons and their followers, settlers sailing across from northern Ireland where they had ruled the kingdom of Dalriada. Now they made a 'greater Dalriada' spanning the sea, and for some centuries there existed a common Dalriadic kingdom stretching from northern Argyll down the Kintyre peninsula and across into what is now County Antrim in Northern Ireland.

The Romans had called the inhabitants of Ireland 'Scotti'. Soon this name was extended to the new settlers in Argyll as well. In the late sixth century, the two parts of Dalriada began to separate politically (if not in language and culture), and after a meeting at Drum Cett in Ireland in 574, Argyll Dalriada became effectively independent.

That is how 'Scotland's story' begins in the school books, and some of it at least is true. The tale of Fergus may be invented, but Dalriada existed. Probably some kind of common society inhabiting north-eastern Ireland, the Argyll mainland and the islands between them had come into being far earlier than the sixth century, a Gaelic-speaking Atlantic world connected rather than divided by the sea. In those times, travel by water was relatively easy while travel by land – across the spine of mountain, forest and bog which walled east and central Scotland off from the west – was hard and dangerous. But something happened to shift the political balance around the sixth or seventh centuries AD. Almost certainly, it was nothing like a mass migration or full-scale invasion of Argyll from Ireland. Instead, the change may have been no more than a change of rulers, the arrival of one small warrior band or family seeking power in a bigger landscape.

This band – perhaps Fergus mor mac Erc and his sons – took control of the local communities they found in Argyll and organized them into a coherent Dalriadic polity. Later chroniclers wrote that the new Dalriada was divided into three regions named after the sons of Fergus. The Cinel (kindred group) Loairn ruled in the land which is still called Lorn, north of Crinan Moss. The Cinel Gabran took the Kintyre peninsula. The Cinel Angus took the fertile island of Islay. Later, in or before the eighth century, the Cinel Gabran divided and a fourth kindred appeared, the Cinel Comgall, controlling the steep peninsula of Cowal to the south-east. For all these clan warlords or kinglets, the navel, high place and capital of this confederation was almost certainly Dunadd.

In the time of Fergus, the future Scotland was divided into three main regions. In the west, Dalriada was a continuation of the Gaelic culture of Ireland; its speech, 'Irish', belonged to the so-called 'Q-Celtic' (Goidelic) sub-group of languages. In the east, stretching down from Shetland and Orkney to the northern shore of the Firth of Forth, was Pictland, a confederation of kingdoms with a unique, highly distinctive tradition of decorative art. Nothing comprehensible written in Pictish has survived (or has so far been recognized), and their language is unknown. Those who enjoy the 'mystery of the Picts' like to fancy that they spoke a pre-Indo-European language, but there is no evidence for that, and it is assumed now that their speech belonged to the 'P-Celtic' (Brittonic) family. Alone of these ethnic groups, the Picts appear to 'vanish' from history in about the ninth century. That was the time when the expanding Dalriadic kings established their dominion over 'Alba' (most of modern Scotland) and moved their capital from Argyll to the old Pictish centre of Scone in Perthshire.

In a third region, south of the Forth–Clyde isthmus, lived three main groups of 'Britons', Celtic peoples who seem to have been closely related in culture and language. West-central Scotland was the home of the 'Strathclyde Britons', whose capital-fortress stood on Dumbarton Rock overlooking the Clyde estuary. The kingdom of Rheged covered part of south-western Scotland and Cumbria. South of the Firth of Forth, in the Lothians and on the site of Edinburgh, dwelt the powerful Votadini, the nation who eventually – according to the

Gododdin epic – took refuge in what is now Wales. All spoke versions of 'P-Celtic', the linguistic branch which includes Welsh, the extinct Cornish tongue and Breton. Within living memory, children in rural west Scotland sang a playground counting-out rhyme whose 'nonsense' words were recognizable to philologists as the Welsh numerals up to ten.

A fourth population, however, belonged to a quite different, non-Celtic language community. The Anglians were newcomers, a northern prong of the Germanic invaders – Saxons, Jutes, Angles – who had crossed the North Sea and entered eastern Britain at the end of the Roman period. By about AD 600, they had defeated the Votadini and occupied most of south-eastern Scotland up to the Forth, and their raiding parties were beginning to ravage Pictish territory as far north as the Tay estuary. If the Picts had not slaughtered an advancing Anglian host at the battle of Nechtansmere, near Forfar, in 685, they might well have conquered the whole of Scotland east of the Highland mountains. All north-eastern Britain would have become part of England, in the course of time, and the kingdom of Scotland would never have been born.

The twentieth of May 1985 turned out to be a fine day. But the Society of Antiquaries of Scotland came well equipped with umbrellas, green wellies and tweed fore-and-aft hats, just in case. As we climbed out of our hired coach at Dunnichen, the modern name for Nechtansmere, there was already a small crowd on the green. We and they had come to witness the unveiling of a monument to what had happened here exactly 1,300 years before. The minister of Dunnichen church was standing ready with the Provost of Forfar wearing his chain of office, and the pipe band of the local branch of the British Legion. Several dozen local inhabitants stood around on the moist grass, waiting to see what would happen. Honour was to be done to the deed of Bridei mac Bile, commander of the Picts, who on this spot (or somewhere near it) fed to the ravens

King Ecgfrith of the Northumbrian Anglians and most of his soldiers.

We had brought sandwiches. But before we could unwrap them, or feed them to the carrion crows loitering on the fringe of the ceremony, we noticed a van distributing leaflets and stickers. There was to be a Pictish Free State, the leaflets proclaimed, and 'Dunnichen Day' was to be a national holiday. 'Up to now it has been celebrated almost privately by dedicated Pictophiles and folk who happen to be sitting near them . . . The Pictish Cultural Society ask you to be courteous to the folk living in the neighbourhood and give them no cause for complaint.' It turned out that several hundred people had attended 'Pictish' ceilidhs and discos over the past few evenings.

The antiquaries marvelled. One said, 'I thought we had come to visit the seventh century, but I see we have reached the nineteenth century already. My, does time fly!' She was correct. The Pictish Cultural Society belonged by right to that epoch in Europe when buried nations were being dug up, when new and romantic ancestries were invented and when small, unfree peoples were surprised to be told by poets that they had an heroic past and epic virtues. Cultural societies redecorated the identities of the Czechs and the Irish, the Flemings and the Germans, the Serbs and the Scots and the Welsh and a dozen others. Here at Dunnichen was a latecomer.

Was it a joke? Not entirely. Like many straight-faced jokers, the New Picts disliked being laughed at. They were Scottish nationalists, but they wanted a different, clean-sheet past on which to paint their nation. Enough of John Knox and the Jacobites, of Mary Queen of Scots and Flodden Field and Highland regiments – enough of that history sodden with tragic failure, treachery and guilt! The Picts, in contrast, were virgin land. They offered a greenfield site on which – because almost nothing was known about them for certain – a new palace could be raised for a new and stainless nation.

The memory of the Picts has repeatedly been melted down and cast in new, unexpected shapes, to suit the changing needs of Scottish self-assertion. During the life-or-death struggle to defend Scotland against English conquest, in the thirteenth and fourteenth centuries, it seemed crucial to proclaim that Scotland had a longer line of unbroken royal succession than any other nation – including England. Accordingly the Pictish king-lists were spliced onto the lineage of the Dalriadic dynasty, carrying the predecessors of Fergus mor mac Erc back through some forty (sometimes up to seventy) shadowy Pictish names to 'Fergus I', Fergus mac Ferchar, who was supposed to have reigned in the time of Alexander the Great. At the same time, the patriotic chroniclers began to gloss over the Irish connections of Dalriada, suggesting that the Picts and the Scots had always shared the same land – and sometimes that the Scots had arrived there first.

After the Reformation, Irish origins were associated with Roman Catholicism and became even less desirable. Sir Walter Scott, that stoutly Protestant patriot, almost totally suppressed the Irishness of the early Scottish kingdom in his *Tales of a Grandfather*, and wrote as if Picts and Scots had shared the lands north of Hadrian's Wall since the dawn of history. And as recently as 1971, the fine historian Isabel Henderson could write that 'if we Scots like to think of ourselves as something distinct from an Irish colony, then it is the spirit of the tribes who went to make up the Picts that we must invoke'.

Now the Picts are being painted Green, a race of caring New Agers who believed that small was beautiful. One of the leaflets handed out at Dunnichen urged that 'the New Picts should be an example of gentle nobility'. The Presbyterian minister, when his turn came to speak, solemnly called for forgiveness and reconciliation, for respect to the memory of the dead and their widows and orphans, linking the commemoration to the recent ceremonies for the fortieth anniversary of victory in the Second World War. But where is the evidence that the Picts, even though they had accepted the Gospel from St Columba a hundred years before Nechtansmere, understood Christianity as a religion of mercy?

A few miles away from Dunnichen stand the Pictish sculptured stones of Aberlemno. One of them is pretty evidently a monument to the victory at Nechtansmere. On one side, it carries a superb 'Celtic' cross, embedded in carved animal interlace. The other side, however, is military. It displays scenes of battle, arranged in a strip-cartoon sequence of battle, defeat and then slaughter. The fight is between bare-headed warriors and riders in Anglo-Saxon helmets, and the final relief shows a bird devouring the face of a fallen Anglian prince – probably Ecgfrith. This carving has been shown to illustrate a text from the Book of Revelation, 14:17: 'And I saw an angel standing in the sun, and he cried with a loud voice, saying to all the fowls that fly in the midst of Heaven: Come and gather yourselves unto the supper of the great God, that ye may eat the flesh of kings and the flesh of captains, and the flesh of mighty men, and the flesh of horses and of them that sit on them . . .'

Gentle nobility? The relationship of generals to Holy Writ has always been that of a hangman selecting the right shape of tree. Peering at the Aberlemno Stone, I was reminded of London's most revolting memorial, dedicated to the Machine-Gun Corps in the First World War. It bears a text from I Samuel, 18:7. The passage reads: 'Saul hath slain his thousands, and David his ten thousands.'

Not long ago, scholars talked about 'the problem of the Picts'. By this, they meant that almost nothing was known about their culture or language, and that they leave the historical record quite abruptly. But research in the last fifty years has changed that. Air photography, excavation and a systematic re-examination of written sources have dispelled most of the mystery, leaving only dozens of unanswered questions. The Picts were an unusual society; their political structures were more sophisticated than those of the Dalriadic Scots, and their artistic tradition and craftsmanship in stone and silver were extraordinary (one of the most painful open questions is whether they may have also developed a literature which was destroyed in the course of their assimilation with the Scots). But they were probably part of the broader Celtic-speaking family of peoples; they were not aliens from some sunken pre-Indo-European world. And their sudden departure from the scene is not as strange or ominous as it once seemed.

In 842, Cinead mac Ailpin, King of Dalriada, left Argyll and established his royal centre at Scone in Perthshire, imposing his authority over much of Pictland. Cinead (better known as Kenneth MacAlpin) in effect founded the dynasty which was to rule the kingdom soon renamed 'Alba', later 'Scotland'. Pictish customs were suppressed, and little more is heard of a Pictish people. The Gaelic language, brought from Argyll, was soon in use throughout what had been Pictland and much of southern Scotland as well.

The Picts had always been the target for tall stories; not long after Nechtansmere, a Norwegian chronicler had written that 'they little exceed pygmies in stature; they did marvels in the morning and in the evening building walled towns, but at midday they entirely lost all their strength and lurked through fear in little underground houses'. Now their sudden disappearance licensed much nonsensical speculation in the centuries that followed.

After the Dalriadic conquest, and up to modern times, it was widely believed that the Picts had been massacred by Cinead in an act of systematic genocide. This is certainly untrue. Instead, it was probably a case of what German scholars of the early mediaeval period like to call '*fiktive Ausrottung*' – fictional extermination.

Conquering kings in that period led clan societies based on bonds of family or adoption rather than on anything like a state structure. They preferred to rule apparently homogeneous populations which could be represented as extensions of their own lineage. If that sort of 'adoption' could not be managed, then the conquered society could be at least induced to vanish behind a myth of extermination. In return for physical survival, a population might consent to abandon its language and cultural identity and – silently – to be complicit in a fable of its own death by the sword.

Something of this kind was accepted by Romanized Gauls, after the Frankish conquest. Something less explicit but even more complete was accepted by the post-Roman British who came under Anglo-Saxon domination. But none of these sudden mass disappearances, staged under the terms of a variety of bargains, was more than an illusion. The Picts – learning to speak first Gaelic and then the Anglian dialect which became Scots, adapting themselves to new laws and ceremonies brought from Dalriada – are still in some sense hiding in the population of Scotland.

4

[Dunadd] rises less than two hundred feet from the swamp, the first enclosed fields at its feet, but in its setting it crouches like a great lion. A causeway leads to it through the winter-sodden fields, a pot-holed farm track down which have gone the feet of spear-men, riding-ponies, pack-horses and royal chariots, for it was once the high road to a capital.

Marion Campbell, *Argyll: The Enduring Heartland*

The last time I climbed Dunadd was in September, at the end of that summer of hospitals and funerals. The first time I climbed it, I was a small boy in a zip-up jerkin and grey woollen stockings, racing ahead of my mother to reach the top first. From her grave, you can see the hill of Dunadd in the distance, sometimes black against the green of the Moss, sometimes grey in a grey landscape behind veils of rain.

This September day changed every few minutes from darkness to brightness, as blue holes opened in clouds racing in from the south-west. The River Add was brimming after recent rains. The party climbing out of the minibus at the foot of the hill looked at the sky and buttoned up coats against the wind.

Dalriada had come to meet Dalriada. The night before there had been a gathering which was partly a scholarly debate and partly a ceilidh, to celebrate a visit from Northern Ireland. Over there in north-eastern County Antrim, where the sick citizens of Ballycastle are cared for in the Dalriada Hospital, they have begun to talk about the links which once connected them to Argyll and to plan ways to renew them. On this side, after a long alienation made longer by the thirty-year Troubles which began in 1969, the same interest has awakened. The Mid-Argyll Gaelic Partnership had organized the meeting at Ardrishaig on Loch Fyne to mark the 1,500th anniversary – as it could roughly be, assuming it ever happened – of the arrival of Fergus mor mac Erc and his kin from Ireland.

We began to climb. There were two Northern Ireland archaeologists, from Belfast and Coleraine. There was a councillor from Moyle in County Antrim; a giant with silver hair *en brosse*, he was magnificent in an Irish plaid and kilt as he handed out brochures for the new yacht marina at Ballycastle. An equally huge figure in a blue cloak, cassock and neck-torque introduced himself as 'Merlin' from Glastonbury, but we were invited to call him George. A young woman from Edinburgh, a

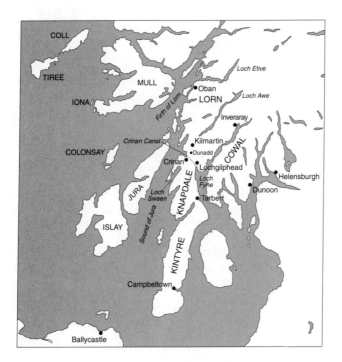

ARGYLL

producer of 'world music', turned out to be the sister of a
Kintyre clan chieftain. A steady, quiet lady with fair hair was
one of the senior figures in Historic Scotland, the agency which
now owns and rules the upper slopes of Dunadd. A blind lady
with a sweet smile was helped up the steep path by a woman
companion, who talked to her in Gaelic. And there was our
guide and leader, the Glasgow archaeologist Ewan Campbell.

Nobody knows the place better. Ewan Campbell led the
1980–81 excavations here. He and his team were allowed by
Historic Scotland to open up only a fraction of the site. But
what they found transformed knowledge of what had happened
on the hill. They revealed a seventh-century metalworking
industry, which had produced magnificent high-status brooches
of gold, silver and copper. Imported pottery and beads provided
evidence of widespread maritime trade links reaching as far as
the Mediterranean. And a single crumb of orpiment – a brilliant
yellow mineral from the Mediterranean basin used for pigment –
suggested the presence on or near Dunadd of a *scriptorium*
where manuscripts were written and illuminated. Campbell
dug into the fallen ramparts, and was able to provide some
dating for the concentric drystone walls which ring Dunadd.
Even better, he used his own imagination to reconstruct how
the fortress must once have looked, and how those who entered
it may have been moved and awed by what they saw. Campbell
often stood brooding at the windy place with the basin, boar
and footprint, and interrogated the landscape below. How
might the standing stones and burial cairns dotting the plain,
the weird race-track outline of a Neolithic cursus to the north-
east, the jagged horizon of hills, have inspired an early medieval
prince with his shoe in the footprint?

Dunadd is the passion of this wiry, emotional man. Campbell
belongs to the line of scholars, scientists and dreamers who
have been reinventing Dalriada for a century and a half. The
process is still going on, as ebullient fantasy and merciless academic deconstruction fight it out. It is hard to realize that by

the nineteenth century, Dalriada had almost been forgotten. So had the significance of Dunadd, diminished to a crag with some ruined fortifications and curious scratchings which stood on the estates of the Malcolms of Poltalloch.

The last reference to Dunadd in early medieval times comes in the *Annals of Ulster*, dated to 736. Its political importance fell away in the ninth century, when the Dalriadic kingdom transferred itself to Scone. But there are hints that something of the hill's magic as a seat of power lingered on for much longer. In 1436, a document records that one John MacLachlan of Dunadd was appointed 'seneschall and *thoissachdowra*', a mystifying title which seems to mean the post of hereditary custodian over a sacred site. And in 1506 a meeting was called at Dunadd to compose the feuds of the Hebrides. The Earl of Argyll issued a proclamation dated from Dunadd, and a few days later there was a 'summit conference' there with the Bishop of Argyll, the Bishop of the Isles, the Earl of Argyll and royal officials appointed by King James IV. As late as the sixteenth century, it seems, Dunadd was still an appropriate place to discuss matters affecting landward Argyll and its relationship with the isles – the ancient extent of Dalriada. After that, silence falls.

It was not until 1850 that the pioneer of Celtic studies in Scotland, William Skene, gave a famous lecture at Poltalloch in which he declared that Dunadd had been the acropolis-fort of the Dalriada kingdom, and the first capital of Scotland. Historians and journalists took Skene on trust, and the old tale of the migration of the Scots from Ulster was written back into Scotland's past. Dunadd was surveyed, and more carvings were discovered as the turf on the summit was peeled back. Local antiquaries invented an age-old tradition that Ossian had lived at Dunadd and stamped his footprint on it. (This tradition was news to most Mid-Argyll people. As Gaelic speakers, they still shared the ancient myth culture of Ireland; many could recite tales and poems from the *Fenian Cycle*, the deeds of the band of

heroes led by the warrior Finn Mac Cumhal which included the
bard Oisin or 'Ossian'. But they first learned about Oisin's visit to
Dunadd in the pages of a Victorian tourist guide to Ardrishaig.)

In 1904, David Christison carried out the first excavation,
destroying almost as much evidence as he found in a pick-and-
shovel campaign which dug under old walls and heaved over
the earth in search of 'finds'. A violent, creative row followed.
Lord John Abercromby, Secretary of the Society of Antiquaries
of Scotland, had paid for Christison's operations out of his own
pocket. But he was so disgusted by Christison's methods, especially by his failure to record the position or strata levels of his
finds, that he resigned from the Secretaryship, cut off Dunadd's
funding and instead used his money to endow the Abercromby
Chair of Archaeology at Edinburgh University – still the senior
academic post in Scottish archaeology.

The next investigation was in the wet summer of 1929.
W. F. Craw was a seasoned archaeologist, but a pessimist. He
assumed that the areas he dug into had been so churned up by
Christison twenty-five years before that the soil was just back-
fill and the objects in it a random scatter. Accordingly he did
not bother to record where he found things. Unfortunately
Craw was wrong, and he had been turning over undisturbed
layers without knowing it. As the book *Dunadd* by Alan Lane
and Ewan Campbell gloomily records, 'Craw did not label any
of the finds and therefore paradoxically we know even less
about the provenance of the 1929 finds than those from
1904/5.'

It was left to Ewan Campbell and his team to do a profes-
sional job. But Historic Scotland, now the owners, were
grudging. As a 'cultural resource manager', the agency has a
bias in favour of preserving everything at the expense of 'intru-
sive' research. The rationale is that as much as possible must be
kept intact for a future in which archaeology, using technologies of a delicacy beyond our imagination, will be able to
extract every molecule of information from a site while scarcely

cutting a turf. Archaeologists, who think they know institutional possessiveness and inertia when they see it, do not take that entirely seriously.

Campbell was allowed only the narrow remit of investigating the remains of the fortifications and if possible dating them. But he achieved far more. The finds allowed him to declare that 'Dunadd was a major high status residence in the seventh century engaged in manufacture and long distance trade with surplus wealth expended on exotic luxuries and elaborately decorated personal jewellery'. And he also established that there were rich, undisturbed layers of deposit from human habitation and production to be investigated. But, twenty years on, he is still waiting for permission to dig again.

We halted on the terrace just below the summit. Ewan Campbell wanted to show us that Dunadd had been designed not just as a fortress and royal place, but as a theatre of power. Visitors would have reached the terrace through a tall, narrow gateway formed of a natural cleft in the rock and built higher on each side by drystone walls. From there, looking upwards, they could have seen a group of human figures above them outlined against the sky, standing by the basin, the footprints and the wild boar.

Nobody knows the ritual by which a king of Dalriada was inaugurated. But there are hints from other rituals in ancient Ireland. A priest or abbot, perhaps from Columba's great monastery on the isle of Iona, might have used water from the basin to anoint or to bless. The new king would have placed his foot in the footprint, making his bond with the living rock and earth of the land he ruled – as later kings of Scotland made their symbolic allegiance to the land when they were lifted onto the Stone of Destiny. Below, shielding their eyes, the warlords and priests of Dalriada watched the figures above them move against the clouds.

With his foot set in the mark, the new king looked north

and – if the day was clear – might see snow glittering on the double peak of Cruachan, the holy mountain marking the furthest limit of the land of Lorn. Looking over his shoulder, he could see two more peaks, the Paps of Jura, rising from an island in the territory of his kinsmen of the Cinel Angus.

It is strange that these Argyll footprints, real and imagined, all seem to be striding northwards. A few miles away from Dunadd, on the rocks on either shore of Loch Crinan, there are 'footmarks' which are the elongated traces of bursting lava bubbles formed as the planet began to cool. They are known as 'Pharaoh's Daughter's Footprints'. This recalls several strands of those Scottish origin myths which tell that Gadelus travelled to Egypt from Scythia and married Pharaoh's daughter Scota. They sailed on to Spain, Scota bringing with her the Stone which had been Jacob's pillow in the Egyptian desert, and from Spain northwards again to Ireland, whence his descendants were to make the final move to Scotland. The 'feet' of the lava bubbles also head north.

Perhaps there is a resonance with the much-loved legend of St Columba's voyage into exile, which is also about facing north – or at least turning one's back on the south. A noble of the Ui Neill line (and thus a kinsman of Fergus mor), he was commanded to atone for his sins by leaving Irish Dalriada for ever and serving God as a missionary and monk beyond the sea. He was ordered to sail northwards up the Argyll coast until he found a place from which he could no longer look back and see his homeland. There is another stone footprint at Southend, at the tip of the Mull of Kintyre, where Columba is supposed to have made his first landing. But this was only a few miles from the cliffs of Antrim across the water. His next landfall is said to have been at St Columba's Cave, near Ellary on the Sound of Jura: a dripping cavern hidden in a wood of scrub oak at the head of the shore. But from the hill above, he could still see Ireland. The stories tell of more vain landings until in the end, in the year 563, he reached the low-lying isle of Iona. Columba and his companions climbed to the top of Dun I, the island's little hill, and looked back. Now the horizon was empty. They raised a cairn of stones and gave it a Gaelic name meaning 'The Back Turned towards Ireland'.

On the top of Dunadd, our group broke up and we wandered about. There was time to talk a little with the two Irish archaeologists, and it was clear that their approach to such places was not the same as Ewan Campbell's. On the Scottish side, the word for the kingdom is pronounced 'Dalreeada', with the stress on the second syllable. These Antrim men called it 'Dalri-*adda*'. The Irish pair had an instinct to understand rich early medieval sites as at least partly religious, looking for connections to monasteries and abbots. Campbell thinks in terms of kings and traders, of secular power and its symbols. And then there was the matter of Dalriada itself, and they disagreed on that, too.

Ewan Campbell is a dramatic revisionist. For some ten years, he has been insisting that the sixth-century migration of Scots from Ireland never happened. To see how shocking this has been, you only have to read the version sanctified in Scottish school textbooks ever since the time of William Skene.

The Story of Scotland for Junior Classes, by H. W. Meikle and published in 1936, begins:

> Long, long ago, so the old, old stories tell, there came sailing to the Green Isle a king, a queen and a great host of warriors. The queen was called Scota, and so dearly did the king love her that he and his fighting men called themselves 'Scots' . . . When they stood on the northern shores of Ierne [Ireland] they saw across the waters a new land lying dim beneath the clouds . . . So some of the warriors passed over the sea to that new country. There they fought many battles with the men of north Britain, and beat them. Therefore these Scots dwelt there, they and their children.

The enormously popular *Scotland's Story*, written for Edwardian children by H. E. Marshall in 1907 and republished often over the next half-century, has Scota in Egypt marrying Gathelus, son of a Greek king, and following the same route through Spain to 'Hibernia'. (On Ireland, Marshall lets Caledonian prejudices show and makes the civilized Scots teach the ignorant natives 'to sow and plough and reap, how to build houses, how to spin . . .') But then a prince sails north-wards and seizes the islands nearest to 'Hibernia', and soon 'the Scots . . . sailed over from Hibernia in greater and greater numbers, bringing their wives and children with them'.

The reluctance of these earlier children's writers to use the awful word 'Ireland' is striking. Later schoolbooks use the right name for the place, but are much less effusive about the whole episode. J. I. W. Murray's *Scotland through the Ages: to 1603* merely states that 'in the beginning of the sixth century a people called the Scots, from Ireland, had settled in what is now Argyllshire and the islands around it'. I. M. M. MacPhail's 1954 *History of Scotland for Schools* says that 'it was towards the end of the fifth century that groups of Scottish invaders came across the sea from Ireland . . . the new immigrants were followed by others from Ireland'.

To overturn this sturdy tale takes determination. Campbell's argument has two prongs. The first is that the historical evidence for a mass migration comes mainly from later interpolations into older manuscripts; the earliest chronicle texts do not record it. Secondly, the archaeological evidence not only shows no trace of such an invasion but – if anything – suggests that cultural change flowed in the opposite direction, from Argyll to Ireland. Scottish Dalriada may have arisen from internal change, perhaps from a small warrior group which crossed from Antrim to Argyll in the sixth century. But that change took place within a single Gaelic-speaking, sea-going society which had already inhabited Argyll and northern Ireland for centuries, quite possibly for millennia.

The Irish archaeologists at the Ardrishaig conference disagreed. Colm Donnelly, whose roots are in the Glens of Antrim facing Scotland, challenged Ewan Campbell with complex data about the distribution of ogham inscriptions, the dating of crannogs (artificial islands in lochs) and the building of raths (ring-shaped enclosures with turf ramparts). For Donnelly, the latest work tended to confirm the older version of events: a culture-flow from Ireland into Scotland. He added, accurately: 'Archaeologists these days don't like migrations. Yet many historical migrations did happen!'

Disputes like this do not go on in a vacuum. The Dalriada revival has a social and political context on both sides of the water. On the Irish side, it is one of the incredibly rare ideas which have both Protestant Unionist and Catholic Nationalist support. For the Presbyterian establishment in County Antrim, it brings Northern Ireland back into contact with the roots of the Ulster Plantations, the colonizing of Ulster in the sixteenth and seventeenth centuries by Scottish Protestant settlers. At a more practical level, the reopening of the ferry connection between Campbeltown in Argyll and Ballycastle offers a way out of economic isolation and a new source of tourist revenue. For Catholics, on the other hand, the revival celebrates a time when Irish Christianity united Scotland and Ireland in a single culture from Iona to Clonmacnoise. And it powerfully promotes the learning of the Gaelic/Irish language, once spoken throughout Dalriada and now defiantly taught as part of the cultural tradition of Catholic nationalism in Northern Ireland. In other words, the two tribes of Ulster both rejoice over Dalriada, but on grounds which are mutually exclusive.

In Scotland, the new attraction of Dalriada is a fluid mixture of motives. Ewan Campbell, speaking at Ardrishaig, kept up his migration denial and twitted the Irish – of all people, given their past – for wishing to have been a colonial power. But he spoke of the 'artistic and cultural explosion' which his work at Dunadd had revealed, and suggested that 'this kind of cultural explosion could happen again; I hope that this is one of the things that the Argyll Gaelic Partnership is trying to bring about'.

The Partnership is only one of many groups in Gaelic-speaking Scotland, especially in the Hebrides, which have turned back towards Ireland after centuries in which harsh Presbyterian prejudice kept the two nations apart. Their campaign to save the language and the music now brings a procession of visiting Irish bands and singers to the isles. There is an annual contest between Argyll shinty players and Irish hurley players. And since the 1970s there have been successful efforts to copy and introduce the West of Ireland model of 'community cooperatives', designed to restore life to remote and declining townships.

A few years ago, the President of the Irish Republic – then Mary Robinson – made an enthusiastic pilgrimage around the isles, including the Columban sites of Iona. Conservative Protestants in Edinburgh and Glasgow scowled and suggested she was up to no good, but the people of the isles were touched. When had a President or indeed a monarch last journeyed to see them – as opposed to their scenery?

Fascination with Dalriada in the rest of Scotland, south and east of the Highland Line, is less practical. Plainly, it is one aspect of the general cultural slither backwards in time, away from 'school history' and towards names and peoples magnified by distance and sheer obscurity. But, seen in another light, this is also a singular and maverick turn in Scottish opinion. Here is a real freak in the annals of European nationalism: a celebration of ethnic disunity.

For nearly two hundred years, the patriotic writers of the world have devised evolutionary, 'progressive' histories. The primal ethnic soup steadily coagulates. The polyglot debris left by successive 'waves of invaders' melts, blends and solidifies, age by age, until the nation passes through the oven heat of the industrial revolution and attains its destiny as a single substance, '*unie et indivisible*'. And in fact this is how Scottish history was written and taught until quite recently (to the very limited extent that it was taught at all).

It is true that, according to this biscuit-factory line of history, Scotland had to pass through two 'oven' stages rather than one. Scotland (in this view) achieved a primary, internal unity by the end of the Middle Ages, as it emerged from the furnace of the independence wars against England. But this was only the necessary condition to fulfil an even higher destiny, a second fusion, as Scotland entered the 1707 Union with England and the two kingdoms melted into one in the heat of industrialization and empire-building.

That interpretation could hold as long as Great Britain remained convincingly great – and as long as the historical evidence was not looked at closely. Now those conditions have ceased, and the idea that Scottish society in any sense 'fused' with England has been rapidly unpicked by historians in the last few years. So has the 'first fusion' theory, the notion that Scotland itself had some kind of primary unity. Again, historians in the last ten years have emphasized that a state-structure known as the Kingdom of Scotland existed long before anyone alluded to a 'Scottish people'. The old need to show Scotland evolving 'naturally' from tribal diversity into a single respectably united nation seems to have withered away. Instead, at the moment when a devolved Scottish government has taken conscious charge of its own culture, the current of opinion has reversed.

Regionalism is in fashion. Twenty-five years ago, the assertion of distinct, unruly identities in Orkney and Shetland, in the Gaeltacht of the West and in north-eastern Scotland, seemed a threat to Scotland's revival. These days, it is welcomed. One reason may be a sort of relief. Back in the 1970s, during the first, unsuccessful surge towards self-government, there were cultural pessimists who warned that 'Scotland' might have quietly rotted away as a credible polity during the three centuries of the Union. All that remained, they went on, was a handful of disparate provinces held together by strings radiating from London, and when the strings were cut they would simply fall apart. But the pessimists were wrong, about the past as well as the future. The notion of state authority in Scotland had been conserved by the survival of the Scottish legal system, by landed gentry acting as 'managers' for London Cabinets and – after 1885 – by government through the Scottish Office in Edinburgh. In 1999, the revived Scottish Parliament took over authority for most domestic affairs. All went smoothly; no province seceded; Scotland survived.

Scotland entered the twenty-first century reassured that regional diversity was no threat. But what about ethnic diversity? This small European nation, now retrieving the power to govern itself, had a grim and persisting record of religious intolerance and discrimination. Scots who had campaigned for self-government – a relatively tiny group of politicians, intellectuals and community leaders – were well aware of this history. They faced the possibility that this intolerance might be extended to the waves of immigrants, principally Asian and English, who had settled in Scotland during the last decades of the twentieth century. In celebrating the rich ethnic salad of Scotland's origins, they were also making a statement of hope that old sectarianism and new racialism would fail to take root in the future.

The worst problem these optimists faced was Scotland's refusal to acknowledge past realities. There was a dogged public assumption that racial prejudice was an English problem to which the Scots – for reasons of social history, for reasons of superior native intelligence – were immune. Historically, Scots are accustomed to think of themselves as a donor nation in migration terms. Since the sixteenth century, population had flowed out of the country at a sometimes terrifying rate: first to Poland and the Baltic countries and then, after the Union and above all in the nineteenth and early twentieth centuries, to Canada, New Zealand, Australia, South Africa, the United

States and across the border into England. Emigration, at first represented as a token of Scottish energy and enterprise, became part of the national victimology as political consciousness revived and the British Empire declined. The Highland Clearances, sometimes a matter of voluntary emigration but often the result of brutal dispossession by landlords, had always been remembered as a tragedy, but in the twentieth century they came to be regarded by many Scots as a major crime against humanity. In the 1960s, when the net annual population loss was equivalent to the inhabitants of a medium-sized town, the Scottish Office considered its main purpose to be staunching the outflow and creating job opportunities which would keep young Scottish families in Scotland.

This emigrant tradition meant that until recently most Scots had almost no experience of 'inward' settlement: the arrival and presence of strangers. Where it had taken place – the settlement of Lithuanian miners in the Lanarkshire coalfields between the 1870s and 1914, the coming of the Italian families who transformed small-town life in Scotland by opening ice-cream cafés and fish-and-chip shops, the spectacular sojourn of a Polish army in eastern and southern Scotland during the Second World War – a comfortable hindsight recalled that these had been reasonably happy encounters between tolerant hosts and grateful guests.

But this was a prettified version of history. The Lithuanians had at first run into a wall of hatred from the Scottish working class who perceived them, not entirely without reason, as cheap foreign labour brought in to collapse miners' wages. The Italian community was utterly unprepared for the ferocious anti-Italian riots which flamed through Scottish towns and cities in June 1940, when Fascist Italy joined the war on Hitler's side. But the central flaw in this self-congratulatory myth, the grand denial of the blatantly obvious, was the matter of the Irish.

Irish immigration into Scotland, the flight from hunger and hopelessness towards the booming industrial cities of Scotland, reached its peak after the Great Famine of the 1840s. By 1851, there were some 250,000 Irish-born immigrants in Scotland: 7.2 per cent of the population, compared to only 2.9 per cent in England and Wales. Most settled in Scotland, bringing up Scottish-born families, but the rate of new immigration kept up at the same rate until the eve of the First World War. Today some 14 per cent of Scots describe themselves as Roman Catholic, as against 10 per cent in England and Wales, and the great majority of them are the descendants of Irish immigrants.

In his latest book *The Scottish Nation: 1700–2000*, the historian Tom Devine, who has done more research into this immigration and its impact than anyone else in Scotland, makes two points which few Scots care to admit. The first is that most of the immigrants came from Ulster, the Irish province where the devastation of the Famine was not as extreme as in the south and west. The picture of ragged, starving hordes heading for Glasgow is largely myth; the most desperate survivors from southern Ireland to reach Britain mostly went to England through the port of Liverpool. Devine's second forgotten fact is that a very substantial part of the immigration into Scotland – between a quarter and a fifth – was not Catholic but Ulster Protestant. He writes, 'The regional origin of the migrant streams was deeply significant because it meant that the tribal hatreds of Ulster were transferred to the industrial districts of Scotland, and faction fighting between Orange and Green sympathizers became a routine feature of life in several communities in Lanarkshire and Ayrshire in the nineteenth century.'

In other words, one source of the enduring anti-Catholic prejudice in Scotland is an import from Ulster, not a native product. But Orangeism easily made common cause with the fanatically anti-Papist tradition of Scottish Calvinism; Protestant Ulster, after all, was created by the descendants of those Presbyterian Scots who had been encouraged to dispossess the native Catholic Irish and settle there in the seventeenth century. As generations passed, institutionalized job discrimination and verbal or written abuse became the normal experience of the Irish Catholic community, above all in Glasgow and the industrial West of Scotland. In turn, the community withdrew into its own world of Catholic parish care, Catholic football teams and Catholic schooling (which survives as a distinct institution within the state-funded educational system). A century ago, when the Protestant working class was still accustomed to voting for the Liberals as the party of the Reformation, the new-born Labour Party put down its roots in the excluded Catholic masses of the Glasgow conurbation. That alliance, though much eroded, is still a huge factor in West of Scotland politics.

Race prejudice and sectarian prejudice are the same beast. As in Northern Ireland, there has always been a physical, visceral aspect to religious distinctions in Scotland, and a day arrived when this truth came home to my own viscera.

Educated in southern England, I had always thought myself remote from those 'Danny and Billy', Green-and-Orange vendettas at home. But one day in London I found myself talking to a Scottish friend about the dire skin diseases which Clydeside children endured when we were both young. My four-year-old sister, I remarked, had picked up impetigo when we were living in Greenock. How was that, asked my friend. 'Oh, she got it swinging on the rails of the Catholic school; she'd been told not to.'

He looked at me, and then he burst out laughing. It took me a second to register just what I had said. Here I was, a much-travelled journalist with left-wing opinions and a Cambridge history degree. And, nevertheless, for almost all my life I had never questioned that if you touched a railing used by small boys of a particular religion you would probably acquire a disfiguring disease. Now I saw what disease I carried myself, not a skin bacillus but a tiny virus hibernating in the marrow.

In the 1920s, the virus infected the Church of Scotland. The

Kirk had always been grimly anti-Catholic, but the new epidemic was frankly racialist. In 1922, the Church and Nation Committee of the General Assembly accepted a disgraceful report entitled *The Menace of the Irish Race to Our Scottish Nationality*, which (in Tom Devine's words) 'accused the Irish Roman Catholic population of taking employment from native Scots, of being part of a papist conspiracy to subvert Presbyterian values, and the main source of intemperance, improvidence, criminality and much else besides'. The report called for mass deportations. There followed a turbulent period in which extremist Protestant organizations attacked Catholics, led anti-Irish riots and formed political parties which fought municipal elections in Glasgow and Edinburgh with considerable success.

After the Second World War, the Kirk decided to drop this semi-Fascist episode down the memory hole, from which it was disinterred a few years ago by journalists and a shocked younger generation of Church of Scotland ministers. And it is true that the situation of the Irish Catholic community has improved radically since then. Its integration into mainstream Scottish life has moved steadily ahead. The collapse of traditional Scottish heavy industry and mining, especially under the Thatcher government in the 1980s, disbanded the enormous work forces in which job discrimination by religion had become institutionalized. In 1982, Pope John Paul II visited Scotland, kissed Scottish soil (or tarmac) as he arrived and encouraged Catholics to take a full part in the revival of the nation.

But mutual suspicion, occasional violence and petty discrimination still haunt the land. As recently as 1987, a journalist friend of mine who was not called Teresa Lynch but something with the same ethnic resonance went for a job interview with one of Scotland's biggest daily papers. The managing editor, who knew her work well, was genuinely embarrassed. 'Ach, Teresa, what are you thinking of? It's not just that you're a woman – look at your name!'

Every few years, somebody in Scotland announces that sectarian bigotry is dead at last. And every few years, revolting incidents surface to demonstrate that the old monster is still alive. In the summer of 1999, just as the first Scottish parliament for three hundred years was starting work, the monster grunted again. Donald Findlay, a prominent lawyer who was Rector of the University of St Andrews and vice-chairman of Rangers Football Club, was taped singing the bloodthirsty Orange anthem 'The Sash' at a private party and the tape reached a newspaper. The same night, by impure coincidence, a Celtic fan coming away from an Old Firm football game had his throat cut by Rangers supporters, while another was shot through the chest with a crossbow bolt.

Findlay and his friends were amazed at the uproar. Catholics were oversensitive, they said. Bigotry had long ago faded out of the scene, they said, as anything worse than a light-hearted allusion. If Findlay had been bellowing out those lines about wading through Fenian blood, then he was merely observing a harmless cultural tradition.

The row expanded. James MacMillan, Scotland's most famous young composer and himself a Catholic, gave a devastating speech at the Edinburgh Festival that August about 'Scotland's Shame': not just 'the palpable sense of some threat and hostility to all things Catholic in this country', but the bone-headed denial that the hostility existed or, if it did exist, that it mattered. The public wrangle that followed was so muddled and inflamed that it would be hard to call it a debate. But some voices raised a wider, more ominous point. For the first time since the coming of the Irish, fresh waves of immigration were entering Scotland to settle. How would the new Scotland, with this deep flaw of ethnic intolerance inherited from the past, behave to the newcomers? How could a humane society emerge as long as this entrenched complacency insisted that 'there was no racialism in Scotland'?

The future does not look promising. In contrast to English

cities, Scotland has received almost no Afro-Caribbean settlement. The takeover of small foodshops and newsagents by Asian families, mostly Moslems from Pakistan or Bangladesh, took place many years ago in England but is still fairly recent in Scotland. Racist attacks on Asian immigrants became more common in the last years of the century, and in 2001 tensions in Glasgow broke into open crisis.

In the previous year, thousands of asylum-seekers from the Balkans, Kurdistan, Afghanistan and other zones of conflict (decanted northwards by the Home Office in order to get them out of London) were resettled in Glasgow. Beatings and intimidation began. In the summer of 2001, violence broke out in the inner-city tower blocks of Sighthill; a young Kurd was murdered and others were attacked by gangs of local youths. There were turbulent protest demonstrations and counter-demonstrations, and the tabloid *Daily Record* took the opportunity to accuse the dead man, on shaky evidence, of faking his request for asylum. The great and good flocked to Sighthill, whose deprived 'natives' complained that their own poverty had been ignored for years. Although the wave of full-scale race riots which hit the cities of northern England that summer did not reach Scotland, Sighthill put an end to Scottish complacency over race and immigration.

Harder to assess is the new phenomenon of English immigration into Scotland. Much of it originates in the 1980s, when very different groups began to seek an escape northwards from the social turmoil of Thatcherism. Redundant industrial workers used their severance money to buy houses or small businesses in Scotland. Younger idealists, especially from the northern cities of England, sought refuge in the Highlands and Islands to become 'neo-peasant' crofters in places they supposed to be beyond the reach of market forces. Social workers who had lost their jobs in the purge of local-authority services migrated up in search of work (the 'caring professions' in

Scotland remain heavily anglicized). The new cultural bureaucracy which was formed to manage Scotland's arts was largely
recruited in the south, as funding cuts blocked career prospects
in the galleries, museums, theatres or orchestras of London
and the Home Counties.

Are the English unwelcome? There is certainly growing
resentment, especially where the use of money to buy land or
rural houses is concerned. There have been a very few acts of
violence, none of which can be exclusively traced to the
Englishness of the victim, and a few allegations of discrimination against English job applicants. But on this matter people
keep their ill-feelings private, accessible to family and friends
but not to strangers. Scotland likes to think of itself as a polite
and hospitable country, and the English have been the first
people to praise those qualities. Except at football matches,
openly anti-English behaviour is held to be very bad behaviour.
And Anglophobia, to self-critical Scots, implies something
unflattering about Scotland. As a character famously says in
the film of Irvine Welsh's *Trainspotting*: 'It's shite being
Scottish. Some people hate the English; I don't. They're just
wankers, but we were colonized by wankers. We couldn't even
find a decent country to be colonized by.'

The popular English assumption is that Scottish nationalism
is about hating England. Fortunately this is quite untrue, a
judgement which reveals a lot about English self-centredness
but nothing else. The Scots are self-centred too; they are concerned with Scotland, and the absence of England from most
conversations about their country's future can seem uncanny.
None the less, there is a gnawing anxiety in Scotland about the
prospects for ethnic tolerance in a country which has already
found such difficulty in accepting a multicultural society. This
is why it has become important to excavate Picts and Gaels,
Anglians and Norsemen, and to argue that Scottish identity
has never been simple or single.

*

In December 1992, Edinburgh was host to the summit meeting of the European Community. Earlier that year, the Conservatives – against most predictions – had won their fourth general election in a row. John Major, as prime minister, had made clear yet again that devolution and a Scottish parliament were out of the question. But he was aware of the desperate resentment and impatience building up in Scotland, which had been voting impotently but with ever-increasing majorities for Labour since 1979. Perhaps, he thought, the Scots needed a bit of attention. When Britain's turn came to occupy the European presidency, he decided that Scotland should get the summit. Then the Scots would feel wanted, and might calm down.

What happened was quite different. Those few December days became the most important moment in the history of Edinburgh since the visit of King George IV in 1822. Europe had come to Scotland. The city felt like a capital again, and returned to life. It was as if Scotland, even if only for a moment, had been given the chance to take an equal place among nations, to push past London and speak directly to the supreme authority of Europe.

The town jostled with delegations, meetings to pass resolutions for the heads of government, petitions for the Commission. Scottish fishermen tried to reach the summit with 'Save Our Fishing Industry' banners. Old men in kilts and Glengarries marched behind pipe-bands through Princes Street Gardens: 'Save the Scottish Regiments!' The prime ministers and presidents were invited to a score of hastily arranged rallies and theatre performances and concerts of traditional Scottish music (they stayed in their security zone, and went to none of them). In the Meadowbank stadium where the international media gabbled into its mobiles and gulped down lovingly prepared dishes of salmon, scallops or Rannoch venison, every desk was loaded with appeals translated into French, German and Spanish. Welcome to a European nation where the will of the people is ignored at every election!

Welcome to a country with its own laws but no parliament to change them!

On the last day, there was a demonstration, a march 'for Scottish Democracy'. As a member of 'Common Cause', one of the organizing groups, I had not expected a big turnout in chilly December weather. Twenty years in the ranks of the devolution campaign had taught me that Scots would rather vote for constitutional change than walk for it. But as soon as I joined the marchers tramping up the Mound with their banners, I saw that something had given way. The procession was immense. Some 30,000 people, touched by the sense that Scotland was under the eyes of Europe, made their way to the Meadows and asked for their country back.

Out of many speeches, I remember only one, and snatches of it are still quoted by many others who remember. The novelist William McIlvanney is the one writer whose face is recognized in any Scottish street. He is a witty, elegant West of Scotland man, a working-class teacher and orator whose Kilmarnock ancestors came from Catholic Ireland. McIlvanney looked out over the faces stretching away towards Salisbury Craigs in the distance and he said: 'Let's not be mealy-mouthed about all this. The Scottish parliament starts here, today!'

When the clapping died down, he went on: 'We gather here like refugees in the capital of our own country. We are almost seven hundred years old, and we are still wondering what we want to be when we grow up. Scotland is in an intolerable position. We must never acclimatize to it – never!'

And then, in a tone of tremendous pride, he said this. 'Scottishness is not some pedigree lineage. This is a mongrel tradition!' At those words, for reasons which perhaps neither he nor they ever quite understood, the crowd broke into cheers and applause which lasted on and on.

After that December mobilization, the game was up. The Tories knew that they were doomed; Labour knew that they must deliver Scottish self-government as soon as they came to power. McIlvanney was right: the parliament had started that day. And yet what survives from those moments on the Meadows are his proclamation of Scotland the mongrel, and the joy those words released.

5

For long after the Union, as we have seen, the English and Scots did not work well together. Most people in Scotland believed that the Union had been a mistake, and that the country would have been more prosperous had it never taken place. In the second half of the eighteenth century, however, Scotland began to make such progress that all but a few persons became convinced that the Union had been a good thing after all. They began to see that England and Scotland were really one country, and that the more prosperous the one grew the better it was for the other, and from this time onwards both Scotsmen and Englishmen realized they were like partners in the same business and had both the same interests.

P. Hume Brown, *A History of Scotland for Schools*, 1907

[We] teach that the 1707 Union was a marriage of convenience. It suited both partners, but for different reasons. That marriage is no longer convenient, in its present form.

Professor David McCrone, addressing 600 Scottish schoolchildren
in the McEwan Hall, Edinburgh, 20 February 1998

Hume Brown was the grand Establishment historian of his day. On the title-page of his book *A History of Scotland for Schools*, after his name and degrees, is entered: 'Fraser Professor of Ancient (Scottish) History and Palaeography, University of Edinburgh; and Historiographer-Royal for Scotland'. His Unionism was solid and unchallenged, anointed with a royal title.

He also wrote, in the concluding words of that confident volume: 'At some future time the Scotland of to-day will no doubt appear as strange to the men then living as the Scotland of the cave-dwellers appears to us.' But after less than a century we are entering that future time, and Hume Brown's Scotland, if not a cave, is a strange, shuttered palace with willowherb and young rowans already growing up round its windows.

The distance between him and Professor McCrone, also of the University of Edinburgh, is one long lifetime. It corresponds closely to the lifetime of my mother. As a tiny girl, she and her sister were taken to see King Edward VII's funeral in London. The gun-carriage was followed by many kings, and Scottish regiments, Highland and Lowland, stood proudly in the ranks of imperial soldiery lining the route. (The nanny had sewn black mourning ribbons into my mother's knickers. My grandmother, irritated, ordered the ribbons to be unpicked again as soon as she noticed them.)

Her holidays were spent at Crinan in Argyll, where the country people spoke Gaelic and where the landscape, from horizon to horizon and then (if you climbed the most distant ridge) to the horizon after that, belonged to the Malcolms of Poltalloch. The evidence of the 'partners in the same business' that was Great Britain was all over the landscape. The churches were decorated with marble plaques commemorating the sons of Campbell lairds who had fought at the British storming of Havana in 1762, in the American War, in the Peninsular War against Napoleon, at Waterloo in 1815 or in the battles of the conquest of India. The great mansion at Poltalloch, completed in 1859 to replace a traditional Scottish tower-house over the hill, was designed in the English Jacobean style and its grounds were stocked with exotic trees and shrubs from every corner of the Empire and beyond.

The Malcolms themselves had risen on the soaring escalator of Britishness and Empire. Like many of the minor chiefs and gentry of Argyll, they had sent sons out to manage and own sugar plantations in Jamaica in the late eighteenth century. From sugar and their share in the £20 million compensation to slave-owners after Abolition in 1833, later from ranching and land development in South Australia and finally from shrewd investment, they amassed enough money to pass the take-off point into serious wealth by about 1850. In the next hundred years, the Malcolms were to be ambassadors, generals, imperial civil servants, politicians and patrons of the arts (the core of the British Museum's collection of Old Master drawings is a Malcolm bequest, and George Malcolm of Poltalloch was one of the founders of the Edinburgh International Festival in 1947). For generations, Argyllshire politics were based on the rivalry between the Dukes of Argyll, traditionally Whig and then Liberal, and the Malcolms who stood in the Tory interest.

In the last years of my mother's life, when she looked out of her door across Crinan Moss, almost the only thing which had not changed in this rural landscape was the familiar outline of the hills. Even that was not entirely stable. The Malcolm estates in Knapdale had been sold to the Forestry Commission long ago; the hills changed colour from the bright green of summer cattle pasture to the dark blue-green of Sitka spruce, and the skyline grew fuzzy with their tips. Gaelic was no longer to be heard, and no more than a handful of the original inhabitants remained. Some of their houses dwindled into heaps of stone half-hidden by bracken and nettles; others became holiday homes so expensive that they were out of the reach of local people who, when they grew old, were resettled in council houses on the outskirts of Lochgilphead or Ardrishaig. Poltalloch, the great house whose magnificence and stately routines had outclassed even Queen Victoria's neo-baronial castle at Balmoral, was a roofless ruin. The Malcolms, superb spenders defeated by the pitiless economic climate of the twentieth century, had sold all their land except for the fields immediately around them and had retreated into the old castle at Duntrune on the shore of Loch Crinan.

Mellow nostalgia and the sigh for what has gone are all too
easy in Scotland, a refusal to engage with Scotland's modern
history. That Mid-Argyll society which seemed in my mother's
childhood so steady and timeless was in fact a broken remnant.
It was the debris of a much older Highland culture, collapsed
by a century of famine, mass emigration and clearance – and by
planned 'improvement'. The ancient joint-tenancy system, settlements whose people held them in collective tenure, was
brought to an end by landlords who could raise little rent from
them and wanted the land for sheep. The hills were depopu-
lated, as the families from the little upland townships left for
the industrial Lowland cities or were pressed (sometimes
coerced, sometimes offered 'assisted passages') to emigrate to
North America or Australia. Most of the fertile soil was redis-
tributed into efficient farms. The incoming tenants were
seldom local men but more often experienced Lowland farmers and shepherds brought in from Ayrshire or the Borders.

The key to understanding Scottish modern history is to grasp
the sheer force, violence and immensity of social change in the
two centuries after about 1760. No country in Europe, and perhaps no country on earth until the European explosion into
the interior of North America and Australia, underwent a social
and physical mutation so fast and so complete. Tidal waves of
transformation swept over the country, Lowland and Highland,
drowning the way of life of hundreds of thousands of families
and obliterating not only traditional societies but the very
appearance of the landscape itself. Only England underwent
change on a comparable scale. But in England the industrial
and especially the agrarian revolutions – the annihilation of the
peasantry and the flow of population into new industrial cities –
were a more gradual process. The unique feature of the
Scottish experience is its pace.

  In 1600, Scotland had a population of about 1.5 million, of
whom only 3 per cent lived in towns with over 10,000 people –

one of the least urbanized nations in western Europe. By 1850, that figure was 32 per cent, while the population had reached 2.5 million. Only England and Wales, with 40.8 per cent, were more urbanized, but there the increase had been slower from a higher base, a seven-fold multiplication as opposed to Scotland's eleven-fold urban growth. The main leap came in the century between 1750 and 1850, as the speed of industrial expansion sucked in rural population from both the Highlands and the Lowlands until by 1850 over half the inhabitants of the ten largest towns were migrants. Until about 1830, the new machinery was mainly imported from England, and powered factories were almost exclusively producing textiles: cotton, wool and linen. It was not until the early nineteenth century that the Scottish iron and steel industry took off into heavy engineering and shipbuilding and towards a period when Scottish mechanical and scientific innovation became a world legend.

Entirely new urban landscapes appeared. At the time of the American War of Independence, Glasgow had been a prosperous little port-city doing well out of linen exports and tobacco imports. Now it swelled into a blackened megalopolis surrounded by flaring furnaces and shrouded in smoke. As early as 1800, chemical effluent was eating through the copper-sheathed hulls of ships in the Clyde, while the Scottish and Irish migrants cramming themselves into Glasgow's new stone tenements soon endured the most overcrowded and disease-ridden housing in northern Europe.

Other landscapes disappeared. The clan society of the Highlands, based on mutual loyalty, dissolved. As Tom Devine has written in *The Scottish Nation*, 'in less than two generations, Scottish Gaeldom was transformed from tribalism to capitalism'. But Devine's achievement as a historian has been to show that the transformation of the Lowlands was equally complete. A countryside of open, hedgeless fields, with tenant farmers and cottars living in small communities of a dozen or so families known as 'ferm touns' now came abruptly to an end. Between 1760 and 1830, in Devine's words, 'a recognizably modern landscape of trim fields and compact farms, separated by hedges and ditches, had emerged to take the place of the confused mixture of strips, rigs and open fields of the old order'.

The improver landlords swept away the cottars (tenants of small plots of land in return for labour services) and took over the common lands which had provided the communities with peat and rough grazing. As the old field system was broken down and replaced by large modern farms, so the 'ferm touns' and their intimate mix of rural people were abandoned and replaced by tall, stone-built individual farmhouses. Within a generation, the very place-names and locations of the 'touns' were sinking out of memory, as if a new map had been laid over the whole surface of the land.

Robert Burns spent much of his life on new, single-family farms (his father was the tenant of 130 acres near Tarbolton in Ayrshire, and Robert and his brother Gilbert rented 118 acres at Mossgiel in 1783). But he was one of the last people to know the warmth of the older rural world as it faded into extinction. As he rode across the countryside on farm business or in search of songs, Burns delighted in the human mixture of those tiny settlements: small farmers, usually literate and argumentative and sometimes with pretty daughters, the cottars with their stock of oral tradition and the shoemakers or blacksmiths who lived in the same huddle of buildings:

> *I'll aye ca' in by yon toun,*
> *And by yon garden green again,*
> *I'll aye ca' in by yon toun*
> *And see my bonnie Jean again.*

*

Some things, however, did not change, or at least they stayed recognizable. It depended on who you were. Most people in Scotland experienced the arrival of capitalism as the onset of an obliterating, scattering cyclone. By the early twentieth century, the way their grandparents had lived as children had become unimaginably remote, transmitted in family memories of places, customs and types of community which seemed as distant as Galilee in the time of Jesus. But if you were an advocate or a minister, a university lecturer or a banker, it was different.

For the professions and for Scotland's small middle class, the cyclone was no worse than the bracing Edinburgh wind which sent their hats birling away down the Lawnmarket or across the pavements of the New Town. The streets they walked down, the tall stone buildings they worked in, the houses they lived in and often the jobs they performed would have been familiar to their fathers and grandfathers. For this minority, there was a continuity about what they did, and what they thought they were doing.

In 1994, Lindsay Paterson wrote a book which blew away many myths about Scotland's condition during the three centuries of the Union. *The Autonomy of Modern Scotland* absolutely rejected the picture of Scotland as an occupied or colonized country, or even as an informally 'penetrated system' whose strings were pulled from London. The Union had abolished Scotland's formal statehood and removed its parliament. But it had left essentially intact the three structures of Scots law, the established Church of Scotland and the educational system. Paterson pointed out the extent to which the Scottish elite, working through these institutions, had continued to run Scotland according to their own view of the nation's needs with only occasional – and often unsuccessful – interference from England.

This was simple enough in centuries when government was 'small' and London asked little of its subjects beyond loyalty to the Hanoverian dynasty, a supply of recruits in time of war and excise duties on tobacco, wine and spirits. But in the twentieth century government intervention and regulation expanded

rapidly throughout society, culminating after 1945 in the gigantic British bureaucracy of the Welfare State.

As a centralized project aiming to unify living standards
throughout the United Kingdom, the Welfare State seemed
superficially to threaten the grip of those old elites on the management of Scotland. Lindsay Paterson showed that – on the
contrary – the Scottish middle class and the Edinburgh-based
Scottish Office easily met the challenge and emerged as the
controllers of a new 'bureaucratic autonomy'. The Welfare
State in Scotland administered itself and found its own, often
non-English solutions to Scottish problems in health, housing,
schooling and local government. Once again, it was usually able
to beat off objections or unwelcome proposals from Whitehall.
The only real change was that 'bureaucratic autonomy' was
operated by a much less exclusive group. After about 1960, the
post-war boom in free higher education supplied thousands of
working-class graduates as recruits for the new bureaucracy –
and for Scotland's peculiar equivalent of a middle class.

But this 'St Andrew's Fault', the deep discontinuity between
the experiences of the 'hurricane survivor' majority and the
'healthy breeze-blown' minority, is still there, and still gives off
deep subterranean tremors. The wholesale uprooting of
Scottish society within a few years and its forcible replanting in
physically transformed landscapes, in new industrial cities or in
other hemispheres altogether, has left a persistent trauma. If
the nineteenth-century equivalent of what Scotland went
through is the white settlement of interior North America or
Australia, then the twentieth-century parallel is the uprooting
of Russian and Ukrainian society in the thirteen years between
Stalin's first Five-Year Plan and the Nazi invasion of 1941. The
lasting, disabling impact of that period became all too clear
after the collapse of the Soviet Union in 1991, as the Russian
people backed away from capitalist reform with its promise of
yet more upheaval.

The Scottish trauma is to do with self-doubt (sometimes

masked in unreal self-assertion), with sterile speculations about
national identity and – as I guess – with suspicions of 'other-
ness' which so often poison relationships between Scottish
neighbours. But above all, the trauma shows itself in a chronic
mistrust of the public dimension. The invitation to 'participate', especially to offer critical comment in public, touches a
nerve of anxiety. This derives partly from the instinct that to
disagree with another person before witnesses is to open a serious personal confrontation; the English or American
assumption that 'free, open discussion' is non-lethal and even
healthy is not widespread in Scotland. The Presbyterian tradition contributes to this reluctance, with its binary
right-or-wrong approach which leaves little room for compromise or 'agreement to differ'. More fundamental is the notion
that constituted authority is alien and lacks legitimacy, and
therefore that its offer of safe-conduct for critics should be
treated warily. In the small world of my own profession, the
contrast between daily editorial conferences on Scottish and
English newspapers has often been comic: the English meeting
long, argumentative but aiming for consensus; the Scottish one
brief, ritualistic and consisting of little more than the recital of
the day's news and features schedule as the desk chiefs gravely
nod their heads.

Lindsay Paterson observes: 'Scotland is not the only place
where a claim for independence reawakens angst: only the
secure middle class can easily afford to weaken the safety net
which an efficient bureaucracy has seemed to offer.' Here,
exactly, is the contrast between the people of the hurricane
and the people of the breeze. The first group presents an
apparent paradox: individuals often powerfully opinionated,
and with an outspoken sense of equality, who submit every
day of their lives to authoritarian styles of management. The
second group, 'the secure middle class', includes most of those
who have spent thirty years pushing for independence or a
devolved Scottish parliament and inviting the majority to

identify with this project in the name of democracy. The hesi-
tation of the majority to sign up with this cause – or, more
accurately, to sign up with their version of the cause – has
always baffled and distressed the 'breezy' faction, which has
little sense of Scottish discontinuity.

By now, a Scottish Parliament has been at work for several
years, and faces its first re-election in 2003. A strong tide of
public opinion brought it into being between 1997 and 1999;
the Scottish middle class, or governing stratum, or intelligentsia
or whatever one may call it finally succeeded in rallying the
majority into decisive political action. At the same time, the
division has not gone away. The minority is pleased and proud
at much of what the Scottish Parliament has done, while admitting to its severe teething problems. The majority are much
more reserved about what the Parliament may do to change
their lives now and in future. Polling suggests that while they
voted decisively in 1997 for a Scottish Parliament, this may not
be the particular model of parliament that they want. Their
support for it is astonishingly tepid.

The deep geological fault running underneath national self-
confidence is still there, in short, and from time to time it
makes itself felt. When it does, the confident few who lead
political change feel misunderstood and betrayed. In Bertolt
Brecht's words about the leaders of the former East Germany,
they feel tempted to dissolve this people and appoint another
one. I need only cite the agonized cries of Jim Sillars.

Born the son of an Ayrshire railwayman, Sillars has been the
most spectacular and unpredictable politician in post-war
Scotland. Starting as the young star of the Labour Party, his
impatience with doubters led him to found his own socialist
breakaway party in the 1970s, to join the Scottish National
Party as its most powerful orator and then to storm out of a
leadership he accused of feeble gradualism in the struggle for
independence. His vast confidence in Scotland's destiny is only
matched by his amazement that others do not share it. As the

voters 'bottle out', Sillars's rhetoric about the inherently democratic or cooperative bias in the Scottish psyche suddenly gives way to bitter words about 'fearties' (cowards) or 'ninety-minute patriots' (the length of a football game).

The Fault has produced several recent tremors. The teacups rattled in their saucers in the general election of 1992, and some cracks in the plaster could be noticed after the Westminster elections of 2001 which gave Tony Blair his second term as British prime minister. But the last major *temblor* to rise from St Andrew's Fault took place at the Labour government's first attempt to give Scotland self-government, during the devolution referendum of 1979. Many palaces of expectation fell down then, and I was one of those under the rubble.

6

By 1 March 1979, the day of the referendum, I had been the Scottish Politics correspondent of the *Scotsman* for almost four years. This was not my first stint with the paper. I had worked as its Commonwealth correspondent in 1959–60, under the London editor Eric Beattie Mackay, before going off to cover Germany and east-central Europe for the *Observer*. Back then, I had learned to like and respect Eric Mackay for his sheer moral obstinacy.

We came under fire together in 1959, at the time of the 'Nyasaland riots'. Nyasaland (now Malawi) was a British protectorate in Central Africa which had been the focus of Church of Scotland missionary work ever since the time of David Livingstone. Now the British government was attempting to stuff Nyasaland into an ill-conceived 'Central African Federation'. This would have left the overwhelmingly African populations of Nyasaland and Northern Rhodesia (Zambia) under the control of the white-settler minority in Southern Rhodesia. There was much hypocritical prattle about how federation would create a higher inter-racial harmony, transcending mere head-counting democracy. But Africans correctly recognized the blueprints for a second *apartheid* South Africa.

Widespread demonstrations of protest broke out in Nyasaland. The response of the Conservative government was to declare a state of emergency in the protectorate, clamp down a news blackout and brief London journalists about a fictional 'murder plot' by native agitators to assassinate a list of white men and their families. Eric Mackay, well aware of the Kirk's steadfast resistance to federation, decided to ring up the missionaries.

Telephoning Nyasaland in those days was no simple matter, even before the emergency. It took two days and nights for the call to come through, but finally – as the London staff left their desks and crowded round the editor's door to listen – Eric Mackay found himself talking to his old Aberdeen friend the Reverend Andrew Doig. What he said completely debunked the official version of the 'riots' and the murder plot, and day after day Doig and his colleagues at Blantyre or Livingstonia dictated long dispatches about police repression and the united but peaceful rejection of federation by the African population.

With the borders closed, no other paper had such a source. As at the time of the Ice Age story exactly a century before, the *Scotsman* had a world scoop. The government was appalled. Eventually Eric and I were summoned to Whitehall, where Lord Home, the Commonwealth Secretary, roamed up and down a vast, dim room wringing his hands and begging us to abandon this harmful scribbling. 'I appeal to you, as fellow Scots!' he said. I glanced at Eric next to me on the ornamental sofa, his melancholy, handsome features stiff with fury. We left, and carried on publishing our stories. A few years passed before the awful federation project collapsed, but after Nyasaland it was doomed. Those *Scotsman* reports hammered in its first coffin-nail.

Now, in the 1970s, Eric Mackay was the paper's editor in Edinburgh. He sat in his magnificent office in the old *Scotsman* building on North Bridge, his feet crossed on the desk, his fingertips pressed lightly together, his hooded green eyes contemplating private thoughts. Perhaps he was visualizing a Scotland proud and free. Perhaps he was replaying his last wrangle with the management over squeezes in the editorial budget. Maybe he was just wanting his tea. He was not an easy man to read.

Eric never fully disclosed his own political views to us – or at least to me. This was a necessary discretion. The paper's line was discernible: support for the idea of a directly elected Scottish assembly within the United Kingdom, scepticism about the Scottish National Party and its demand for full independence, respect for the middle-class Edinburgh oligarchies (our core readership) as long as their jobbery stayed within the bounds of the law. But the balance was a delicate one. The paper was now owned by Thomson Regional Newspapers, an English-based chain of Conservative outlook. It would not do for the *Scotsman* to give unqualified, enthusiastic support for the devolution cause – let alone for Scottish independence.

But Eric's journalists were almost all enthusiastic supporters, 'nationalists' rather than Nationalists. They had to be watched carefully, allowed to write with passion but restrained when their loyalties became too obvious. Luckily, there was a screen behind which to retreat. The paper had adopted a Whig or Liberal allegiance many years before. This allowed the leader-writers to evade a provocative choice between Tory, Labour or SNP by espousing the small Scottish Liberal Party and its harmless dream of a pan-British federation.

My job was to cover the unfolding devolution story. At times I tried Eric's patience severely, above all in 1976 when I became a founder-member of the 'Scottish Labour Party' (SLP). This was the breakaway from the Labour Party led by

Jim Sillars, then Labour MP for South Ayrshire. The SLP stood for a more full-blooded and powerful version of Home Rule than the hesitant Labour Party offered, coupled with a commitment to 'radical socialism' and – rare on the British left in those days – a call for full Scottish membership of the European Community. The enormous uproar which followed the split brought my own impartiality into question and at moments threatened to compromise the paper's credibility. But Eric, though upset, stood by me. In return, I was able to use my own knowledge of Central European politics and history to show that the problems raised by the Scottish 'national revival' had all been encountered before by Czechs or Poles, by Hungarians or Germans, and that solutions had been found to most of them.

When I returned to Edinburgh in 1975, Harold Wilson was prime minister, soon to be replaced by Jim Callaghan. The Labour government was still in shock following the general election of October 1974, when the Scottish National Party had returned no fewer than eleven MPs to Parliament.

In 1970, the first of the huge oil and gas fields in the North Sea had been discovered. Since most of them lay under the 'Scottish sector' of the sea, the SNP suggested that an independent Scotland could be not merely viable but wealthy on the scale of Kuwait. But the SNP breakthrough had begun well before that, in the late 1960s, and the slogan 'It's Scotland's Oil' merely accelerated the party's growth. Wilson decided on rapid action to pre-empt the spread of the SNP. He revived Labour's half-forgotten commitment to devolution – a Scottish legislative assembly with limited powers, within the United Kingdom. But, to Wilson's annoyance and surprise, Labour in Scotland were reluctant. They suspected that any concession to Home Rule would play into the SNP's hands, but they were pounded into compliance at the battle still remembered as 'Dalintober Street', a special conference held in Glasgow in August 1974. Dalintober Street left wounds which did not heal.

As Andrew Marr remarked, in his 1992 book *The Battle for Scotland*, it was 'a victory for fix and fear, not a triumph of principle'.

Wilson emerged from the October 1974 election with a majority of only four in the House of Commons. Another SNP surge would destroy him. He pressed ahead with the devolution plans. But his own forces were ominously weak and divided, and they ultimately betrayed his successor, Jim Callaghan.

The weakness was not just the split in Scotland between the minority of convinced Labour devolutionists (some of whom soon followed Jim Sillars into the SLP) and the sullenly reluctant mass of the party. Many Labour MPs, English and Scottish, were also hostile. Some objected on pork-barrel grounds, like the group from north-east England who resented 'unfairly' favourable treatment for Scotland. Others on the left of the party made a crude equation between nationalism, racism and fascism; they regarded all concessions to Scottish demands for constitutional change as betrayals of socialism. And a third group – or rather an awkward squad of tirelessly argumentative individuals – rejected the whole devolution strategy on its own terms. Tam Dalyell, the MP for West Lothian, and George Cunningham, a Scot representing the London constituency of South Islington, became famous for insisting that devolution was unworkable. Far from pre-empting the SNP, they said, this plan for a half-baked sub-parliament was a slippery slope leading straight into confrontation between England and Scotland and so to the break-up of the United Kingdom. Between independence and the status quo, there was no halfway house.

In the end, these Labour rebels not only destroyed the devolution project but helped to destroy the Labour government itself. All through the five years of struggle to get the Scotland and Wales bills through Parliament, they exploited the fragility of Wilson's and then Callaghan's tiny Commons majority to delay, distort and discredit their own party's legislation. In February 1977, they helped to defeat the first Scotland and Wales Bill by voting down the 'guillotine' procedure for limiting the time spent on debate. It was replaced by separate bills for Scotland and Wales; these were passed, but the rebels forced through an amendment providing for a referendum before the Acts could be put into effect.

In 1978, George Cunningham managed to insert an extra provision. A simple majority in the referendum, which asked the electors to vote Yes or No to Labour's plans for an elected Scottish assembly, would not be sufficient. The 'Yes' vote would have to amount to 40 per cent of the registered Scottish electorate. To abstain, in other words, would have the effect of voting 'No'. And as the electoral register was old and unrevised, those who had died since it was compiled would also in practice be registering a 'No' – the cemetery vote.

In my diary, I recorded the inglorious beginnings of the 1979 referendum campaign. On the 'Yes' side, its main feature was the spectacular failure of Labour and the SNP to overcome their mutual hatred and cooperate. 'Yes for Scotland', supposed to be the grand platform upon which Home Rulers of every tartan would rally together for the nation, was boycotted by the leaders of all the main parties. Labour's party secretary in Scotland, Helen Liddell, infamously declared that 'We will not be soiling our hands by joining any umbrella "Yes" group.' The SNP tried to stop its best speakers from appearing on platforms with 'people who are normally our opponents'. In spite of this, a number of impressive men and women – politicians, trade union leaders, actors (including Sean Connery) and figures from the churches – ignored these pressures and campaigned with 'Yes for Scotland'. But most of its energy came from Jim Sillars, whose eloquence grew more splendid as his party – the breakaway SLP – dwindled into terminal decline.

By now Jim was involved with an orator and crowd-puller as

hot-hearted and theatrical as himself. It was five years since
Margo MacDonald of the SNP had staggered Labour by seiz-
ing their decayed inner-Glasgow constituency of Govan at a
by-election. At first, journalists celebrated a 'blonde bomb-
shell'. But Margo, as she became the most familiar face
in Scotland, turned out to be a witty, tough politician in love
with all the intricacies of committee work and amendment-
drafting. Like Jim, she was working class through and through.
And like him, she was unmanageably independent.

In mid-January, the pair of them summoned me and a
Scotsman colleague to meet them in Edinburgh. I recorded the
day in my diary.

> Chris and I met Jim and Margo for tea at five, in the
> Rendezvous. They do seem to be a couple. They constantly
> contradict each other's politics, and end up breathing heav-
> ily and glaring at one another over spare ribs and mugs of
> Pimm's. They wanted to convince us that Labour won't
> really fight, that 'big cheeses' in the party are putting it about
> the grapevine that they will vote No, that Callaghan and the
> Scottish Council [of the Labour Party] want the referendum
> to fail.
>
> The first part is a gross exaggeration; the second I don't
> believe. Helen [Liddell] seems genuinely terrified of a Yes
> majority below 40 per cent, which might plunge the party
> into chaos at its Scottish conference a week later, with the
> Noes seeking to reverse the whole devolution commitment.
> Such a result would be immensely damaging to Labour in
> Scotland, and to drop devolution would rend the party now:
> too many of the young and keen activists – as opposed to the
> placemen – are now caught up in the socialist possibilities of
> the Assembly. Bitterness and alarm about the proportion of
> double entries in the electoral register are spreading . . .

I spent a day phoning round the Constituency Labour Parties

(CLPs), to see if they were going to support their own government's Yes campaign.

> Helen Liddell had told me that only five had refused to form a Yes campaign committee, while five others would allow one to be formed only on an unofficial basis. The real figure turns out to be at least twenty refusals – out of seventy-one CLPs.

Meanwhile the 'Labour Vote No' committee, whose most prominent figure was Robin Cook, was doing excellently. Its poster-sites were being rented for it by the Tory-backed, tycoon-fronted group 'Scotland Says No', with money laundered through an anti-devolution trade union.

Those winter weeks were punishing to the campaigners, as blizzards and steely frosts alternated with gushes of sleet. Two days after that tea with Jim and Margo, a huge cloud of hydrogen-sulphide gas poured upwards from the Grangemouth refineries when the flame on a flare-off tower blew out. Trapped under a layer of temperature inversion, the cloud spread sideways over the whole Central Belt from Fife to Greenock, reeking of bad eggs and knocking the weak-lunged to their knees. Nervous, I noted it as 'a gruesome, ominous event'.

I would have done better to look at omens from south of the border. The hard weather was coinciding with a set of intractable trade-union disputes which clogged the English cities with uncollected trash, closed schools, stopped some public transport and, in a few cases, delayed the burial of the dead. Compared to the crises of the early 1970s, when inflation reached double figures and winter strikes left much of Britain stumbling about unheated houses by candle-light, these were minor inconveniences. The only commodity which ran out in my part of Edinburgh was cat-litter. But the political impact was out of all proportion. The media raised lamentation about what was afterwards called the 'Winter of Discontent'. When Jim Callaghan flew home from a Caribbean conference and denied, reasonably, that there was 'mounting chaos', the journalists monstered him into a callous imbecile out of touch with the nation.

Today, every account of that period explains the fall of the Callaghan government in 1979 by a reinvented, substantially phoney version of the Winter of Discontent and its supposed privations. What matters is why that myth gained such public currency. And the answer is that the government was dying, and the English (rather than the Scottish) public needed a solid reason to kill it off.

The sense that the government was weakening haunted the referendum campaign. Andrew Marr, in his book *The Battle for Scotland*, summed up that moment well. 'In 1979 devolution carried the stigma of a failing government. It had been imposed on a doubtful party by a London leadership for purely electoral reasons. It had been legislated for in a fog of internal dissent and confusion. It was campaigned for by divided parties at a time of economic chaos. In some ways it is surprising that so many Scots voted for it.'

The twenty-fifth of January was Burns Night.

Comedy yesterday, as both Margo and Labour independently kidnapped Robert Burns. Margo called the press together in the Covenanter [under the Yes offices in the High Street], and gave them haggis pies and whisky in the morning. Then she issued an exuberant statement about 'Such a parcel of rogues in a nation' and 'the coward few', 'bought and sold for English gold' and so on.

That night, Labour's party political broadcast began with a rendering of 'A Man's a Man for a' that'. The singer assured Helen Liddell that Burns had been a nationalist with a small 'n', but of course an internationalist too. Helen asked him to confirm that the Lad from Kyle would never have voted for 'Separation' – No, never! Willie Ross, Labour's previous

Secretary of State for Scotland, then spoke against a red back-
drop about Burns, about Scotland's chance of democracy, about
how the Scottish people had been working for devolution for a
hundred years (this surprised the historians). Apart from
Helen's careful interruption about Separation, the whole tone
of the broadcast was one of noble, elevated patriotism.

Next day, Eric Mackay came into the room where I worked
and flung down a copy of the *Daily Express*. 'Have you seen
this?' He managed a bitter smile. The whole front page and
centre pages were covered with No propaganda: Vote against
the Break-Up of Britain! There was a cute picture of Miss
Edinburgh dressed in nothing but a Union Jack.

Five weeks before the vote, opinion polls showed the Yes
vote declining and the Don't-Knows rising.

> Went to see the 'Yes for Scotland' office, just over the
> Covenanter pub . . . The usual despairing group of boys and
> girls round a half-stripped duplicator, the usual dirty win-
> dows, biting cold and – as always – a great cardboard carton
> containing dusty bundles of undistributed leaflets from the
> previous organization to rent the room.

I went for beer and mutton pies at the Covenanter with two Yes
workers. One told me that he had phoned the Labour agent
for Berwick and East Lothian to ask when his campaign
dates were, so that 'Yes for Scotland' could avoid splitting pro-
devolution audiences.

> But [the agent] refused to tell him! This is carrying Helen's
> 'Let's not soil our hands' to crazy extremes!

At the time, I was writing an article series for the *Scotsman* in
the form of fictional letters to his wife from a member of the
future Scottish assembly. I named him 'Andrew Fletcher', in
memory of the erratic, brilliant Fletcher of Saltoun who had led

the opposition to the Union Treaty in 1707. The articles went down badly, partly because they were thought vaguely patronizing and partly because my account of imaginary crises in the assembly was judged by the Yes camp to be alarmist.

A few days after the series ended, I received an angry letter headed 'Saltoun' and signed 'Andrew Fletcher'. Unknown to me, the family was still at home three hundred years on, and still interested in politics. This Andrew Fletcher, however, was a No man. I rang him up, and enjoyed a conversation with a rather shy, determined gentleman who was anxious not to overdo his protest into impoliteness. Soon afterwards, I wrote an article on the three-hundredth anniversary of the murder of Archbishop Sharp of St Andrews on Magusmuir; a brutal, messy killing by Presbyterian fanatics led by one Hackston of Rathillet who rode his horse over the dying bishop's face. Within days, I opened a letter from Hackston of Rathillet complaining that I had misunderstood his ancestor's motives. I found these eerie continuities somehow comforting.

In mid-February, I set out on a reporting journey, starting in the Western Isles. It was a chance to visit beautiful places like the township of Iochdar in South Uist, which I had last seen twenty years before, to walk on the deserted silver strand and watch the flocks of little brown birds – fieldfares? – squirming in the stubble on the machair. But politically, only two weeks before the poll, nothing was happening.

No campaign of any sort exists, and no information has been sent out. The *Daily Record* is the only place to find concise accounts of the Scotland Act. Loyalty to Donald Stewart [the patriarchal SNP MP] is very strong, but not so much to the SNP. Suspicions of Edinburgh rule, of Lanarkshire ways to be imposed [by an assembly] on the Isles. As in Shetland, party politics are only seasonal. What counts is the man, the most impressive person who can fight the Western Isles case at a distant capital.

In the early winter dusk, there were crescents of flame in the dark hills: 'muirburn', the seasonal burning of heather. I thought of Hugh MacDiarmid, who had died the year before, and his poem 'Why I Became a Scots Nationalist'. Has any other poet compared his own country to a reluctant woman in bed? But MacDiarmid knew what he was talking about:

> . . . Like Pushkin I
> . . . Am happy, when after lang and sair
> Pursuit you yield yoursel' to me,
> But wi' nae rapture, cauldly there,
> Open but glowerin' callously,
> Yet slow but surely heat until
> You catch my flame against your will
> And the mureburn tak's the hill.

From the Uists, I went north to Lewis. I drove across the island, through moors the colour of a golden eagle, streaked with snow, to Ness, a string of crofting townships along the Atlantic coast road.

In a converted schoolhouse, I talked to Annie MacDonald, the community education officer. A schoolmaster-writer named Norman was there, and a trembling man who seemed to be a piper. Then there burst in a delegation of school-children come to *demand* an all-week youth club. They were confident, noisy, in bright anoraks. They talked in Gaelic but wrote down their list of requests in English for Annie, beginning with 'leaders' and going on through table-tennis and basketball to cookery. Is this confidence what the community cooperatives can do for the Isles? A good decade for the Isles: the coming of their own all-purpose authority, Comhairle nan Eilean, their courageous choice of Donald Stewart [as MP], the unique success here of job creation, the arrival of the co-chomunn idea.

When Annie asked them, the children all said No to devolution. But they wouldn't say why; only giggled and caught
each other's eyes.

In Stornoway, I talked to Sandy Matheson above the sta-
tionery shop he owned, a stout, easy-going fellow who was an
ex-Provost and the Labour parliamentary candidate. Some of
his cronies drifted in. Sandy told me that he would disregard
any instructions and vote No, because he believed that to be
the best way to smash the SNP. Trying to forestall them with
devolution was a mistake.

I drove out to Melbost, to look for the poet Murdo
MacFarlane. His township lay beyond the airport, where black
Phantom fighters were hurling themselves about in threes.
Blue, icy wind, the sea running across the bay. I asked for him.
'Ach, the Bard . . .' And he appeared, hooded in an old blue
anorak.

The smell of his croft house brought back childhood: that
compound scent of sour milk, peat-smoke and old clothes.
Upstairs was his eighty-five-year-old brother, who groaned
loudly as he was helped about the house. The Bard, at seventy-
eight, had an eager, sharp face with white stubble and blue
eyes. He shouted all the time, always enthusiastic, a socialist
who emigrated to Canada in the thirties, somebody who might
well have heard John Maclean speak when he was an appren-
tice on the Clyde in 1919.

The Bard had mislaid his Gaelic song calling for a Yes vote.
This was what I had come for, but my plane was leaving and
the only other copy was at the *Stornoway Gazette* being set up in
type for the next issue. I drove back furiously to Stornoway.
Swerving through congregations pouring out of the churches, I
persuaded two *Gazette* journalists to desert their dinner and
snatch a proof of the song from the case-room. I caught the
Inverness plane by a few seconds.

In Perthshire, I found campaigning conducted on both sides

by estate-owning magnates. 'Scotland Says No' was run by the Tory colonelocracy, with a token Labour councillor on the platform. 'Yes for Scotland' was led by Lord Perth, assisted by Colonel Lyle. Lord ('Eddy') Boyle, the plump and enlightened Tory who had been Minister of Education, was brought up from the south to declare that 'the Imperial Parliament [i.e. Westminster!] should recognize the spirit of nationhood and the strong element of national pride in Scotland'.

In Stirling, little was happening. All I saw was one man wearing a Yes stickie, and another with an antique 'Keep Britain United' badge. Dunblane was no more alert. I met the inevitable citizen who didn't even know there was a referendum. 'Reffy-whit? Naebody telt me aboot that . . .' She was a cheery young woman, the sort of person who sits in the classroom back row happily letting it all pass over her.

From Dunblane, I drove up to Sheriffmuir which was under heavy snow. (This was the site of a famously indecisive battle during the 1715 Jacobite rebellion.) I passed the Macrae monument to the clan dead, very black and carrying a savage inscription. Then, at a turn in the track, I saw in front of me an immense grizzly bear chasing a girl with yellow hair through the snow. The bear was gaining on her.

But this was not a shadow of the coming glaciation. A man appeared trudging through the drifts after Beauty and the Beast. A bear-tamer. He and the young woman turned out to be a couple, well known to Scottish journalists, who ran the dilapidated Sheriffmuir Inn. They were voting No, because the local SNP branch had apparently said that it was cruel to keep a bear on Sheriffmuir. The bear, the couple added, intended to go down to the poll and vote No as well.

By now, a new twist was appearing in the No campaign. On 14 February, Lord Home (formerly Sir Alec Douglas-Home) had appeared on television to say that pro-devolution Scots could vote No with a clear conscience. By so doing, he promised, they would not destroy the project of self-government.

Quite the contrary: they would obtain a better, stronger Scotland Act from the Tories, an assembly armed with taxation powers and elected by proportional representation. He implied that Mrs Thatcher, who would be prime minister if the Conservatives won the next general election, had a new Home Rule plan of her own.

Why that honourable man made this statement remains a mystery. As events soon showed, no such plans existed and Mrs Thatcher had not the slightest intention of offering the Scots self-government. But Lord Home, an ex-prime minister himself, was widely respected and his words offered a fatally comfortable escape route for thousands of waverers. The substantial pro-devolution minority among the Scottish Tories collapsed, and confusion spread.

In his youth, Sir Alec had been a junior minister at the side of Neville Chamberlain, when he went to Munich and abandoned Czechoslovakia to Hitler. Now the historian Christopher Harvie was able to deliver the cruellest thrust of the whole campaign: 'He began his career by betraying one small nation, and ended it by betraying another.'

Within a few days, other leading Scottish Tories were taking up the Home line. In Lanarkshire, my next destination, I saw the impact.

The No side have no fresh arguments, or at least the four or five they laid down in December – cost, extra tier of government, more bureaucracy, 'separation' – have stopped making converts; the Yes side is now demolishing those arguments. But the 'vote no and get a better Act' ploy is new . . . Mass defection to No by Labour councillors, regional and district . . . Many now work for [the Tory-run] 'Scotland Says No'. In their dim minds, this is less disloyal than working for Tam Dalyell and the 'Labour Vote No' campaign.

Margo MacDonald rang me up and said: 'This battle is for

the soul, Neal!' By now the Yes campaign was at last in high gear. At Bathgate, in West Lothian, I watched one of the best-organized teams (run by an unknown SNP youngster called Alex Salmond, who was later to become the party's leader) deftly sliding its message into local papers and radio stations. This group was a coalition of SNP, Tories, Liberals, Communists, the National Union of Mineworkers and some of the brightest survivors of the 'Sillarsite' SLP. They took turns at haranguing the shoppers in the Steelyard at Bathgate, who took pains not to be impressed:

> The farcical sight of people pretending not to listen to the speakers: turning their backs, staring into empty shop-windows – très écossais!

My last stop was Aberdeen. I met Chris Ramsey, the champion Yes fly-poster, and at six one morning watched him climb the Wallace Statue and hang a 'Wallace Says Vote Yes!' banner on his sword. The statue was slippery with rain; wind tore at the banner, and I had to retrieve it from the gutter and stand on the bottom rung of the ladder as Chris put it back. This was invigorating. But friends warned me that the Labour movement in the city was staying out of the campaign, and at the Trades Council building I saw what they meant.

> Through the locked glass door of each trades union office, piles of Yes leaflets and posters could be made out lying on the carpet – never to be distributed . . .
>
> In the evening, a No rally in the hall of Harlaw Academy . . . Bob Boothby [the most convivial and outrageous survivor of Winston Churchill's cronies] and Iain Sproat [a leading Tory No man of rabidly right-wing outlook]. Considerable audience of old ladies; some Yes people, led by Chris Ramsey, much stared at.
>
> Boothby, in his superb port-and-biscuits growl, began: 'I

consider it my duty, frail, shaky and drunk as I am, to come and make my last political speech . . .' The eyes of the old ladies bulged. The speech turned out to be mostly about what he had told Hitler in 1933 after several large brandies, and hardly at all about devolution. But he did observe: 'The world is Scotland's oyster! If you want to reduce her to the status of a limpet, go ahead!'

*

The campaign was over, and I went home to a large Victorian flat on East Preston Street in Edinburgh, where four of us lived in shabby comfort with several cats. We spent good years there and, looking back on them, I can see that the world may have been our oyster. It did not feel like that on the dank morning of 1 March 1979, Referendum Day.

We went and voted in East Preston Street School, in the morning. Later, unable to sit and wait, I went to the local 'Yes for Scotland' office in the Communist shop on Buccleuch Street and did a series of posters in Polish. '*Polacy! Za naszą wolność i waszą* . . . for our freedom and yours, we appeal to you in the name of forty years of Scottish–Polish friendship for a Yes.' I put one on the door of the Polish Hearth in Drummond Place, and others in shops and in our local butcher's on West Preston Street. To my relief Mr Zawadzki, the butcher, was pleased with the poster. 'As long as it's nothing to do with Communism . . .!'

But in the *Scotsman* offices, I found depression. Arnold Kemp, the deputy editor, was sure that the referendum was lost. The turnout had been high in middle-class districts, low in working-class areas. I remembered a discussion on referendum coverage we had had with Eric Mackay a few weeks before. Arnold had been silent, then suddenly exclaimed: 'When I see someone on North Bridge wearing a No stickie, I feel like telling him: You fucking traitor!' Then he burst into loud, uneasy laughter.

That evening prospects improved for a moment. At home,

we watched the MORI poll on television, taken as the voting was going on and usually accurate. This predicted a very sound majority for Yes, although possibly just below 40 per cent of the electorate. I remember raising a large whisky and shouting: 'We've made it!'

Next day I arrived at the office late, in time to meet the disaster slowly emerging from the radio. There had been a healthy start with the Western Isles and then Central Region voting Yes. But then Borders showed too big a No majority, and when Tayside went No, the trouble was plain. I listened to Donald Dewar, as one of the radio panel, conceding even before the result that the Act could not be put through on these figures.

The result came out steadily as a three-way split: Yes just ahead by 71,000 votes with 33 per cent, No at about 31 per cent, the remaining 36 per cent abstaining. At first sight, it was the worst of all possible results. Lothian, where the Yes majority should have been large, showed only a hairline victory. Highland bucked the trend by going Yes, and Grampian's No majority was far less sweeping than expected. But in the office, the sense of failure was suffocating.

Among the feature writers, Julie Davidson led the others in cursing the cowardice of the Scots who wouldn't put their vote where their mouth was. Julie said: Jim Sillars was right, the Scots are fearties. We all remembered the Sillars litany about how this referendum was the one and unrepeatable chance, about how Scotland would be the laughing-stock of Europe, about how no Scottish wish would ever be taken seriously by the outside world again.

At some point that afternoon, I rang Tom Nairn, Scotland's most influential political philosopher and one of my flatmates. But Tom was astonishingly cheerful. He pointed out that where the working class voted, they had voted for the assembly: this was very clearly the evidence from people who had been inside the counts at local level. It was the middle class which had ratted. And this also ensured that when self-government did come, it would be in a more radical form, not merely a painless removal of the Establishment into a new building.

I was impressed, and the pain began to ease. Tom's proposition was convincing: the assembly which would just be a harmless rearrangement of the furniture had died on 1 March. And it was true, after all, that the Yes option had won. They had at least been more numerous than the Noes. But the Labour backbenchers at Westminster, opposed to devolution all along, were now going to use that 40 per cent Cunningham Amendment to declare the victory invalid.

For years, one of the *Scotsman*'s most pertinacious letter-writers, Mr Archie Birt of Mathie Crescent, Gourock, had been asking the editor: 'What will the Scots do if England says No?' Now we would find out. But I suspected that, in spite of the defiant rhetoric, they would do little but mutter.

In my diary, I wrote:

> What happens now? A lot of 'we will fight on' talk, a lot of hope for the radical independence-or-nothing wing of the SNP. But I don't think the public will be interested. They have had enough for the moment . . . I think devolution – which certainly won't 'go away' – will recede now for a long season, here as well as in London.

*

Everything now came apart. The Labour government disintegrated, and in May 1979 Margaret Thatcher and the Conservatives were elected with a huge majority. They were to stay in power for eighteen years.

The SNP took a shattering defeat; from eleven, the number of their MPs fell to two. But Labour's result in Scotland was startling. In England, the swing to the Tories washed the Labour MPs away. In Scotland, by contrast, Labour won three more seats and emerged stronger than before. A trend had emerged which was to grow more blatant for the rest of the century: Scottish voting patterns now diverged from those in the rest of Britain, and Labour's majority of Scottish seats increased at each successive general election.

A few days after the 1979 election, an SNP friend of ours sent a telegram to Gordon Brown, one of the rising stars of Scottish Labour: 'You are the Nationalists now!' In the short term, this was a false prophecy. The phalanx of Scottish Labour MPs returned to Parliament in the next two decades looked impressive north of the border, with nearly three-quarters of the Scottish seats. But at Westminster they were an irrelevant minority. They had to watch in impotence as Mrs Thatcher demolished Scotland's steel, engineering and mining industries, decreed the sale of council housing on which Labour's local power depended and used Scotland as a testing-ground for the disastrous poll tax – the flat-rate levy on each registered citizen which led to mass refusals to pay and eventually to rioting.

The reviving SNP mocked the Labour MPs as 'the feeble fifty'. This taunt went deeply home, and hurt. After the first few years of Tory government, it seemed obvious that a Labour-dominated assembly at Edinburgh could have defended Scottish working people against at least some of the social devastation imposed by Thatcherism. Minds changed, and by about 1985 most of Scottish Labour's doubts about self-government had melted away.

In the same way, the complaint that the Conservatives had 'no mandate' to impose unpopular policies on Scotland – at first dismissed as a mere nationalist whine – slowly spread to become a cliché of Scottish political oratory. 'Every time we vote for a Labour government, and every time we get a Tory one.' It was true. Much less true was the expectation before each successive Tory election victory that the Scottish people would finally lose patience with this mockery of democratic rights and rebel in a 'Doomsday scenario'. Nothing of the sort happened. There are things ordinary Scots will march for, but constitutional change is very seldom one of them. Feelings about the nation are private, not to be flapped around in view of the neighbours. That was the significance of the unique Edinburgh demonstration for democracy in 1992. The difference that time was that it wasn't the neighbours who were watching but Europe and the world.

The years after 1979 were bleak. At my desk on North Bridge, the steady inflow of political handouts, reform plans, party statements and counter-statements which had been running for the previous five years dried to a trickle within weeks of the referendum. Much more upsetting was the impact on my own friends and acquaintances.

During those years, they had grown accustomed to the idea that Scotland was to become an exciting, lively little country in which their talents would be needed. In the diary, I wrote: 'The future existed for many years; people became used to it as a background; now it has vanished and there is a blankness only.' People seemed to shrink and fade. Many turned to alcohol, some to hard drugs. Many more fell back into the old assumption that Scotland was a dead-end ('there's nothing for young folk here'), and they left for London, America or continental Europe. The failure of self-government ruined many lives, and they were not the lives of politicians.

We were not immune at the *Scotsman*. A sort of high-spirited desperation settled over us. That summer, the promotions department organized a fund-raising parachute jump at Strathallan, and suddenly the whole features staff, men and women alike, was volunteering. We agreed that we would all leap into space shouting the paper's motto: 'For You, For Scotland!'

To my shame and relief, I was persuaded to pull out and spare my slipped disc. But the others soon found themselves clinging to a wind-battered spar above Perthshire, one foot on the wheel-spat and the other waving in nothingness. Some jumped screaming; one had to be pushed.

The casualties were proportionately worse than at Arnhem.

Fred and Henry broke their legs. The features sub-editor fell
through a roof, nearly tearing his foot off. Julie landed in a pig-
pen; Harry made a crater in a cornfield. David twisted his knee
sinew. They were all rounded up by ambulances and came to
rest in a row of hospital beds at Bridge of Allan.

Eric Mackay was angrier than I had ever seen him, and there
were hard words about Walter Mitty delusions. But perhaps
that leap of self-immolation was a way of purging the heart.
Those who jumped almost all stayed in Scotland and worked
on. Unlike them, I decided that I must get away from Scottish
politics, at least for a time, and took a job with the *Observer* in
London. It was almost twenty years before I came back.

Why did the referendum fail? (And it did fail: the result, though
wickedly gerrymandered, was too feeble to support the assembly we were offered, and our 'We won!' reaction was, in
retrospect, unworthy.) I have told the story of the campaign as
I lived through it. But the weakness of parties or politicians was
not the underlying reason. The explanation, I think, goes back
to the 'St Andrew's Fault'.

One of the strangest facts about Scottish politics is that party
allegiances do not match constitutional attitudes. Labour is a
Unionist party, committed to maintaining the United Kingdom.
The Scottish National Party, although it now acts as the official
Opposition in a devolved Scottish Parliament, is committed to
an independent Scottish state. And yet – as poll after poll has
shown – nearly half those who support full independence are
Labour Party voters. More predictably, a substantial minority
of SNP voters do not want independence, but prefer self-
government within the United Kingdom.

One way of putting this is to say that party and class loyalty
is far stronger than feelings about self-government. In 1979,
many thousands of men and women voted No or stayed at
home in order to 'dish the SNP', although in fact they wanted
a devolved or even an independent Scotland.

But there is another explanation. Much popular nationalism in Scotland is inaccessible to politics – even today, after the revival of a Scottish Parliament. Love of one's country has been held to be a private and intimate area rather than a public one.

Here the Fault is plain to see. The new political elites, the intellectuals and the rapidly expanding middle class with university education, are much less inhibited about expressing patriotism. But others, lacking their confidence, keep their feelings to themselves. The children of the hurricane remain wary about the way the children of the breeze wrap housing reform, improvement in social services and Home Rule into one gleaming manifesto package.

But the mismatch between popular feeling and party programmes goes further. For at least thirty years, it has suited the Labour Party, especially, to present devolution and independence as if they were mutually exclusive. Either you want a Scottish sub-parliament within the United Kingdom, or you are a 'separatist' out to wreck the devolution settlement. In the same fashion, the SNP – in its fundamentalist moods – has presented devolution as no more than a Unionist sabotage plot to render independence impossible.

This choice is fraudulent. The Scottish people do not see their future in this binary way, as an either–or. They simply wish Scotland to run its own affairs, as other nations do. For most people, devolution and independence are little more than different uniforms which can be buttoned over the single reality of self-government. Most Scots would prefer not to leave the United Kingdom, but if that is the only way in which self-government can be made real, then so be it. This wish is widespread, of rather low intensity and rather vaguely formulated, but absolutely persistent.

Here, I think, is the key to another mystery. For decades, opinion polls have suggested that around 30 per cent of Scots want an independent Scottish state (the figure can sag below that, and very occasionally shoot well above it). In any 'normal' country, the fact that a third of its citizens rejected the constitutional order would be a terrifying alarm signal. In Scotland, however, life carries placidly on, and the SNP have learned that those poll choices have little or nothing to do with the size of the Nationalist vote at elections. Why? It comes back to that caution about public life engrained by the blows of recent history, and to that self-preserving instinct to keep patriotism out of politics.

In 'The Lay of the Last Minstrel', Walter Scott proclaimed his own patriotism as a rhetorical question:

> *Breathes there a man with soul so dead*
> *Who never to himself hath said:*
> *This is my own, my native land?*

Scott, for all his regrets about the passing of an older Scotland, was not about to be blown off his roots by the hurricane of change. He was not just the son of a Border dynasty with powerful Edinburgh connections; he was himself a member of that impregnable oligarchy which is the Faculty of Advocates, Scotland's legal elite.

Norman MacCaig, a twentieth-century poet, came from the other side of the chasm. His Gaelic-speaking family were crofting people who remembered the wounds of the Clearances. His poem 'The Patriot' runs:

> *My only country*
> *Is six feet high*
> *And whether I love it or not*
> *I'll die*
> *for its independence.*

*

The years passed, an interminable government fell, and once again there was to be a Scottish referendum on devolution. It was 1997. I sat in my mother's house, and she asked me how I thought she should vote.

I knew that this was a rhetorical question. She had made up her mind, and was simply lining me up, like a golfer settling the ball on the tee, before she told me. None the less, I had no idea what she would say.

Why do people vote as they do? I remain baffled by this basic question. The preferences of abstract lumps of Scottish opinion – regional, class-based, sectarian – have sometimes been predictable. Individuals are the trouble. Some, even now, approach the polling booth with Biblical solemnity. When I was a boy, an old forestry gamekeeper used to take me on long, discursive walks to put me right on matters like long-forgotten disputes about the usage of Gaelic pronouns. 'At election time,' he once told me, 'a man should go into the hills alone and hearken to the voice of his own conscience.' Others stay on the low ground and hearken to any old impulse which pops into their head.

My mother, like Eric Beattie Mackay, was not easy to read in this respect. Neither was her family. For some years, my grandfather and his son had lodged comfortably in a farmhouse a mile or so from Crinan Moss. My uncle, a retired colonel of Royal Scots, was a sceptical but loyal Tory who could be relied upon to offer his car to drive local Conservative voters to the polls. My grandfather, however, would tease his son at election times by sonorously telling visitors that he was a lifelong Liberal. No doubt he was. Nevertheless, he waited until he was in his nineties to tell his family about it. My uncle grumbled but my mother, who enjoyed surprises, laughed a great deal.

My mother was nostalgic for the old order of society, and impatient with chatter about equality. At the same time, she was an instinctive rebel and in no sense a 'bankable' Tory. As she grew older, she grew more suspicious of the Mid-Argyll Conservatives, whom she accused – sometimes unfairly – of being middle-class English settlers determined to treat the West Highlands as if they were an extension of suburban Surrey. She complained that local people, whose grandmothers and grandfathers she remembered, would soon have no voice in their own land.

I think she voted SNP at one election in 1974, helping to put Iain MacCormick into Parliament. Much later, she came to support Ray Michie, as Liberal-Democrat MP for Argyll. In both cases, heredity counted strongly for her; she had little respect for either party or their programmes. Iain MacCormick was the son of John MacCormick, the Argyll man who had been the leader of moderate nationalism in the 1940s and 1950s, and who became Rector of Glasgow University. Ray Michie was the daughter of John M. Bannerman, another famous Gaelic-speaker with Argyll roots who had spent his life campaigning for economic and social development in the Highlands. 'I kent his faither' was anything but a dismissive comment for my mother, who liked her politicians to have 'background' and lineage.

Now I explained to her why I thought she should vote Yes. I trotted out the usual reasons, to do with democracy and responsibility and the evils of long-range government from London. But I could feel that she was restless with this stuff, which she had heard or read a hundred times before, and I prepared to hear protests about the importance of the Union or the noxiousness of Tony Blair.

Instead, she said: 'I am voting No. And I am voting No because a Scottish parliament will make Scotland more English!'

For the first incredulous moments, I thought she was provoking me. But then I saw that she was not. At the age of ninety-three, she had sensed the tangled ironies and cross-dressings which are inherent in any national revival. Reaction can dress itself up as Revolution. Or, on the other hand, a cloudy programme of reviving past glory can conceal the hurricane of modernization which uproots a nation's real continuities. Scotland longed to 'join the world', to take charge of its own gates and fling them wide open. But what if that meant opening Scotland far more widely to the nearest bit of world – England?

I did not agree with my mother. But I came to understand what she meant.

7

I wonder my blood
Will you ever return
To help us kick the life back
To a dying mutual friend?
Do we not love her?
Do we not say we love her?
Do we have to roam the world
To prove how much it hurts?

The Proclaimers,
'Letter from America'

When I think of the 1980s in Scotland, those lines from 'Letter from America' are the ones I remember. The mutual friend was in a bad way, not a well lady at all. Native politics was an abandoned city, in which a few prowlers picked up fallen stones, weighed them in the hand and then threw them back into the ruins. Scotland's industrial landscape also became archaeology. Where cranes had swung over acres of assembly halls, there were soon cinder-plains growing nettles in spring, purple willowherb in summer and brambles in autumn. Collieries where a thousand men had laboured for a hundred years became silent fields around a concrete shaft-cap. The furnaces were quenched one by one.

These ways of working had long ago become part of Scotland's self-definition. Now a third identity-question was added to 'When was Scotland?' and 'Who are we?' It was: 'What do Scots do?'

The Proclaimers (skeletally thin, bespectacled, expression-less) had an answer to that. Scots emigrate, as their forefathers had done. Their song took a familiar Gaelic lament for lost places and added new ones – truck assembly plants, shipyards, new towns:

> *Lochaber no more . . .*
> *Skye no more*
> *Bathgate no more*
> *Linwood no more*
> *Methil no more . . .*

But Scots who stayed in Scotland did a great deal of singing, writing, composing and painting in these years. With the political leadership lying face-down in the rubble, there was nobody to preach about the art required by a renascent nation. As a result, an explosion of creativity took place, much the most remarkable period in culture since the 'Scottish Renaissance' of the 1920s. If these novelists, painters, dramatists or pop bands expressed any political views, they were usually coloured by an angry, undifferentiated nationalism. The binary division between 'ethnic' or 'civic' nationalism beloved by academics is unreal; all nationalisms partake of both. But feelings in Scotland during the 1980s certainly registered in the 'ethnic' half of the spectrum. Resentment spread, some of it tinged with dislike of 'the English' as personified by Mrs Thatcher. Each successive opinion poll showed more people defining themselves as Scots and fewer feeling 'British'. And yet little of this upwelling of national emotion flowed to the SNP, whose vote stagnated through most of the decade. Parties and election results were not what this mood was about.

When politics did revive, it was 'unlicensed'. Change came from outwith the party structures, driven instead by what Andrew Marr has called 'Scotland's anti-establishment estab-lishment'. Jim Ross, a retired senior civil servant from the

Scottish Office, was backed by an impressive group of professors, public-sector executives and church figures when in 1987 he launched the idea of a Constitutional Convention to draw up proposals for a Scottish parliament. The group soon produced the 'Claim of Right', asserting that the 1707 Union Treaty had been 'eroded almost to the point of extinction' and that the Treaty had not deprived the people of Scotland of a residual sovereignty to determine their own future.

The main parties, at first reluctant, were drawn towards cooperation with the Convention. Only the Tories would have nothing to do with it. At the last moment, the SNP also backed out, although some important Nationalist figures disobeyed party orders and participated. The core of the Constitutional Convention was an alliance between the Labour Party and the Liberal Democrats, made possible by Labour's astonishing and historic concession that a future Scottish parliament should be elected by proportional representation. But the beef of the Convention, the strength which impressed the parties into taking it seriously, was the concerted support of Scotland's civil society – the trade unions, the churches, the Gaelic lobby, the army of single-issue leagues for the reform of this or that, the ethnic minorities, the educators, the planners.

The Convention held its first meeting in March 1989. In the Assembly Hall of the Church of Scotland, on the Mound in Edinburgh, fifty-eight out of Scotland's seventy-two MPs signed a declaration affirming 'the sovereign right of the Scottish people to determine the form of government best suited to their needs'. This was an absolute rejection of British constitutional doctrine, which lays down that sovereign rights in the state belong exclusively to the House of Commons at Westminster and certainly not to any 'people', Scottish or British. But in the surge of excitement, nobody seemed to care.

The declaration was also an answer of sorts to that 'Archie Birt Question' which had haunted the *Scotsman* correspondence columns back in the 1970s: 'What Happens if England Says

No?' Canon Kenyon Wright, the august Episcopalian who was the Convention's chairman, had evidently been a *Scotsman* reader. We all recognized the Archie Birt echo when, on behalf of the Convention, the Canon sent a defiant message to Mrs Thatcher: 'What if that other single voice we all know so well responds by saying: "We say No, and we are the State"? Well, we say, "Yes, and we are the people."'

She did say No. But the Constitutional Convention set to work, and over the next few years designed a 'modern' parliament for Scotland which abandoned many of the pointless traditions of the House of Commons. To begin with, the choice of a proportional voting system would almost certainly lead to coalition governments, with no party commanding an absolute majority. This un-British and 'European' scenario led to another Continental innovation: most legislation would be drafted and debated in powerful parliamentary committees, rather than in the plenary sessions preferred by the archaic Westminster tradition. Members of the Scottish Parliament (MSPs) would work in normal daylight hours, allowing them a family life, rather than following the eighteenth-century manner of night debates after a good dinner at a London club.

There was a certain unreality about all this. Nationalists had always argued that a Scottish constitution should be devised and approved in Scotland rather than in London. This was now taking place. But the facts of British life meant that nothing whatever could happen until Britain as a whole voted to remove the Tories and replace them with a Labour government committed to devolution. Given the massive English preponderance in the United Kingdom, Scottish public opinion by itself could be ignored.

In 1992, it seemed to many journalists and politicians that the hour of destiny was approaching. John Major had replaced Mrs Thatcher two years before, and the Tory government was beset by scandal and failure. Labour was plainly reviving, and as the April 1992 election drew nearer, feverish optimism infected the Scottish scene. Deceived by freak poll results, one of which put support for independence at 50 per cent, Alex Salmond, leader of the SNP, announced that this would be the 'independence election'.

All these predictions shrivelled on polling day. To universal astonishment, the Conservatives won their fourth general election in a row. They lost ground badly in England, but in Scotland the Tory vote actually registered a slight increase. Labour in Scotland won its usual massive but impotent majority, while the SNP gained only a fifth of the popular vote.

There was a moment of appalled disillusion. Jim Sillars delivered one of his memorable volleys of abuse against 'ninety-minute patriots' who 'bottled out'. But this was not to be a repeat of 1979; the despair was transient. Within days, new cross-party groups were being set up to back the Constitutional Convention and agitate for Home Rule.

The most effective of these was 'Common Cause', a fusion of Church of Scotland radicals with an assortment of writers and academics who came together in a passionate meeting at the Kirk centre of Carberry Tower. The most heroic was 'the Vigil'. As the election results emerged, a handful of enraged men and women made their way to the old Royal High School on the Calton Hill in Edinburgh, the building expected to house the Scottish Parliament, and sat down outside it. They put up a hut next to the gate, under a 'Democracy for Scotland' banner, and announced that they would stay there for as long as it took. So they did, enduring rain, gales and biting winter frost around a brazier of coals while passers-by stopped to debate with them or to offer them pokes of chips or (occasionally) bottles of whisky. Significantly, the police made no serious effort to remove them. The Vigil, which became one of the sights of Edinburgh, remained at the gates for over five years until the referendum on 11 September 1997 released them from their oath. They had been there for exactly 1979 days and nights, a neat exorcism of that year of failure almost two decades in the past.

The Convention itself rapidly recovered its nerve, and returned to work. And, on the other side of the 'St Andrew's Fault', public opinion grew angrier and more sharply focused on the notion of a Scottish Parliament. Only a few months divided the April election from the December 1992 demonstration at the Edinburgh Summit. But in those months Scotland changed and acquired fresh confidence.

There would be a next time. No government could last for ever, and the parliament was now inevitable. The project was too widely supported and its plans too advanced to be resisted indefinitely. The setback of 1992 soon came to be regarded as a mere *accident de parcours*, the insertion of a few more wasted years before the future could begin, and on 1 May 1997 the day of reckoning finally arrived.

The Conservatives suffered the worst election defeat in twentieth-century British politics. Scotland and Wales became 'Tory-free zones', as the Conservative Party lost every single parliamentary seat in the two nations. But the decisive shift was the collapse of the Tory vote in its rural and suburban English heartlands. 'New Labour', now led by Tony Blair, crowded into Westminster with an absolute majority of 179 seats, even bigger than the historic 'Labour landslide' of 1945. And the new government kept its promise. Within weeks, the outlines for Scottish and Welsh devolution were published, the proposals for Scotland reasonably faithful to the plans drawn up by the Constitutional Convention.

The new government had no intention of repeating the mistakes of the 1970s. This was to be a fast-track process. The devolution bills would be brief. Adopting the model of Gladstone's Home Rule bills for Ireland in the 1880s, they would list only the powers to be retained at Westminster.

There would be another referendum – but this time before the Scotland Bill was introduced into Parliament rather than after it had been passed. It turned out to have two questions rather than one: a Yes or No to the Scottish Parliament itself, and a second question on whether the Parliament should have marginal taxation powers (to vary the basic rate of income tax by up to three pennies in the pound). But this referendum was to be decided by a simple majority of votes. There would be no 'Cunningham Amendment' to twist the balance against Yes by turning abstainers into Noes.

The White Paper 'Scotland's Parliament', laying out the framework for devolution, was published in July 1997. Donald Dewar, Secretary of State for Scotland, announced that 11 September would be referendum day. And yet, behind the confident government statements, fear began to crawl. If the Yes majority was very narrow and the abstentions were massive, would the government be justified in pressing ahead with the Scotland Act? And what would remain of the whole project if the voters accepted the Scottish Parliament but denied it taxation powers? The scars of wounds inflicted in 1979 began to itch.

I fingered my own scar, and felt some of the same fears. Scotland had certainly become a more assertive place in the eighteen years of Tory rule. In pubs and buses and in Scotland's rusting, draughty trains, people spoke more easily about their feelings for their country. But were they ready to risk acting on those feelings? The veterans of the long struggle for self-government had an almost immaculate record of getting public opinion wrong. The great Fault of misunderstanding dividing the garrulous few from the distrustful many was still there.

Could the politicians conducting the referendum campaign cross that gap? If they dared to abandon the wooden, bureaucratic language of Scottish party discourse and show their emotions, they might connect. Otherwise, there was a danger that they would bore the country to sleep. A few years before, in the Tory epoch, I had witnessed an agonizing example of this lack of oratorical resource. The occasion was a 'Great Debate' on Scotland's political future, held in the Royal High

School, which confronted George Robertson (then Labour's shadow Secretary of State for Scotland) with Alex Salmond, then leader of the SNP.

The principals made their speeches. Then there were questions from the gallery. All droned predictably on until a black-haired young woman from Inverness named Lorraine Mann put her own question. 'We all know what the first choice of you gentlemen is, between independence, devolution or the status quo,' she said. 'But what's your second choice?'

A small, cruel smile appeared on Salmond's face. The question, naturally, gave him no problems: his second choice was devolution, as a stepping-stone towards independence. Then he turned to enjoy the spectacle of George Robertson under torture. The status quo? But Labour was committed to the slogan that 'the status quo is not an option'. If Robertson chose it, then he would seem disloyal to his party, or unpatriotic as a Scot, or a crypto-Tory – if not all three at once. Independence? But Labour was committed to maintaining the Union, and independence was the policy of the enemy SNP! George squirmed, blethered, puffed. He grew pink with fury but found no words, no formula of escape. Soon the audience began to laugh at him, and then to interrupt. He was helpless.

The moral of this scene is not that George Robertson (now Lord Robertson of Port Ellen, and Secretary-General of NATO) had nothing in his belly but party formulae. He had fire in there too, including hot feelings about his own country and the injustices of its history. The point is that he had been trained to keep those feelings off the platform. He could have replied that, while he wanted neither of those two alternatives, independence was marginally the less repellent – except that Alex Salmond was peddling it. Perhaps that is what he really thought. But the rules of a political lifetime gagged him: it was unsayable.

Remembering Robertson in the Mann-trap, I was reminded of another European country in which decent social-democratic

politicians found it impossible to say what they felt. I had been
a foreign correspondent in West Germany at the time of the
1965 elections. Chancellor Ludwig Erhard, a Christian
Democrat, was being challenged by the Social Democrats
(SPD) under Willy Brandt. Privately, the SPD leaders had passionate views about inequality, workers' rights, the lack of
contacts with Eastern Europe and the survival of old Nazis in
the civil service and judiciary. But they had drilled themselves
to say none of these things in case the SPD was pilloried as
'Red' and soft on Communism. The campaign was no more
than an auction of banalities: 'Safe with the CDU', 'Security
with the SPD'.

But then a novelist lost patience. Günter Grass was at the
height of his fame. A few years before, he had astounded
Germany with *The Tin Drum* and *Cat and Mouse*, and he was at
work on *Dog Years*. These were political novels, each in its own
way designed to break the congested silence about the Hitler
years, to celebrate the earthy vigour of plebeian life, to mock
the conformism of West German public behaviour.

Grass decided to enliven this dismal election campaign. If
the SPD would not make their own case properly, then he and
his friends must make it for them. A bunch of fiction-writers,
dramatists, critics and other assorted intellectuals was recruited
to travel about the land in a bus, avoiding the big cities and
touring the small towns of provincial West Germany. At each
stop, a local 'Citizens' Initiative' was set up to hire a hall for
speeches, lay on a party with booze and music for the population, and organize beds in which the visitors could rest their
beer-fuddled heads.

The campaign called on the people to vote for Willy Brandt
and the SPD. But it did so with raucous, satirical abuse of
the Bonn Establishment which terrified the Social Democrat
leadership (except for Brandt himself, who was privately
delighted). Grass was the main speaker; a powerful graphic
artist as well as a writer, he had his speeches printed and flung

around in cheap leaflets illustrated by himself. They became the only words worth remembering from the whole stolid contest.

Chancellor Erhard was not accustomed to being laughed at, and he lost his temper. The chubby 'Father of the Economic Miracle' let his mask slip and snarled that this band of *Pinscher* (yapping terriers) had no place in German politics. This shocked respectable Germans, who in those times still venerated their intellectuals.

None the less, Erhard won the election comfortably. There was no evidence that Grass had shifted many votes, but he told me afterwards that he was surprised by the success of the journey. 'I was pleased that the Chancellor played so nicely into my hands. He could have shown a bit more self-control, but there you go. At least we made people think: not just that they should vote SPD, but that they should bother to vote at all.' The audience collections in the fourteen towns he visited amounted to 14,189 deutschmarks and 43 pfennigs. To the outrage of the Defence Ministry, Grass and the novelist Uwe Johnson spent this money on buying libraries for Bundeswehr barracks: 'Technical books, pulp crime stories, classics – it doesn't matter. Who knows what will happen when soldiers start reading?'

And there was one more point to the 'Citizens' Initiative'. Germany has its own Fault, inherited from the past, and a very Central European one. This division is about geographical space as much as about contrasts in historical experience. It runs between the semi-divine class of city-dwelling intellectuals and the mass of small-town and village Germans. The language is full of sneers about 'benighted provinces' and 'dreary back-country'. If the provincials have looked up to urban thinkers and creators with exaggerated awe, the intellectuals have despised the provincials as ignorant, superstitious, ugly, reactionary and unworthy of notice.

Grass thought that the bus journey could be a two-way

experience. It would open 'the province' to sophisticated wit and persuasion. But it would also introduce those metropolitan intellectuals to their own country – that other Germany which they had practically never seen, let alone taken seriously. The bus party's task was to listen as well as talk: to preach, but also to discover what ordinary people thought and to put questions back to them – something almost unheard of in German politics. After the speeches and the discussions, the intellectuals would drink beer with the chemist and the surveyor, eat the town's own thick soup and rye bread with an SPD local councillor, walk by the river with argumentative schoolchildren from the Gymnasium, and maybe end the evening in a bar with the Lutheran minister's daughter.

The flair and high spirits of the bus party, its complement constantly changing as people rode for a day or so and then gave way to others, shone out in the greyness of the campaign. The media, starving for colour and incident, were fascinated. The lessons in democracy were reported. And the intellectuals learned elementary truths, meditated on their encounter with 'real' people and emerged all the readier to plunge into public action during the upheavals of the late 1960s.

I thought Scotland needed something like this. In the summer of 1997, as the referendum began to take shape, the Home Rulers shuddered at what they saw. This threatened to be one more party-bound, lifeless exercise, conducted mostly by the same old faces mouthing the same old formulae on television. With the exception of the SNP, which had abandoned its sulky neutrality and was now mobilizing to fight for devolution, there was no sign that local party branches intended to make a serious effort to go round the doors and canvass for a Yes. Labour Party members muttered that they had been exhausted, physically and financially, by the exertions of the May election. The terrible danger was that too few people would vote Yes to register a morally convincing majority.

In 'Common Cause', I had argued for a long time that some new way of engaging with the people, an imaginative raid into democracy, must be found. That summer, 'Common Cause' agreed to resurrect the Günter Grass experiment, adapted to Scotland. There was no time to set up 'Citizens' Initiatives' in the towns we would visit. But Willie Storrar, the young minister whose energy kept the group moving, saw that the radical Kirk people gathered around Carberry Tower could use their network of contacts to make the local preparations. Some money came in; a small blue bus was hired. But where was our Günter Grass?

There was only one possible name for the job, and he agreed. William McIlvanney, apostle of Scotland's 'mongrel tradition', had all the qualities. His many novels – *Docherty*, *Laidlaw*, *The Big Man* among them – are read throughout Scotland. TV dramas scripted by him or based on his work are watched by millions. As a television personality, his face is instantly familiar – and it helps that it is a handsome face. Best of all, Willie McIlvanney has the gift of oratory. He jests and charms, and men and women trust him with their laughter like a brother. He turns serious, and they find his anger in their own hearts. It is a rare, heavenly gift, and like most of those who have it, its display leaves him melancholy.

Summer approached its end, and we made our final preparations. And then, in a Paris underpass on the last day of August, a princess died.

8

'They don't deserve a nation like this,' said the woman in the Mall. 'They' meant the Royal Family, the reigning House of Hanover and Windsor. And by 'nation' she meant not Britain but England.

Among the millions of flowers, the thousands of teddy bears and the hundreds of handwritten messages which were stacking up against the walls of St James's Palace, the gates of Kensington Palace, the railings of Buckingham Palace and the trees of the Mall in London, one flag was everywhere. But it was not the Union Jack, the emblem of state and the United Kingdom. Instead, the crowds clutched small red-and-white paper flags with the cross of St George. Where I saw a Union flag, in the vast, strolling encampment which had taken over the parade streets at the heart of London, I usually found a Canadian tourist, or a tearful lady from Australia.

Why that flag at this moment? History is made out of countless shreds of memory and pellets of data; these coagulate into impressions which in turn are dried, cleaned and carved into narratives. Perhaps the London tourist stalls had simply sold out of Union Jacks the week before, and fallen back on English flags instead. I can't exclude that. But there were other, more convincing explanations. The crowd was angry because the Queen and Royal Family had chosen not to interrupt their Balmoral holiday for Diana's death, and because of a flag. The Royal Standard was not flying over Buckingham Palace at half-mast. This was held to symbolize cold indifference by the Royals to their crushed English Rose, to the young woman whom Tony Blair a few hours before had called 'the People's Princess', to England's outpouring of remorse and love.

In 'Diana Week', the Kingdom for a moment came unstitched. The English suddenly glimpsed themselves as a nation, and during that brief moment they understood that nation, state and monarchy were three separate beings standing under three separate flags. People spoke as if there were a war of the palaces: between Diana's home at Kensington Palace, the court of feeling and compassion, and Buckingham Palace where young, warm hearts were frozen into lifeless obedience. 'Thank you, Diana, for loving the broken even in your brokenness,' said one note tied to a bunch of flowers. Another cried: 'You were worth all the other Royals put together.' And another – moist with the week's weird mixture of guilt, grief and superstition – read: 'Diana, as children we often have our favourite toy taken away for not treating it properly, in order to learn our lesson. I know I've learned my lesson. So when are you coming back?'

It was the monarchy's worst moment since the Abdication in 1937. In some ways, it seemed more serious. The people had not taken to the streets to defend Edward VIII and Mrs Simpson, but the talk of these crowds showed that support for the Crown had become perilously conditional by the end of the twentieth century. 'They don't deserve a nation like this . . .' That could be read as a threat to have the Windsors' favourite throne taken away for not treating it properly.

It was also one of the worst moments for Britain's tabloid press. The people on the Mall had no doubts about who had killed Diana. 'She was hounded to death by the media,' they told me, over and over again. If the camera pack had not chased Diana and her lover across Paris in their usual way, she would still be alive. They were right, of course; the facts that the driver was not sober and that Diana had courted publicity when it suited her were rather beside the point. But you could not find a syllable of this huge popular verdict in the tabloid news-papers. Terrified, the editors suppressed it and changed the subject to the failings of the Royal Family.

On the Mall, I ran into a historian who knows Poland. We remembered John Paul II's first visit there as Pope in 1979, the year before the Solidarity revolution. Then, too, there had been flowers, vast crowds wondering at their own temerity, a sense of rulers losing the confidence of the ruled. My friend said: 'I think this may mean the end of the monarchy – and probably of the United Kingdom as well.'

He was mistaken, at least in the short and medium terms. The Queen was induced to return to London, and the funeral became a triumph of improvised British pageantry watched on television by the entire world. To general astonishment, the popularity of the Royals not only recovered but in the next few years reached new heights in the opinion polls.

All the same, something had changed. Those families all over England who had sent one or more members down to London to lay flowers for Diana had made a discovery: the Union Jack was the standard shown to foreigners, but the Cross of St George, the flag of England, was the flag of the heart. In this sense, my historian friend had not been wrong about the portent for the United Kingdom. The re-emergence of English national consciousness, long predicted by Scottish and Welsh students of the 'Ukanian' state, was under way.

Diana's death had instant political consequences for Scotland.

Public grief was more temperate; although flowers piled up on the steps of many town halls, there was nothing resembling the scenes in London. But all campaigning for the referendum was suspended until Sunday, 7 September. Referendum Day was the following Thursday. Neither the Yes nor the No camps had made much effort by the time that the princess and Dodi Al-Fayed were driven into the tunnel at the Pont de l'Alma. In effect, the vote had to be sought and won in only four full campaigning days – just under a hundred hours.

On the previous Thursday, a week before the poll, I had been called to see Donald Dewar, Secretary of State for Scotland and the designated First Minister if the referendum succeeded. Why he wanted to see me I never discovered. We had often met over the years, and I knew that he had liked some but certainly not all of what I had written. It seemed that this lonely and yet gregarious man just wanted a chat.

The Diana outburst baffled him. 'What's it all about? Is it anti-Windsor? They were certainly extremely ill-advised not to come south at once.' He knew that women were very pro-Diana; his personal assistant had told him so long ago. But he was shocked by the venom of that morning's tabloid attack on the Royals. As for the Westminster Abbey funeral, 'Do you think I should be there? I hate all that sort of thing. Of course, I know that Alex Salmond will go.'

I said that I thought he must go, or at least attend some parallel ceremony in Glasgow. He changed the subject, and for a while we gossiped about Mid-Argyll people and places we both knew. Then I asked the question haunting many campaigners: would Diana's death produce a surge of Unionist sentiment in Scotland and affect the outcome of the referendum?

'The figures are still good,' Donald said, looking anxious, 'and I think we can win both questions. Anyway, all is not lost if there is a No majority on the tax question. Perhaps we should not have added taxation powers to the project, with hindsight.

But John Smith wanted that, you know. He was keen on the Parliament having financial responsibility.'

This was not encouraging. I told him about our bus-party initiative, and he cheered up and became enthusiastic. But I left with an uneasy feeling that Donald – who knew all too much about the morale of Scottish Labour and its will to fight – was preparing himself for a result which was indecisive or worse.

The Yes campaign held its launch 'rally' that Sunday, in the Royal High School. It was not a rally at all, in the sense of a public mass meeting. Instead, it was a gathering of all the leaders and worthies whose followers were committed to the Parliament cause. But it was an entirely amazing gathering. For the first time in my life and (I have little doubt) the last, the supporters of self-government put aside their differences and embraced.

Coming in from the yard, where our bus stood fuelled and ready to depart, I could not believe what I saw in the debating chamber. Winnie Ewing of the SNP, the 'Madame Ecosse' of the European Parliament and her party's senior politician, sat high in the convener's chair under a 'Yes/Yes' poster. Alex Salmond settled beside Henry McLeish of the Labour Party, Jim Wallace, leader of the Scottish Liberal Democrats and Nigel Smith of the 'Scotland Forward' movement, among ranks of MPs and candidates from all the parties save the Tories. On the front bench, looking nervous, was Sean Connery. We pretended not to stare at him.

Winnie, white-haired and draped in a tartan scarf, spoke first. She praised parliaments based on cooperation across party lines, like the European Parliament where she had worked for so long and the Scottish Parliament now coming to birth. There would be no place in the new Scotland for the adversarial pattern of Westminster.

Sean Connery stood up and read from the Declaration of Arbroath. He had no time – to my regret – for its majestic myth of origin: 'The which Scottish nation, journeying from Greater

Scythia by the Tyrrhene Sea and the Pillars of Hercules ...'
Instead he read the familiar passage: 'For so long as a hundred
of us are left alive, we will yield in no least way to English
dominion. We fight not for glory nor for wealth nor honours; but
only and alone we fight for freedom, which no good man surrenders but with his life.'

Connery's thick voice faltered on those last words. He
stopped for a moment, then said: 'That was written 677 years
ago. The Scots are not usually known for their patience. Well,
we may have patience but we don't have time. There's just a
hundred hours to go.'

Henry McLeish was next. He complimented Winnie for
speaking about cooperation and, unexpectedly, invited the
SNP to join Labour in preparing a reform of Scottish education.
'I trust the people. So does Alex Salmond, so does Jim Wallace,
so does Sean Connery. For the sake of John Smith and everyone concerned for Scotland, let's finish the unfinished business
on Thursday.'

Could I be listening to a Labour MP and minister? The
dream-like hour of truce went on, as the other politicians took
their turns. Finally Willie McIlvanney added a few barbed sentences comparing Scotland's revival as a nation to an
'intermittent serial' overdue for its final episode. He was sorry
he could not speak longer. 'But now I've a bus to catch.'

We stood up and filed out. And the meeting, that improbable
congregation of temporary saints, gave us a round of applause.

A small mob was surrounding the bus as we emerged from
the Royal High. It was already crammed with luggage and wads
of paper; television reporters from Breakfast TV and Channel 4
were clambering in and out of the doors in search of writers and
celebrities. The big banner meant to hang along the bus's
flanks had blown away, hooked off by the wind on the journey
in from Carberry Tower. This wasn't going to work. We
replaced it with another, nailed to a long spar of wood, to
be unfurled only at halts and meetings: 'The Bus Party: Talk-

ing about Scotland with William McIlvanney and his friends'.

A few yards away, the Vigil people in their hut sized us up. The scoreboard next to their door registered 1975 days and nights spent waiting for 'Democracy for Scotland' on the public pavement. They looked tough and weatherbeaten. If it needed another five years of sentinel duty on the Calton Hill, they would do it. In contrast, we were frail eggheads, unused to campaigning through Scythian frosts and addicted to our own beds at night.

The bus party changed all through the journey, as it was meant to. But there was a permanent core. McIlvanney himself was the lead performer, and the red-haired minister Willie Storrar was our manager. He was helped by Audrey Hart from Fraserburgh who worked at Carberry. I was there, and an old friend of mine, Danus Skene, drove the wagon. Margaret Macintosh was a wise and witty retired headteacher, seen off at the Calton Hill by her husband, Farquhar, who had himself been the 'heidie' of the Royal High. The critic Joyce MacMillan rode with us, and so did Alison Elliot from the Church and Nation committee of the Kirk. And in the back, huddled beside his instrument, was a young boy named Fin Moore who played the sweet-toned 'smallpipes', the little indoor bagpipe which survives in the Gaelic-speaking settlements of Atlantic Canada.

We drove over the Forth, the bridges glowing in a brilliant evening light, and Joyce was haranguing a puzzled woman from Breakfast TV with extracts from the cultural gospel. This was the chapter about how the 'tartan monster' of phony Celticism had entombed the land under Royal Stuart shortbread and false consciousness. Yes, but . . . I couldn't listen to this and not join in. Never mind Scotland the Brave, what about the 'Caledonian Antisyzygy' – Gregory Smith's old theory of Scottishness as an interlace of opposites, grinning gargoyles with kneeling saints? What about the intellectual substitute for tartanry which had claimed that each

Presbyterian Scot was not one fellow but two fellows, Stevenson's Jekyll and Hyde or James Hogg's Robert Wringhim and Gil-Martin from *The Confessions of a Justified Sinner*, dual spirits wrestling in one body for the pleasure of the Great Elector in the sky? Or the *Trainspotting* notion that Scottish identity might be just passivity, a prone consent to be colonized by one set of confident wankers after another?

The van was loud, but McIlvanney was silent. I knew enough about him to know that he thought this sort of debate was crap. Was this a serious conversation, or were Joyce and I talking to ourselves, putting on a display to overwhelm the poor Breakfast woman who had to get a few minutes of comprehensible television out of this trip? The truth was – and I had to admit it – that the fashion for debates about Scottish identity was over anyway. Self-accusation was for the moment a finished business, and people wanted to move on to the unfinished business of inventing a country fit to live in, whoever the hell its inhabitants thought they were.

Silence fell, and I leafed through a relic found in a drawer: the Labour Party's 'Speaker's Notes' for the 1979 referendum campaign. The section on 'Doubts' was instructive. 'The Assembly will make Scotland the most overgoverned country in the world.' It will be 'too unstable to survive' and push us all down 'the slippery slope to independence'. It will reduce Scotland's influence at Westminster. People 'are just not interested in devolution' and 'an Assembly will undermine the unity and solidarity of the Working Class struggle'. Were any of these doubts extinct? Probably not, and we would soon meet them all again.

We made for Dundee. The Bonar Hall was crowded; political debate turned into a ceilidh punctuated with poetry and songs. We picked up more bus passengers: Billy Kay, promoter of the spoken Scots language; Rod Paterson, song-writer and singer; Matthew Fitt, poet. From St Andrews came two professor-poets, Douglas Dunn and Robert Crawford. Dunn said: 'One of my greatest hopes from a Scottish Parliament is the advance of education to the point at which my Scottish students would speak to me.'

Dundee was a festival for the converted. Next morning we drove on to Arbroath and worked the streets, pushing for a 'Yes/Yes' vote but asking people what difference, if any, the Parliament would make. Almost everyone admitted that they would probably vote; almost nobody said how. They were surprised but then pleased to be asked for their own opinions. These were unpredictable. One boy said, after a second's thought: 'A Scottish Parliament should help wee-bitty Third World companies to compete with multinational companies and not be destroyed. And it should make mair flags!'

We found our way back to the bus, outside the red Abbey where the Declaration of Arbroath was signed, and agreed that the response looked hopeful. Audrey reported one old man who had yelled at her that he would vote No and No again, and that he wanted the poll tax brought back. Willie McIlvanney raised his eyebrows. 'And you let him *live?*'

After Arbroath we moved up the east coast to Stonehaven. All I remember now is the bus party crowding into The Haven, the chippie which had just won global notoriety for inventing the deep-fried Mars Bar. There was laughter and music in there; Fin contrived to wield his pipes in the throng and play Hamish Henderson's 'Freedom Come All Ye'. People sang until the house speciality came sizzling over the counter and stopped their mouths.

Billed in the world press as the most unhealthy snack ever devised by man to plug his arteries, the Bar turned out to be intensely delicious but so rich that none of us could get beyond three mouthfuls. In old times, the killer dish was a black bull's head, whose appearance was the signal for armed men to spring from behind the arras and slaughter the guests. This new delicacy has a future as the finale of state banquets offered by the president of a Scottish republic to foreign heads of state: *Beignet au lingot de chocolat à la mode d'Ecosse.*

The next stop was Mintlaw Academy. Inland from Peterhead, this is a big comprehensive school in rural Buchan. I had not been there since the 1979 election campaign, at a moment when the Scottish Tories realized that the Labour government was dead on its feet and that their party was on its way back to power.

I had found Albert MacQuarrie, their local candidate, standing in a field at Turriff wearing his three-piece pinstripe suit and staring into the sky. He was waiting to welcome Mrs Thatcher, who presently swooped down from heaven in an obliterating convoy of helicopters. The SNP were about to lose all their three seats in the north-east. But Hamish Watt, the SNP member for Banffshire, was still full of optimism and punching back at the wicked landlords. 'Folks, fat's sauce for ta goose is sauce for ta gander!'

In those days, Mintlaw was nicknamed 'Fort MacQuarrie'. But by 1997, nobody remembered that. The seat had been recaptured for the SNP by Alex Salmond himself, ten years before; the defeated Mr MacQuarrie had been comforted with a knighthood, and no prophetess in a fiery chariot came down to rescue his successors. Peterhead, the hard old burgh on the North Sea which had once sent its sons out to catch whales, command Russian armies or colonize Poland, was in a poor way as the oil boom receded and the fishing grounds grew barren.

At the Academy, the boys and girls in the assembly hall astonished us. It was not local politics or the lack of jobs which they most wanted to talk about. Instead it was language – the right to express themselves in Scots. This delighted Billy Kay; as a broadcaster and as the author of *Scots: the Mither Tongue*, he had done more work than anyone to publicize the plight of the language and agitate for its introduction into the school curriculum. The rest of us in the bus party knew about the language campaign, but we had not suspected that it had reached beyond patriot intellectuals to the school pupils themselves.

Buchan is the biggest surviving stronghold of spoken Scots, the tongue known variously as 'braid Scots', 'Lallans' or – in these parts – as 'the Doric'. Its origins lie in the northern version of Anglian, enriched by the Scandinavian speech of the Viking colonization. After the Kingdom of Scotland established itself, this tongue (first known as 'Inglis' to distinguish it from Gaelic) diverged away from southern Anglian to emerge as the official language of Scotland by the fourteenth century.

'Classic' literature in Scots had a glorious but short life. It emerged in the late fourteenth century with John Barbour's epic poem 'The Brus', and began its steep decline less than two centuries later at the time of the Reformation. No full translation of the Bible into Scots existed; John Knox and his colleagues adopted the Geneva English version, and chose English as the language of the Kirk and its new metrical psalms. From then on, as Billy Kay has said, 'God spoke English', and written Scots began to lose status and disintegrate.

This first Scots literature reached its zenith between the late fourteenth and mid-sixteenth centuries. Its masters and 'makars', William Dunbar, Robert Henryson and Gavin Douglas above all, set out deliberately to enrich the language (to make it 'aureate', as they put it) by inspired word-invention and borrowing from Latin, French, English and Flemish. The crown of this literature remains Gavin Douglas's superb and sovereign version of the 'Aeneid', described by Ezra Pound as the greatest of all works of translation.

These were Renaissance writers, learned in Greek and Roman prose and verse. But at the same time they were in love with the blunt, carnal and comic quality of popular Scots. They drew from it – among other devices – the 'flyting' form of satirical dialogue, a competitive verse exchange of often colossally obscene insults. Dunbar could greet an adversary:

Haill, soverane senyeour! Thy bawis hingis through thy breik.

But, brooding on death as he incessantly did, he also wrote the most perfect summary of the Renaissance spirit I know in any literature:

> *I will no priestis for me sing,*
> *Dies illa, dies irae;*
> *Nor yet na bellis for me ring,*
> *Sicut semper solet fieri,*
> *But a bag-pyp to play a spring.*

It would be wrong to think that the composing of literature in Scots fell abruptly dead during the Reformation. What slowly perished was the innovating drive, the will to maintain and enlarge a single literary language for Scotland. When James VI moved his court to London and became James I of England and Ireland through the Union of Crowns in 1603, the main source of patronage dried up. The new Calvinist orthodoxy was suspicious of all utterances in Scots which were not 'improving', and remained intensely hostile to the theatre. By the mid-seventeenth century, few sophisticated writers in Scotland used the marvellous verbal palace built by their predecessors.

But that did not mean that the work of the 'Golden Age' in the fifteenth and sixteenth centuries was forgotten. It continued to be read by educated Scots with access to good libraries, even though the identities of its authors were sometimes forgotten. Some even older texts had a much wider readership. The establishment of the parish school system meant that reading literacy – as opposed to writing, which was much rarer – was prevalent in Lowland Scotland by the end of the eighteenth century, and small farmers traditionally possessed not only the

Bible but a copy of Barbour's 'Brus' or Blind Harry's 'Wallace'.

Gavin Douglas's 'Aeneid' was republished in facsimile in 1710 for a list of over three hundred subscribers, although it now required the addition of a 'glossary' of obsolete words. English was the written language of the Scottish Enlightenment, and word-lists circulated of 'vulgar' Scotticisms to be tweezered out of the conversation of polished ladies and gentlemen, and yet late medieval and Renaissance texts in Scots were being collected, edited and reissued all through the eighteenth and nineteenth centuries. There was no suggestion that 'ancient' written Scots – even if judged rather barbarous – was an extinct curiosity. The editor of one such collection, published in Perth in 1786, observed that difficulties with vocabulary were due only to 'the mutability of the language, in the space of near four hundred years, an imperfection attendant on every living language'.

The common people of Scotland, south and east of the Highlands, continued to speak this living language in regional variations. But the notion that language became entirely class-determined – that the upper and middle classes switched to English speech while the 'workers and peasants' used the vernacular – is wrong, and misses the cultural complexity of Scotland in the eighteenth and early nineteenth centuries. Grand Polish families at the same period used French in the drawing room and for their letter-writing, but relapsed into their own tongue in the fields, the regiment or indeed the Sejm (parliament). In the same way, Scottish judges often chose to speak Scots on the Bench, while peers occasionally annoyed their English colleagues by speaking their 'incomprehensible dialect' in the House of Lords in London.

Carlyle recalled that the Principal of Edinburgh University, the historian William Robertson (1721–1793), 'spoke broad Scotch . . . his was the language of literature and taste, and of a liberal and enlightened mind'. That was an optimistic tribute. Another view on Scots was that it could convey a sort of intimate brutality which would have seemed impossibly appalling in English. Robert MacQueen, the savage judge Lord Braxfield, informed a defendant that he was 'a verra clever chiel, man, but ye wad be nane the waur of a hanging'. He would never have said that in English.

As well as speaking Scots, the people continued vigorously to sing it. 'Civilized' urban types were familiar with the Border Ballads, and the published collections of traditional songs encouraged eighteenth-century poets – Allan Ramsay the elder, Robert Fergusson and above all Robert Burns – to adopt their forms and to write in the demotic Scots which had been the tongue of their own parents and neighbours (Burns spent much of his later life collecting songs, and he 'aureated' his own Ayrshire vocabulary with loan-words from other parts of Lowland Scotland). Novelists from Walter Scott onwards wrote in English, with Scots confined within quotation marks to the dialogue of rustic characters, but recent research has shown that in Victorian Scotland there was a resurgence of popular newspapers largely written in the vernacular.

Scottish society, in short, remained bilingual at least into the early twentieth century. After that, the relatively small middle class generally abandoned full-blooded Scots, which by then was differentiated into half a dozen local dialects, but the rest of the nation was more reluctant to change. In consequence, wide areas of Scotland today are still essentially bilingual, and that includes working-class Glasgow or the towns of post-industrial Fife as well as more remote rural districts.

Bilinguality, none the less, is usually about context. People with two languages do not simply drop from one into another as the mood takes them; they switch speech to perform different functions. Alsatians talk Alemanisch in private, on the bus and in the café, but they switch to French in the office or the schoolroom – as once they switched to High German when Alsace was under German control. Scots do much the same, even though their English is distinct in its accent and its inclusion of Scots words or tricks of syntax. But the closeness of the two languages only emphasizes the instinct that Scots has a lower status than 'standard English', and that it is not acceptable in the ambition-world of job applications, form-filling or examinations.

The English view has been that Scots is no more than a regional dialect of English, indicating a tartan narrowness among its speakers, and over the past hundred years many Scots reluctantly swallowed this valuation. In Tom Leonard's famous phonetic poem 'Unrelated Incidents', the six o'clock BBC news reader explains that:

> *thi reason*
> *a talk wia*
> *BBC accent*
> *iz coz yi*
> *widny wahnt*
> *mi ti talk*
> *aboot thi*
> *trooth wia*
> *voice lik*
> *wanna yoo*
> *scruff . . .*

In most of Scotland, not only in Buchan, children talk some variant of Scots at home and in the school play yard, but English when they go indoors to the classroom. But the question asked more and more urgently in recent years is whether this bilingualism is really complete. Does standard English remain a 'learned' second language which most learners never totally internalize? And this leads to a second question: whether this linguistic lack of confidence explains the notorious silence of Scottish first-year students, contrasting so sharply with the easy response of English students at Scottish universities. That was precisely what Douglas Dunn meant at Dundee, when he hoped that self-government would make his students talk to him.

There has always been resentment about the sovereignty of standard English. But until now, there has been no militancy. At Mintlaw Academy, though, there was a new mood. Buchan Scots is a rich but very particular dialect with its own substitute consonants and an almost Swedish intonation (my wife went to primary school a few miles from Mintlaw, and even now I find her Doric recitations impenetrable). It survived with its own literature of bothy ballads and local poetry, beating off all attempts to subdue its vigour. Back in the 1790s, the Peterhead minister had moaned that 'The language spoken in this parish is the broad Buchan dialect of the English, with many Scotticisms, and stands much in need of reformation, which it is hoped will soon happen, from the frequent resort of polite people to the town in summer.' As Billy Kay commented, 'Some hope!'

We started the meeting with entertainment. Rod Paterson took his guitar and sang his 'Five-Minute Hamlet in Scots', and McIlvanney read his short story about a Glasgow drunk meeting Frankenstein. Then we broke up into groups, talking about the Parliament and the future and trying to condense each discussion into a set of headlines. In my group, the first to speak (in English, to set me at ease) was a boy who said: 'I want to be proud of what I am. I go into a shop, and why should he force me to use a language that's not my own?' At progressive Mintlaw, 'the Doric' is now taught as an option. But that was not enough for this group. They wanted their own Scots to be the medium of instruction, and the tongue in which the school went about its routines. The headteacher, the astute 'heidie' Mr McWhirr, is in fact a Doric speaker and respected for it. Many of the other teachers, inevitably, were not.

We put together our group report. As we talked, it was obvious that several boys and a girl were from England, probably from families brought in by the oil boom. But the prickly nationalism of the report did not bother them at all. 'We want a firm Scottish culture, but not against anyone else like England.' Scottish history should be properly taught, 'to explain why we are as we are'. The Parliament would only be useful if it had taxing powers, so that Scots could take charge of the economy. There should be equal numbers of men and women in the Parliament. And, coming back to the big preoccupation, 'there ought to be a pride in our language; Scots should be taught; the Scots should not have to apologize for themselves, because Scotland as a nation deserves international respect and recognition from the whole world . . .'

I thought of another time, almost a hundred years before, when school pupils had fought for their language. In May 1901, when Poland was still obliterated from the map of Europe, Imperial Germany had launched a new campaign to suppress Polish identity in its occupied territories. German was declared to be the compulsory language of instruction for religious classes in primary schools. But at the small town of Września, near Poznań, the children went on strike in defence of the Polish language. The Prussian police marched in, dragged the little strikers out of their homes and had them thrashed for disobedience. Their parents instantly joined the protest. Scores of mothers and fathers were arrested and imprisoned, while liberal newspapers all over Europe and America piled contempt on a Germany whose power rested on beefy gendarmes battering the arses of small boys.

Mintlaw is a long way from Września. Scotland is not an occupied country, and the Grampian constabulary – a fine, Doric body themselves – are not going to draw their batons if some teenage loon or quiney says in class that Jesus 'sufert under Poncio Pilat to be crucifeit, to de and to be yeirdit'. All the same, Mintlaw is also a long way from the subdued 'Fort MacQuarrie' of 1979. This angry cultural nationalism, gathered in such a European way around a language, is something which grew up in the politically stagnant 1980s, and it is here to stay.

9

'Powerlessness to the people!' said the social worker. 'Here people just go down and down, month by month.' We were in Middlefield, a big housing scheme on the fringes of Aberdeen. The hall was almost empty. The residents had assumed that Middlefield was one of the places which a Parliament could not reach, and it was hard to blame them. Two or three women sat in a corner, and several small boys circled the crisps and lemonade hopefully laid out on a table. Apart from them, there were a few Church people, a couple of social workers and the local SNP councillor. The bus party outnumbered them all.

Talking about Scotland with the population was obviously not on. Instead, we drew some chairs into a circle in the middle of the emptiness and talked to each other. Willie McIlvanney started to speak about the old Scottish instinct for community and solidarity, which had been tried so sorely during the Thatcher years, and to back his case he quoted the Scottish stock response to injustice: 'It's no fair!' But the SNP councillor interrupted him. 'What's missing from that is: . . . "and what are we going to do about it?"' We listened to sad accounts of Middlefield's passivity and the indifference of its families to designs put together in Edinburgh or Westminster. Again, this passivity seemed understandable. It was not Middlefield's apathy which had brought so many local self-help initiatives to nothing. It was the mistrust of those initiatives by local government, unwilling to allow such community groups to handle money and spend it as they saw fit.

Joyce MacMillan was outraged. 'How can people be at once so divorced from the system and so dependent on it?' We all knew how. Scottish local government, above all in housing, is preoccupied with control, and a condition of silent, divorced dependence is what it prefers from its tenantry. Middlefield was a microcosm of the worst aspect of Scotland – an archipelago of undemocracies, run by power cliques who want as few people as possible to participate in running their own lives.

Most of these power cliques are Labour councils. Labour's overwhelming domination of urban local government in Scotland has been a fact of life for half a century, and the transfer of over half the country's housing into low-rent public ownership became a guarantee that the council schemes would deliver a solid Labour vote down the generations. Dependency on council services and subsidized rents steadily deepened as the houses grew more dilapidated. The change in planning fashion in the late sixties, as Labour councils tore down inner-city housing and decanted its inhabitants into gigantic peri-urban plantations of tower blocks, did nothing to alter this pattern. The tower blocks decayed even faster than the low-rise council houses, and the rapid rise of unemployment multiplied dependency as industrial wages were replaced by income from welfare benefits.

But this is the tale of a tragedy, not of a crime. Three great events in recent history transformed the lives of Scottish people for the better: the Crofting Acts of the 1880s which created a secure Highland and Islands peasantry, the Lloyd

George budgets between 1909 and 1911 which brought in the principle of national insurance, and the Welfare State established by the Labour government after 1945. Nothing can take away from the Labour Party the honour of what was done then, the attempt to realize a vision of socialism which would give ordinary people the means to live according to their needs. And nowhere did that vision glow more brightly than in Scotland, where Labour councils confronted the most overcrowded and degraded urban housing in northern Europe.

They said 'It's no fair!' and they at least knew what they were going to do about it. In 1945, there was no time to wait for the people to take their own initiative, and no plan to let workers manage their own nationalized industry – which is what housing now became. Socialism in post-war Britain was something brought from the centre, to be imposed and maintained by central force and power against local 'vested interests'. In Scottish Labour, this authoritarian, Jacobin view of reform – the centre by definition progressive, the periphery by definition reactionary – survived long after it had ceased to fit the facts of Scottish life. At local government level, its legacy was enduring distrust of the grassroots: who were these awkward squads who thought they knew better than the Housing Department? At national level, faith in 'socialism from one centre' was at the roots of Scottish Labour's instinctive fear of devolution, the fear which was brought to bay at Dalintober Street.

The housing revolution was driven through with uncompromising zeal. Post-war Europe, rebuilding itself after six years of destruction and neglect, was full of 'social housing' experiments. But none of them went as far as Scotland's. By the early 1970s, public-sector housing in Scotland had become so dominant that only 30 per cent of dwellings remained in owner-occupation (in England, by contrast, private home-ownership still accounted for over half the total housing stock). Even in the Communist states of eastern Europe, in Hungary or Poland, the percentage of state-owned public housing was generally well below the Scottish level.

Political loyalty was a matter of gratitude but also of realism. For those who remembered the squalor of the old tenements, the idea of voting for a party which might restore private land-lords was unthinkable. For the next generation, brought up in these housing schemes, living and voting in any other way than their parents had done was unimaginable. A subsidized way of life is a steady way of life, and contemptuous hindsight – the view from the other side of the free-market counter-revolution – is too easy. The withering of Labour's housing empire into a patchwork of urban ghettos governed like penal colonies did not become patent until the 1980s. Until then, for something like thirty years, Scottish working people were able for the first time to live in security and some comfort, with baths, in-house toilets and enough rooms to allow basic privacy. They deserved no less than that, and they knew how to appreciate it. They had come from a far more terrible dependency, whose agents were tuberculosis, hunger, rickets and the rent-collector. To write off the council-house years as a mirage, as a doomed bid to escape from 'the real world' of market forces, is con-temptible. Those years happened, and on balance they were good. The fact that they came to an end, having lasted for more than a generation, does not discredit them.

But the empire did wither, and the first signs of blight were soon visible. The new housing deteriorated much faster than anyone had anticipated, and maintaining it demanded invest-ment far beyond the finances allowed to local government. As the journalist Colin Bell wrote in 1976, 'in ... Dundee, Glasgow, Paisley and Alloa, to cite only the best-known exam-ples, there are post-war estates which have already fallen into ruin, and are scheduled for demolition. What this means is that homes built on money borrowed over thirty, forty, even sixty years have become slums long before their capital cost has been repaid'. It also meant that Scotland's ancestral plague of housing unfit for humans was spreading back across the cities, infecting the low-rise housing schemes and the tower blocks as it had once infected the stone-built inner-city tenements.

To know the true state of a housing scheme, I learned to study doors. In Scotland, until recently, most people lived in apartments off a common stair. The stair may be reasonably clear and clean; the sign to look for is a door with a crushed, bruised look around the lock. It may be hastily repainted, but a door never fully recovers from being opened with a boot. That mark, instantly recognized by everyone on the stair, is the sign that the virus has entered the building. If nothing is done about those who live behind the door, rubbish and worse will appear in the close, uproar will disturb the nights and the other tenants will eventually apply for a transfer – leaving the council to recolonize the stair with more people with 'problems'. In this way, bit by bit, a sound block of council housing begins its downward slide to slumhood.

And the sheer predominance of public housing meant that the segregation of 'disadvantaged' families and tenants went further and faster than in England. By the early 1970s, almost all Scottish towns and cities had 'ghetto schemes' of ill repute, where street-level windows were boarded up, broken glass shimmered in the gutters and bus conductors hoped not to find passengers. In almost all these places, that ill repute was unfair to the majority of their inhabitants, whose crime was no worse than to be poor and unqualified. And many of them (in Glasgow, Castlemilk, Easterhouse and Drumchapel; in Edinburgh, Craigmillar) soon developed remarkable self-help networks, organizing defences against the loan shark, the drug dealer and – not least – the sheriff's officers as they came to seize possessions against debt or evict rent defaulters.

The trouble was that Labour disowned the ghettos. It was an instinctive rejection. The condition of 'exclusion', or 'divorce from the system' as Joyce put it, seemed to challenge the whole social pattern on which the party's local power-structure rested. The provision of public housing at controlled rents was meant to integrate people, not to exclude them, and to marry them happily ever after with a Labour-run system. And Scottish Labour, which had begun as the party of the Catholic Irish minority – the unskilled, discriminated against and excluded – was now the party of the better-off working class who still had work. Increasingly, it recoiled from social failure.

At Keir Hardie House, Labour's Glasgow headquarters in the 1970s, there was plenty of traditional sympathy for the unemployed. But what about the tens of thousands who were not so much unemployed as unconnected? What about those who had grown up in a world where a regular job was no more than a grandfather's tale, who would never belong to a trades union, who fiddled housing benefit or sold heroin in order to keep themselves in cigarettes and feed their children, who were multiple lone mothers before the age of twenty? Was Labour their party too? Or were they too feckless to be included in politics at all? At this question, the party blew its empathy fuse.

As Labour's housing empire began to show these stresses, other parties moved in. By the late 1970s, Scottish political journalists knew that Labour was losing its grip on what might be called 'the lower depths vote' – the most deprived areas in housing schemes. I noticed in Drumchapel, one of Glasgow's biggest peripheral estates, that the SNP had gained a solid foothold in the scarred houses known as 'The Hill'. It was a pattern which was repeated in many places. At first not much came of it, except in the famously volatile Glasgow constituency of Govan. That was because the 'lower depths', though willing to shout anti-English slogans and wave Saltire flags, were pretty unwilling to register on the electoral roll, turn out and vote. But the hint that poverty was becoming an anti-Labour indicator on council estates was startling. This was a crack in the established political surface, and the future began to leak through it.

Returned to power in 1979, the Tories instantly made their own move. Colin Bell's article three years before had noted that 'the attractions of ownership, as every political party recognizes with more or less frankness, appeal to a very large proportion of those at present paying rents to public housing authorities. Tenants do want to buy their own homes, and only a stubborn commitment by the Labour Party to an outmoded doctrine prevents us from mobilizing that reserve of enthusiasm.' Within months of taking office, Mrs Thatcher did what no previous Conservative leader had dared to attempt and decreed that council houses could be sold to their tenants. The outcry was deafening in Scotland, where the new law was said to threaten the whole social and political settlement of the nation.

So it did. That was exactly what Mrs Thatcher intended. In some respects the last Leninist, she meant to destroy the class base of opposition by social engineering. If the masses were to become individual property-owners, she reasoned, then the cultural superstructure of voting for Labour would buckle and collapse. But in Scotland, at least, her calculation did not work out. Thousands of tenants rushed to buy their homes at knock-down prices from sullen local councils. It soon became clear, however, that the upgrade from proletariat to property-owner had not changed their politics at all. Families on Scottish council estates who had bought their homes continued to vote Labour. In fact, they were slightly more inclined to vote Labour than they had been before. It was the Tory vote which continued to shrivel. Even in the Orange Lodges in the industrial west of Scotland, for generations the fortresses of working-class Toryism against the Labour-voting Catholic masses, the party's support collapsed.

If the sale of council houses miscarried politically, its social consequences were more mixed. For some, it was an emancipation. Families whose ancestors had never owned anything more than a spade, a cow, a second-hand Hillman Imp or a colour television now possessed a capital asset theoretically worth many thousands of pounds. The restrictions on resale were complicated, but when they had been navigated, the new owners for the first time could make radical choices about where and how they wanted to lead their lives. For others, however, ownership turned out to be a cruel deception. Maintaining houses and apartments which were already deteriorating when they were sold was expensive, while the market for ex-council houses in run-down areas was almost non-existent. Many buyers found themselves trapped in 'negative equity', owning houses whose market value was far below the price they had paid for it.

A widening chasm now ran across urban Scotland. The luckiest ones moved out into the private housing estates springing up around small towns and villages. The unlucky stayed behind, stuck with worthless property in declining council schemes, as Scotland's public housing – originally designed to offer homes to all working people from the high-earning technician to the unskilled labourer – now diminished to a last-chance safety-net for families in trouble. In Middlefield and places like it, owner-occupiers who could not afford to move away found themselves inhabiting disaster areas of deprivation. The 'inclusive' vision of the post-war housing planners had ended in its opposite: a pattern of excluded poverty-ghettos whose people were isolated from the normal world of working, shopping and politics. The sale of council houses ended in a grand separation with a Presbyterian flavour; the elect were taken up rejoicing to another world, while the reprobate – damned through no fault of their own – were left to fry in sin and misery.

As we left Middlefield, a van drew up, and a squad of young men and women emerged unfurling SNP banners. They shared out bundles of 'Yes/Yes' leaflets and prepared to canvass the scheme close by close. One said: 'There's no evidence at all of Labour campaigning, here or anywhere in Aberdeen. Are they going to try and take the credit for our work, as they did in 1979?'

I looked at him. In 1979, he would have been in a nursery class sticking daisies in a jar. But in Scotland, as in Ireland, political grievances have no sell-by date.

That evening, we parked outside St Machar's cathedral, in Old Aberdeen. The church was full, and the faces welcoming. But the chill of Middlefield still pinched us, and we craved reassurance that we were back in a warmer, familiar Scotland impatient to listen and to talk back. Willie Storrar opened the session with the inmost slogan of what we were doing: 'Don't vote for your fears; vote for your aspirations!' Billy Kay read a Scots poem by Robert Fergusson, the wild and tragic boy who took such delight in the street life of eighteenth-century Edinburgh; Rod Paterson sang 'Birks of Invermay', the ballad which Fergusson chanted to himself as he lay dying in the madhouse straw at the age of twenty-four.

Willie McIlvanney observed that the Scots loved ideas, 'but didn't like to see them wandering around unchaperoned by experience'. Then, because John Barbour had been an archdeacon at St Machar's in the fourteenth century, he read comforting words from Barbour's poem 'The Brus':

> *A! Fredome is a noble thing,*
> *Fredome maiss man to have liking;*
> *Fredome al solace to man gives;*
> *He livis at ease that freely livis . . .*

It was dark outside the cathedral now, and warmer inside; the lights glittered on the roof bosses with the arms of the kings of Europe: Henry of England, Zygmunt of Poland, the Emperor Charles V. But I was still cold inside, and when my turn came to speak, I talked about powerlessness.

Andrew Fletcher of Saltoun, in *An Account of a Conversation*

Concerning a Right Regulation of Governments, says that he 'knew a very wise man . . . that he believed if a man were permitted to make all the ballads, he need not care who should make the laws of a nation'. Once I had loved that saying, but now it disturbed me. In a land as rich in songs as Scotland, it is too popular, too seductive, suggesting that a nation without a state can flourish on its culture alone. The boys and girls at Mintlaw had shown a frightening dissociation between the search for cultural identity and the need for political change, as if the one could be achieved without the other. The songs matter, but it matters more who shall make the laws, and to say otherwise is a wince against the pain of powerlessness.

This dreaming consent to impotence was an aspect of the curse which lay over Scotland. It was the condition William McIlvanney had implied five years before in the Meadows, when he spoke of the Scots still wondering what they wanted to be when they grew up: '. . . an intolerable position. We must never acclimatize to it – never!' And it might be that powerlessness was related to lovelessness, the intimate wound inflicted by so many Scottish fathers on their children which has been about the withholding of praise, the lack of a language in which to tell a child that it is beautiful or clever or deserving. That was another aspect of the curse.

Self-assertion born of self-distrust; that is a formula for the helpless false consciousness which authoritarian governors prefer in their subjects. Germany was plagued by it and became easy prey for the dictator. Using a little imagination, Scots should be able to recognize the Germans' fatal inhibitions about public life, perceived as an alien, dangerous place into which no godly or cultured man should venture. But Schiller, Bach and Luther had not been enough in Berlin in 1933. Burns and the Doric and the 'muckle sangs' would not be enough in Mintlaw or Middlefield.

Three centuries before, when he stood on the scaffold at Edinburgh, the Covenanting martyr James Renwick said:

'There is a great storm coming which shall try your founda-tions. Scotland must be rid of Scotland before the delivery comes.'

The talk-back from the audience at St Machar's lasted into the night. One old man unexpectedly shouted: 'Comparing Scots to sheep is an insult to sheep! Sheep don't have the vote, and if they did, they widnae vote for mutton pie.' The vote, it seemed, could still falter. It was the leaders, Donald Dewar for Labour, Jim Wallace for the Lib-Dems and Alex Salmond for the SNP – who had constructed a common platform strong enough to support them all for a week. But at the grassroots the Yes campaign scarcely existed. The SNP was turning out in many areas, as we had seen at Middlefield, but Labour activists were ignoring appeals and staying at home. Their excuse of exhaustion after an election now nearly five months in the past was not convincing. More probably, their dog-bristling hatred of the Nationalists (a hate which filled the hole where ideology should be) was still too strong. In consequence, the voters were taking their information almost exclusively from staged TV 'debates', the most alienating form of political performance. If they wanted to know more, nobody was on the doorstep to tell them.

Next morning we moved on to Inverurie, and found the same doubts and more at a breakfast meeting with local people. If the second question – on tax-raising powers – were lost, was there any way in which those powers could be granted to the Parliament after a 'suitable interval' or would another referen-dum be needed? Was it healthy in a globalizing economy that Scotland should concentrate on its own affairs ('I don't want to leave where we are for a narrower world')? Would a self-governing Scotland still be attractive to visitors? And there reappeared the old fear that a Scottish Parliament would be dominated by the Central Belt ('We don't want to be governed by a pack of time-served Labour "cooncillors" from Glasgow!').

This had been the main reason for the north-east's rejection of devolution in 1979. We replied that this danger was precisely the reason why this Parliament would be elected by proportional representation, ensuring that any phalanx of West of Scotland 'numpties' – blockheaded time-servers – would be outnumbered by the rest of the country. But the doubt lingered. Scotland is a deeply regionalized society, and government by Edinburgh or Glasgow can seem as remote as government by London.

One of the breakfasters was Malcolm Bruce, the Liberal Democrat MP for Gordon. It was striking, all through the journey, how members of the Westminster Parliament sat in the back rows and listened rather than elbowing their way to a platform. There was no platform; we had seen to that. But another ground for the MPs' reticence was that the bus party faced them with an unknown political species, and they had no idea how to harness it.

Malcolm waited politely for the debate to near its end before he put in a word on behalf of his own party. He had been a member of the Constitutional Convention; the Liberal Democrats there had argued that the Parliament should simply be assigned a percentage of United Kingdom tax revenue and trusted to spend the money as it thought fit. There were nods from the businessmen in the room. They might have reservations about where all this would end, but a Scottish legislature with less fiscal powers than a parish council would have no sense of economic responsibility at all.

One more question came. 'How can we ensure that the MSPs (members of the Scottish Parliament) represent the real talent in Scotland?' It was a plain-sounding question, but Willie McIlvanney recognized the subtext. It read: maybe our small nation of Scotland no longer has the brains, skill and political energy to govern itself. He answered drily: 'It is an act of self-belief to vote for this Parliament.' And that was the bus party's line all through the journey, a line which no politician could dare to take. Yes, of course this is a leap into the dark. Yes, of course there's no guarantee that self-government will not be mugged by gloomy phantoms from the past and end in fiasco, humiliation or mediocrity. We are asking you to take a risk, and it is not a quantifiable risk. As Lech Wałęsa said when the Solidarity revolution began in Poland, 'Our only guarantee is ourselves.'

Outside the Town House at Inverurie, a small pile of bouquets for Di lay on the steps, with cards addressed to the 'Queen of Hearts'. But the people on the streets were smiling, and eager to take our leaflets and talk. In the shops, busy young women suggested that buying something might be the price for their attention. I bought an overflowing cream pancake and two pairs of tight green underpants, and learned that a Scottish Parliament would be quite good, really, so long as it wasn't anti-English.

The bus set off again, heading north past the peak of Bennachie towards the Moray Firth. It was a day of small grey towns: Huntly and Keith, Elgin and Forres. We parked the bus in each main square, unrolled the banner and sent 'Willie McIlvanney and his friends' off down the streets to talk about Scotland. He had a good day; people recognized him in the street, rosy women asked him to sign his novels in bookshops, and everyone wanted to have a few words about Scotland with him. But Margaret Macintosh found herself in a betting-shop in Forres with a handful of young no-hopers who told her, civilly enough, that they were jobless, that several of them had police records, that they had never dreamed of registering to vote and that a Parliament would make no difference whatever to their lives. I encountered people flattered to be asked for their opinions, but strictly unwilling to disclose them. One elderly woman broke discretion so far as to say: 'I need time, but I watched it last night on the television. I think a Parliament might be quite good.'

This guardedness made a startling contrast with the cheery

enthusiasm of English people met on the street, visitors from the south or families from the RAF bases along the Moray Firth. Those who had a vote in Scotland all said they would vote a double Yes. Why not? The Scots ought to run their own show if they wanted. Some thought they already did. 'Look out, or you'll have the same bloody awful sort of government we've had in England for the last twenty years,' said one couple.

We were tired already, after less than three days on the road. Halfway through that Tuesday, we fell into the armchairs of a hotel at Elgin and asked each other what we had learned. That the voyagers should encounter their own country was, after all, part of the Günter Grass design. And the encounter with small-town Scotland had sometimes been disconcerting. Some of us had always believed that Scotland was a compassionate country, more so than England; now we wondered if that was true and, if it was, whether that virtue could survive in times of rampant free-market individualism.

The talk moved to racism, the vice to which Scots like to imagine their country is immune. Several of us knew better, especially Margaret Macintosh. There was anti-English bullying in schools; two of us had seen it in Edinburgh and one of us knew it here in Elgin – though, significantly, not at Forres where English children from RAF Kinloss made up almost half the school. If this anger was an unconscious reaction to the last eighteen stagnant years, or even to Mrs Thatcher personally, would the pleasures of Home Rule drain it away again? We suspected not.

How about the vote? We grew more cheerful. Allowing for reticence, it looked as if there was going to be a widespread Yes – at least to the first question about the principle of a Parliament. But something utterly unexpected was emerging too. All the doubts which had brought the 1979 referendum to grief were still intact.

Like the rest of us, I had been told again and again by

people over the last three days that they were worried about the survival of the United Kingdom, that they feared that the Parliament would be run by Central Belt machine politicians, that big business might decamp from Scotland, that devolution might make Scotland's world narrower at a moment when it should be growing broader. These were exactly the objections I had heard and reported nineteen years before.

Why, then, were they apparently going to vote Yes this time, instead of voting No or abstaining? John Smith, Labour's leader until his unexpected death in 1994, had repeated that devolution had become 'the settled will of the Scottish people'. If that was ever an accurate account of opinion, it needed amendment now. A Scottish Parliament was the 'unsettled' will of the people, who came to it with temperate hopes and intelligent anxieties. The difference lay in just that point which McIlvanney had made at Inverurie: they wished to register an act of self-belief. This was a chance, and also a risk, and they were in the mood to take it. When Willie Storrar had invented his slogan, he had been reading the collective mind. 'Vote for your aspirations, not for your fears' was exactly what the Scots were minded to do.

That night at Inverness, on the edge of the Highlands, there was a solemnity in the people who had gathered in the upper hall of the Town House. We had a purposeful debate about how the federal system worked in Germany, with questioners who knew what they were talking about. But passion was waiting in the hall as well, and it soon broke through. A playwright from the north spoke of what Home Rule meant to him, and ended: 'My crofter father prayed every day of his life for this!'

Then an old man in the front row, grasping his stick, began in a sonorous voice: 'Never again will this chance come. Your fathers and your grandfathers look on at you.' I heard a hiss of indrawn breath all around me. He went on: 'This is a moral and

even a spiritual decision. Let politics look after themselves!'
And the grave men and women in the room began to clap their
hands and to cry out in agreement.

This was the old Highland way of exalting political change
into Biblical terms of grief, faith and the promise of redemp-
tion. The bus party were awed. I remembered James Hunter,
the crofters' historian, repeating his Argyll ancestor's words that
if Mr Gladstone were standing, he would go every yard of the
way to the polling booth on his knees. The Scots, like many
nations, have fancied that they have been led to freedom and
safety by a pillar of fire by night, and that they have survived
under the protection of heaven. Virgil had told how Aeneas,
under the guard and guidance of his mother, Venus, led his
people through many seas and dangers to their destined land.
To read the 'Aeneid' in Scots is to know that Gavin Douglas
had in mind the mythical voyage of his own people from
Scythia through Egypt, Spain and Ireland to the coasts preor-
dained for them by the Lord. And in Psalm 124, in the metrical
'Inglis' of seventeenth-century Scotland, is a message for every
Israel, for every small nation which has seen conquest and
extinction approach:

> *When cruel men against us furiously*
> *Rose up in wrath, to make of us their prey;*
> *Then certainly they had devour'd us all,*
> *And swallow'd quick, for ought that we could deem;*
> *Such was their rage, as we might well esteem,*
> *And as fierce floods before them all things drown,*
> *So had they brought our soul to death quite down . . .*
> *But bless'd be God, who doth us safely keep,*
> *And hath not giv'n us for a living prey*
> *Unto their teeth and bloody cruelty.*
> *Ev'n as a bird out of the fowler's snare*
> *Escapes away, so is our soul set free:*
> *Broke are their nets, and thus escapèd we.*

After Inverness, we packed ourselves into the bus for an overnight journey south. It was hard to sleep. Somewhere near midnight, we stopped at the top of the Drumochter Pass and clambered out into the darkness to smell the heather and bog myrtle and to look up at the stars. It was uncannily clear and cold. The corner star of the Plough was hidden by the hillside, but the Milky Way was laid across the whole north-western sky like a silver fleece. As we stared, a meteor flashed out of the constellations and slipped towards the Pole.

We sensed a good omen, and as the bus moved on we began to recite and sing. I fell asleep, and woke hours later to McIlvanney's tenor voice softly remembering Sinatra ballads.

At Carberry Tower, before dawn, we got a couple of hours' sleep in our clothes. Then on to Biggar in the Lowland hills, where a television crew was waiting to confront us with local No campaigners. They were dogged, but sour with the sense of betrayal. The No camp (feebly named 'Think Twice', for the two referendum questions) were suffering the Yes camp's problems in reverse. The Yes leaders were energetically pushing their case into press and television in Edinburgh and Glasgow, while trying to conceal the weakness of their effort on the ground. The No cause, in contrast, started out with plenty of volunteers in the constituencies (mostly but not all Tories), who then waited with growing frustration to be marched into battle by a weak, untried leadership who assumed the campaign was already lost. So did the Scottish Conservatives, still shattered after being wiped off Scotland's political map at the May elections. They were sick of being abused as 'anti-Scottish', and they declined to grant 'Think Twice' the party's official support. This persuaded a great many folk who considered devolution disastrous to think thrice, give up and go home.

The bus party was changing now, as passengers climbed stiffly off and gave place to new campaigners. At Biggar, the singer Mairi Campbell and her husband, David, came on board with their baby daughter, Ada, who slept on our laps as the bus toiled over the Border hills.

At Lesmahagow High School, I watched Mairi, David and Fin setting up in the hall before the meeting. The speakers prowled at the back of the stage, muttering to their notes. I heard gusts of pipe music, a run of guitar chords and suppressed laughter. Ada stood unsteadily by the wall, watching while her mother – red-haired, with slanty blue eyes – practised a step-dance. Mairi's small tackety boots clattered on the boards. Outside, I could hear the din of approaching children.

Something was about to begin, and we were all ready for it. There are moments when you sense the movement of the earth itself, rolling forward into light. I felt a dangerous tightening in the chest. For some reason I remembered an old Slovak friend who had been with me in the Prague Spring thirty years before, an optimist who carried the blue numbers of Auschwitz tattooed on his arm. His comment, at the high moments and the terrible ones, had always been '*die Welt dreht sich!*' – the world is turning. It was turning here, even in this small, peaceful countryside where the straw bales stood in the harvest stubble.

They had brought in coach-loads from the senior forms of other schools, from Carluke, Biggar and Lanark. A tall boy from Lesmahagow High piped 'Heights of Cassino', with prodigious loudness and skill, as the rows of chairs filled up. We made our music, with fiddle, pipe, guitar and song, and made our speeches. Then there was a roaring of chairs as the hall rearranged itself into debating groups.

'I don't feel put down because I'm Scottish,' said a girl from Biggar. 'English, Scots . . . each just puts the other down in the normal way.' A Chinese boy felt that a Parliament was 'not relevant' to his way of life, but an African schoolmate was enthusiastic: he hated the dereliction of Scottish towns and wanted the Parliament to 'clear up Scotland'. Labour's threat to introduce university tuition fees throughout Britain worried them all. They wanted the Parliament to use its taxation powers and perhaps oil revenue to keep Scottish higher education free.

But when they graduated, what would they find to keep them in Scotland? Out of my group of sixteen, only three were confident that they would get a job of the kind they wanted. Another five were 'reasonably confident' of finding any sort of job at all. The rest shrugged.

Remembering encounters on the journey, I had quoted Yeats in my own speech:

> *Parnell came down the road, and said to the cheering man:*
> *Ireland shall have her freedom and you still break stones.*

In three or four years' time, they would be first-time voters at the second elections for the Parliament of Scotland. If they gave any thought at all to the struggle which had brought it about, they might wonder why it had taken so long, why it had required so many false starts and hesitations, to create something which to them was so normal and so obviously necessary. But some of the boys and girls in this hall would not be voting. They would be like the young men in the betting-shop at Forres: jobless, embittered and excluded.

What Scotland needed was not so much devolution as democracy. To me, self-government and the Parliament and even the possibility of independence have always been means to the end of a deeper 'fredome', a condition in which nobody accepts exclusion and ordinary people rebel every day in their ordinary lives. So much has been written and sung here about universal brotherhood, and the equal right of all to the chance of happiness. At his trial for sedition in 1918, the Clydeside revolutionary John Maclean said: 'We are out for Life, and all that Life can give us!' And yet for three centuries Scotland has been governed on the principle of 'involve as few people as possible'.

10

Peebles is a small town with a name for rectitude. It was thought of as a place where folk kept as far as possible indoors, and where nothing remarkable ever happened. Henry Cockburn, in *Memorials of His Time*, recalled the rising of the radical weavers in 1820 and wrote that 'Edinburgh was as quiet as the grave, or even as Peebles'. A few years later, one of its citizens said that a cannon could safely have been fired down the High Street of Peebles at noon without danger of harming anyone.

This is unfair to Peebles, which has intercepted a great deal of alarming history between quietnesses. Armies tramped through it, sometimes doing much damage. The English sacked the town and burned its churches on several occasions. In the Napoleonic Wars, exotic French officers – prisoners of war on parole – strutted about its streets. In the Second World War soldiers from the Polish Army, also exotic in their cloaks and braided caps, raided Peebles in search of entertainment. But it was the Frenchmen in Peebles, melancholy and romantic figures, who indirectly changed the whole course of Scottish culture.

Most of them came from the prison camps around Penicuik, a few miles to the north. In spite of their fine uniforms, they were hungry, penniless, homesick and lonely. War was not total in those days, and doors in Peebles opened to the 'enemy'. Although the Kirk disapproved, the French prisoners were allowed to open a theatre in an old ballroom, and Peebles women lent their dresses for the female roles. In part this excitement was curiosity about foreigners and about the glamour of French culture. But it was political too. Peebles, quieter than the grave, had none the less been moved by the promises of the French Revolution, and a few years earlier, before the Napoleonic Wars threatened Britain with invasion, there had been radical debating clubs in the town. Now all that had closed down under the threat of trial for sedition.

Even Peebles was bored. Newspapers were hard to get. As a substitute, a town eccentric called Tam went round the doors each evening with an old copy of Josephus's *The Jewish War*, reading from it as if it were the latest bulletin from the war fronts:

'Weel, Tam, what's the news the nicht?'

'Bad news, bad news, Titus has begun to besiege Jerusalem – it's gaun to be a terrible business.'

One of those starving for intelligent conversation was Mr Chambers, a weaver turned shopkeeper who invited some of the foreigners to his home. Close friendships were made, and Chambers, distressed by the poverty of these gentlemen, began to allow them credit in the shop against the promise of repayment when funds reached them from their properties in France.

But his debtors were unexpectedly transferred to other camps. They vanished, and nothing was heard from them even after the war was over. Later, charitable persons in Peebles suggested they might have been killed at the battle of

Waterloo. But Chambers was ruined. The business had to be sold to pay creditors, and in 1814 the family left for Edinburgh. The two Chambers sons, Robert and William, looked around desperately for ways to keep the family afloat. As a temporary expedient, they loaded second-hand books from their own library onto a barrow, which they stationed halfway up Leith Walk, in Edinburgh.

The books sold well. The stall became a shop, then a circulating library, then a publishing business for which William and Robert did their own binding and, initially, their own printing. The brothers wrote books of their own, and commissioned others. These also sold well; the public seized on the Chambers' combination of easy, anecdotal style with valuable instruction. The business rapidly took off, and by the mid-nineteenth century, Chambers had expanded into the biggest popular-education empire the world had ever seen, disseminating universal knowledge with a noticeably Scottish accent. Chambers dominated the English-speaking book market with its encyclopaedia and biographical dictionaries, its history books, its superb popular science series and its much-imitated *Chambers' Journal*, followed by *Chambers' Miscellany*. But the brothers also published collections of Scottish ballads, folk tales, proverbs and popular rhymes, mostly put together by Robert who had brought out his own classic *Traditions of Edinburgh* as early as 1825.

William, the elder brother, went on to become Lord Provost of Edinburgh. His 'improvement' schemes swept away many of the Old Town closes and buildings celebrated by Robert in *Traditions*. But by the time William died in 1883, the Chambers' example had been so widely imitated that Edinburgh had become – after Leipzig – the publishing and printing capital of Europe. The French officers' bad debts were a loss for Peebles, but in the long run a gain for Edinburgh and the world.

It was a hot morning by the time we reached Peebles. We leaned against the warm stones of the bridge over the

Eddleston Water, and felt reluctant to trouble the lieges with politics. Near the bridge, we noticed a large 'Think Twice' sign, but this turned out to be the name of a second-hand clothes shop which was holding its closing-down sale. Encouraged, we started to move down both sides of the High Street and ask for opinions.

One old man snorted: 'They all say "Trust me!" – and would you?' He was a Tory but, in the Peebles manner, he enjoyed having contentious dinners with his SNP friend. Labour was corrupt, and (he was relaying his own table-talk) the Nationalists intended to make devolution run on into independence. Why did they not say so openly, and how dared they call him unpatriotic for voting No?

Off the High Street, a close ran into a small cobbled space named Parliament Square. Here, we were told, the Scottish Parliament had met in the fourteenth century, in bad times when King David II was a captive after a reckless attempt to invade England. An old house on one side of the square had Masonic symbols engraved over its door, where 'French exiles from Napoleon' – more probably, those gallant officer-prisoners – had established a Lodge.

Behind the square, a craftsman was making horn-handled walking-sticks in a barrel-vaulted chamber which had been part of an abbey. Alexander III had established a monastery here in 1361, after 'the discovery of a cross', and there was supposed to be monkish treasure buried under the building. The stickmaker said that a silver arrow had been dug up here many years before, which now, titled 'The Peebles Arrow', is used as a competition trophy by the Royal Company of Archers.

I took a fancy to a fine stick whose head was carved in the effigy of a salmon. But the craftsman was shocked when I offered to buy it. 'That stick took me fifty hours' work to make,' he objected. No further argument was possible.

We drove on towards Galashiels, our last destination. It was a hot afternoon. Sleepily, I tried to remember all the rivers we had crossed on this journey: Forth and Tay, Don and Dee, Deveron and Spey, Ythan and Ugie, Eddleston Water and Gala Water and Tweed. My head began to nod forward. I turned to counting the poets we had quoted along the way: Barbour and Dunbar, Alexander Montgomerie and W. B. Yeats, Hugh MacDiarmid, Shakespeare on occasion, Burns on many occasions, and King David, perhaps, if you attribute the Psalms, and of course 'Anon.'. But this raised a problem worth trying to stay awake to solve, because the song we had returned to again and again (Fin playing its melody on the small pipes, Billy Kay or Rod Paterson singing its words) was the 'Freedom Come All Ye'.

Was that 'Anon.' or was it not? In my own past, when friends in Edinburgh or Glasgow began to chant the song in moments of triumph or despair, everyone knew that it had been written by the scholar-poet Hamish Henderson. They knew it not least because Hamish was often present: tall as a lamp-post, grinning, a glass in his hand. But in pubs and ceilidhs up and down the country, most people sing the words without knowing that he had written them, or even that anyone in particular had written them. The 'Freedom Come All Ye' has been taken up into the great body of traditional song, and Hamish had ascended into the Valhallah of anonymity long before his death in 2002. The melody is from a relatively modern pipe tune, 'The Bloody Fields o' Flanders', and Henderson first wrote the words in a book called *Ding-Dong-Dollar* in 1961. But nobody cares about this, any more than anyone cares how much of 'Thou Hast Left Me Ever, Jamie' is traditional 'Anon.' and how much is Robert Burns.

Several of Hamish Henderson's songs have become *Volksgut* in this way, especially the rousing 'Fare Ye Weel, Ye Banks of Sicily', his last salute to the men he fought with in the Second World War. But the popularity of the 'Come All Ye' is harder to explain. Why do crowds of celebrators with pint glasses in their hands roar out words which declare that Scottish soldiers are

not glorious, but have drenched the world with innocent blood
for the sake of a racialist Empire?

> *Nae mair will the bonnie callants**
> *Mairch tae war when oor braggarts crousely* craw,*
> *Nor wee weans frae pit-heid and clachan*
> *Mourn the ships sailing doon the Broomielaw;*
> *Broken families, in lands we've herriet,**
> *Will curse Scotland the Brave nae mair, nae mair;*
> *Black and white, ane ti ither mairriet,**
> *Make the vile barracks of their maisters bare . . .*

The 'Freedom Come All Ye' is a socialist battle-song. It was
composed at a time when millennial faith in socialism was
beginning to decline in Scotland. But the song lives on because
it also packs an enormous, high-voltage shock of national self-
assertion. It declares that this people, so long misled and
abused, is still strong enough to tear off the alien uniform which
it has been persuaded to think its own, and to regain its true,
noble and universal nature. 'Scotland must be rid of Scotland
before the delivery come.' In the game of identities, this is the
boldest throw of all.

Galashiels seemed deserted. At six on a hot summer evening,
the only sound in the town centre was the fountain clattering
under the silent busts of Scott and Burns. Rookies at managing
the stress of a political campaign, we were in a trough of
exhaustion after that unreal high of emotion at Lesmahagow in
the morning; we found an Italian restaurant open, and slumped
around the table as if we would never rise again. I watched
Willie McIlvanney take some fizzy pills in water. This was our
last evening together.

*callants = young lads; crousely = merrily; herriet = harried; mairriet = married

About thirty people waited for us, lost in the big hall of Gala Academy. Most of them were elderly, and for the first time on the journey I felt that we were talking to what the Covenanters used to call 'the savoury remnant' – the few who had long ago sworn their private oaths to Nationalism or to the devolution cause. They had come with serious matters to raise, mostly to do with takeovers in the knitwear industry of the Borders, but they were not confident that the Scottish Parliament could do much to protect the mills. I felt that my own speech and responses were lagging and leaden. But Willie brought the meeting to life with wit and anecdotes, feeling in his practised way for the phrase which would open hearts. 'Scottishness is a wee bit like an old insurance policy. You never think about it until you need it, and then you can't find it!'

After the talking, we gathered round the school piano in a corner, and a ceilidh developed. A choir of middle-aged Galashiels businessmen sang Border ballads and then urged us to vote Yes and Yes next day. A local poet recited his own work in Scots. Then Mairi Campbell, accompanied by David and Fin, sang 'The Broom o' the Cowdenknowes' in her light, poignant voice, with its refrain: 'Fain wad I be in my ain countree . . .' I saw tears on tough old Border faces around me.

At the end, it had to be 'Auld Lang Syne', but Mairi took up her fiddle and she and Fin played it to the older, prettier melody which Robert Burns first chose for the words. The singing suddenly filled the darkening hall. That night was a passage, not from an old year into a fresh one, but from dead times into newborn times.

It was almost midnight when the small blue bus drew up again on the Calton Hill in Edinburgh. Outside the Royal High School, there were applauding crowds and flaring lights. The Vigil's cabin was covered with flags, and the slate recording the Vigil's days and nights had reached the fateful numeral '1979'.

Plastic cups of whisky were waiting for us, and television cameras from BBC and CNN. Alex Salmond of the SNP was in the crowd, and Jim Wallace of the Scottish Liberal Democrats (who was to become deputy First Minister of Scotland eighteen months later). Friends cheered and embraced, as passing cars hooted in celebration.

Standing with our backs against the school gate, we said our farewells to the crowd and to one another. We agreed that we had learned much, and shared much. Willie McIlvanney made a graceful speech, but we couldn't find the Declaration of Arbroath when he turned to us at the end and wanted to read from it. Like Scottishness, it was not to be found when needed. So instead, on a strange impulse, he recited the oldest and gloomiest poem in the Scots tongue, the lament for King Alexander III whose horse rode over the cliff at Kinghorn on a stormy night in 1286. The poem is about well-founded foreboding, rather than hope, and about one of this small country's many lost leaders. But Scotland had found its own stony path through the wilderness of dangers which lay ahead.

> *Qwhen Alexander our kynge was deid*
> *That Scotland lede in lauch and le,**
> *Away was sons* of ale and brede,*
> *Of wyne and wax, of gamyn and gle.*
> *Our golde was changit into lede.*
> *Crist, born into virgynyte,*
> *Succoure Scotland and ramede,**
> *That stade* is in perplexite.*

It was midnight. Willie Storrar rolled up the canvas banners from the bus and thrust them into our hands, saying: 'These are like the scrolls of the Torah. Keep them!' Fin

*lauch and le = law and security; sons = abundance; ramede = to remedy; stade = held, trapped

raised his pipes and played the 'Freedom Come All Ye' for the last time.

The crowd began to thin out, and the few cars still passing in the darkness were silent now. Quietly, without trumpets, Referendum Day began.

The day was a fine, still Thursday. As the Scots voted, an almost absurd silence fell. The morning papers came out with raucous headlines – 'Vote For Us! Vote Yes! Yes!' and 'X Marks the Scot'. But they were out of tune with their readers. There were no loudspeaker wagons in the street, no demonstrators waving flags, no exultant invitations to celebrate. That evening, television cameras followed the great and good to the Edinburgh Conference Centre, to watch the results come through. But there was nothing stronger than coffee or bottled water to drink there. It was as if all Scotland had suddenly turned wary, appalled at its own boldness.

The results were bold enough. Little remained of the hesitations of 1979. There was a heavy turnout. Three-quarters of the voters said 'Yes' to the Parliament, and 63.5 per cent gave a second 'Yes' to the tax-varying powers. Only two voting regions, Dumfries and Galloway, and the islands of Orkney, voted 'No' to the tax question, and only by a very narrow margin.

In their book *The Road to Home Rule*, Christopher Harvie and Peter Jones declared that 'the Scots did not just agree to their parliament; they thumped the table and demanded it'. But that is a giddy overstatement. There was no thumping of tables in September 1997, and no challenge flung down to Westminster or England. The Scots had weighed the arguments for and against this particular offer of self-government at this particular moment in history, and had concluded that the time for change had come. There were many divergent roads leading forward from devolution. But the strength and decisiveness of the vote meant that there could be no road back.

11

The Highlanders are not a sensitive people.
But exactly the opposite. I am all
For the de-Tibetanization of the Hebrides.
It is perfect humbug to imagine
There's a reservation there for fine forms of consciousness . . .

Yet, my dear, as who upon the Cornish moors
Breaks apart a piece of rock will find it
Impregnated through and through with the smell of honey
So lies the Gaelic tradition in the lives
Of our dourest, most unconscious and denying Scots.
It is there, although it is unnoted
And exerts its secret potent influence . . .

Hugh MacDiarmid, 'The Highlanders
are Not a Sensitive People'

One of my tasks for the *Scotsman* in the 1970s used to be the
reporting of Scottish Labour's annual conference. Most party
conferences took place at Perth. They happened in the same
hall which would be draped with Gaelic slogans for the SNP
conference and then – when the Tories' turn came in mid-
May – stuffed with powdery blue hydrangeas to match
Mrs Thatcher's suit.

At the Labour conference, there was one regular event to
which I looked forward keenly. This was the resolution on
Highland land policy. Each year, the agenda committee would
try to get this resolution dropped, remitted or composited out
of existence. Each year the delegates would overrule the plat-

form and settle down to enjoy some genuine blood and thunder.

The proposers were nicknamed the 'Highland Luxemburgist' faction, after the German-Polish revolutionary Rosa Luxemburg and her habit of putting principle before party discipline. They invariably included Brian Wilson, then the young and furiously radical editor of the *West Highland Free Press*, and the novelist Allan Campbell MacLean. They were usually supported by the militant Skye crofter Margaret MacPherson. The 'Luxemburgists' were utterly opposed to the Labour Government's policy of transforming crofting tenure into owner-occupation. Instead, they demanded that the landlords of all crofting estates be expropriated, and the land be returned to the people to own and manage collectively under a democratically elected Crofting Trust.

Magnificent, incandescent speeches would echo through the hall, punctuated by cheers and glittering with references to Gaelic literature, to the nineteenth-century Land Leaguers and to the battles of Highland men and women against police, troops and landlords sent to evict them. On the platform, Willie Ross, Labour's Secretary of State for Scotland, glowered in disgusted silence. But every year the delegates would ignore the executive's pleas and vote massively for the resolution, before trooping off to celebrate with whisky-and-lemonade at the Salutation or the Isle of Skye.

Nothing much ever came of these resolutions. The Labour government ignored them and went ahead with its plans to allow crofters to purchase their own holdings. In the House of Commons, Willie Ross had to endure the sarcastic congratulations of Tory spokesmen for standing up to his party's extremists and defending the ideals of private property. But I asked myself why those delegates, normally well-drilled and obedient to party discipline, rose so recklessly to the pibroch of the 'Luxemburgists'. Overwhelmingly, that audience came from the industrial Lowlands and the Central Belt: trade unionists and local officials whose background was in the mines or the steel mills or the shipyards. How could the tortuous niceties of crofting legislation, affecting only a tiny section of Scotland's rural population whose way of life and often language was utterly remote from the normalities of Grangemouth, Greenock or Coatbridge, move them almost to tears?

The explanation lies in history. The Highland Clearances, the century and a half of oppression, hunger, exploitation and eviction which the peoples of the Gaeltacht underwent between about 1750 and the 1880s, are now irreversibly a part of Scottish political identity. Many people at those Labour conferences, whose families had lived in the cities of central Scotland for generations, were descendants of Highlanders driven from their homes by the Clearances. Others remembered great-grandparents who had come to Scotland as refugees from Irish landlordism and famine. But there is more to this emotion than family tradition.

Few nationalisms do not incorporate a wound. The icon of national identity is not complete without the scar left by a foreign sword. All Poles look to the Black Madonna of Czestochowa, who bears on her dark, sad face the slashes inflicted by Hussite invaders from Bohemia. The Czechs think of the twenty-seven patriots executed in Prague by Maximilian of Bavaria in 1621; the Israelis remember the Holocaust carried out by German Nazis; the Irish understand themselves through the Great Famine of the 1840s (laid to the account of British misrule) and through Cromwell's atrocities.

Scotland can finger such scars, almost all of them the work of the English over the centuries. But, remarkably, the Scots are not obsessed by the evil which others have done to them. Instead, the iconic wounds are the self-inflicted ones: the massacre of Glencoe, the battle of Culloden (perceived accurately enough as the last act of a civil war within Scotland, even though the core of the army which defeated the Jacobites was English), and the Highland Clearances.

The English are accustomed to being the scapegoats of the

world, blamed for the slave trade, for Ireland, for appeasing Hitler, for the Bengal famine and all the sins of colonialism. Perhaps they appreciate this status. Perhaps foreign blame is England's iconic wound; after all, the whipping-boy has a special sense of superiority. Whatever the truth of that, it is often assumed 'down south' that the Highland estate-owners who drove out people and replaced them with sheep must have been English aristocrats and plutocrats, and that the Scots hate the English for it. But, with a few exceptions, the clearing landlords were not incomers from south of the border. They were traditional clan chiefs, Highland gentlemen or Lowland capitalists and speculators. Scots cleared other Scots, and the Scots know it.

In many ways Scottish nationalism is freakish, and this is one of the ways. The 'other', the aggressor whose black crime sets off the angelic whiteness of national essence, is not out there but in here. This is a national identity founded in treachery – even nourished by it. William Wallace needed Sir John de Menteith, who sold him to the English, in order to be sanctified as a patriotic hero. Robert the Bruce was supposedly betrayed to the English by 'the Red Comyn' (an official myth, spun to excuse Comyn's murder by Bruce and his comrade Kirkpatrick in the sanctuary of a church at Dumfries). Robert the Graham made James I into a martyr king by murdering him at Perth. The Covenanters of the late seventeenth century would now be recalled only as a band of theocratic terrorists, if James Graham of Claverhouse, by hunting them down with royal dragoons, had not transfigured them into emblems of Scottish virtue: honest hill farmers equal in the sight of the Lord and faithful unto death to their beliefs.

In the same way, the Clearances have become a narrative of betrayal which shines a torch on the virtues of the betrayed. The people of the old Gaeltacht are held to have been guided by the principles of mutual solidarity, property shared in common, loyalty and the transmission of identity through song and story. How true that was, or how far that notion belongs to 'the Tibetanization of the Hebrides', is another matter. The first point to make is that those qualities – above all, the sense of collective responsibility – are currently held to be those qualities which distinguish Scotland as a whole from the 'selfish individualism' believed to be prevalent in England. Anyone who listens to political rhetoric in or out of the Scottish Parliament will recognize this, whether the politician is Labour, SNP or Scottish Liberal Democrat. A 'Hebridization of Edinburgh' has taken place.

Those who brought about the Clearances, cash-hungry chieftains or wealthy improvers or brutal speculators, were men and occasionally women who were held to have put their ambitions above the moral norms which define that communitarian Scottishness. One of the great misunderstandings about Scotland, displayed most recently by Mrs Thatcher, is that this is an entrepreneurial society which has always set a premium on individual self-advancement. This small nation has bred plenty of spectacular entrepreneurs, and has seen plenty of colossal advancements. But nationalist values, especially as they developed in the twentieth century, have not found a satisfactory way to incorporate them. Nobody on earth supposes an American to be less American because he has become a millionaire. In Scotland, by contrast, there is an instinct that conspicuous personal success must involve some loss of Scottishness. The young are urged to 'get on', but never quite forgiven for having got on.

At its worst, this amounts to a sardonic 'Partick Thistle' cult of failure in a nation which is never more itself than when it rescues defeat from the jaws of victory. At its best, it is a belief that the Gaelic-speaking society disintegrated by the Clearances was a model for how human beings can live well together in community. In what survives of that society, Scotland seeks to find its own image.

*

The thistles climb the thatch. Forever
this sharp scale in our poems,
as also the waste music of the sea.

The stars shine over Sutherland
in a cold ceilidh of their own,
as, in the morning, the silver cane

cropped among corn. We will remember this.
Though hate is evil we cannot
but hope your courtier's heels in hell

are burning: that to hear
the thatch sizzling in tanged smoke
your hot ears slowly learn.
     Iain Crichton Smith, 'The Clearances'

In the summer of 1848, more than forty people were living at
Arichonan in North Knapdale. The ruins of their homes and
byres are still there, on a high terrace of land several hundred
feet above sea level. There is a long view to the south over the
fjords of Caol Scotnish and Loch Sween. A burn of clean water
runs out of the hill and past the houses. In front of the settlement, the level spaces overgrown with bracken and brambles
were once strip-fields under oats and potatoes.

About ten houses and outbuildings can still be made out. A
tweed-dyeing boiler lies among the nettles, and a broken iron
cauldron nearly four feet across. The last farmer, who lived on
his own among the ruins and built chimneys and gables onto
his own house out of the fallen stones around him, left a metal
bedstead, now lying on the grass in front of his hearthstone.

Arichonan in 1848 was a 'multiple tenancy', the ancient settlement pattern in which a group of family heads jointly shared
the land. The soil was poor and often uneven in its fertility; to
prevent unfairness, the people would usually hold an annual

ballot to decide which family would have the use of each strip (rig) of arable. Each summer, Arichonan's small black cattle would be driven to the hilltop pastures above, joining the beasts from other settlements nearby and watched over by children and young people camping out in the temporary shelters and cabins known as 'shielings'.

Too much is made of the 'organic' difference between Highland and Lowland Scotland. Most of the difference is relatively recent: the result of a divergence between the two regions which began in the Middle Ages. Anyone who goes looking for some equivalent of a clan system in the medieval Lowlands will find plenty of evidence. Basic social arrangements were pretty similar in territories supposedly 'Celtic' or 'Teutonic'. Allowing for worse weather, worse soil and the Gaelic language culture, the Arichonan type of community (*baile*, in Gaelic) strongly resembled the Lowland 'ferm touns' that were swept away in the late eighteenth century. What the ruins do not resemble is a modern crofting township, with its widely separated houses. Instead, Arichonan was a tight, cosy maze of stone walls and buildings, narrow paved closes once overhung by heather-thatched eaves, tiny yards and bothies, secret corners and hiding places. It must have been a good place for small children.

On a cornerstone in one of the ruins, a man carved his name: 'Niel Macmillan'. Two things are known about him: that he was the father of ten children, who lived with their parents at Arichonan until 1848; and that he was evidently literate. A man who could write, even though he was shaky at the spelling of his own name, would have been able to read. But what did he read, and is it possible that newspapers reached Arichonan during the early months of that fiery year?

The papers carried news of revolution, beginning at Palermo in January and spreading to France in February. Monarchies fell and liberal constitutions were granted. By March, the revolution had gripped the German states and Austria; Hungary rose and so did smaller Slav nationalities who feared Hungary as much as they feared the Habsburgs. In the United Kingdom, the 'Young Ireland' movement threatened armed insurrection and a programme of land reform, while that April the Chartists held their climactic, gigantic, futile rally for political reform in London. All over Britain, landowners cleaned their fowling-pieces and nervously watched the night horizon for the flames of arson.

From the hill above Arichonan, on a very clear day, you can just see the shadow of Ireland. Elizabeth Grant of Rothiemurchus, the 'Highland Lady' whose memoirs and diaries are a unique personal record of her times, had begun life as a young girl in Edinburgh and Speyside. Now, in 1848, she had become an expatriate Irish landowner, married to Colonel Henry Smith and managing the big house and estate of Baltiboys, near Dublin. Like many intelligent property-owners in times of political upheaval, she was at first excited by the overthrow of dilapidated regimes. 'This news [of the revolution in France] must have some effect in England, where we are very nearly ready for a similar revolution. The higher classes cannot much longer be allowed to live in idleness principally from the proceeds of the labour of the middle ranks, enjoying peculiar privileges unearned by any merit', she wrote in her diary in March. 'They had quite a right to depose their King if he did not govern them satisfactorily, and if tired of monarchs, as we all shall be bye and bye, they choose to try a republick it is nobody's business to question their wisdom.'

But by the end of April 1848, she was anxious. 'The mob', especially in Ireland, was denouncing landed property itself, not just the privileges which it conferred. Riots spread through English and Scottish cities, and there were hopeless armed risings in the Irish countryside. She still thought that aristocracy should surrender its privileges, but 'the property and the greater part of the intelligence of the country are against any discription of tumult'.

All around her, Ireland was perishing and emigrating in the
fifth year of the Great Famine. Daughter of a chiefly family in
the northern Highlands, Elizabeth Grant had been raised to
believe in *duthchas*, the mutual relationship which linked the
chief's duty of protection to the personal loyalty and obedience
of his people. The Famine faced her with an utterly different
relationship which she was never able to accept: human suffering on a scale far beyond the means of even a benevolent
landowner to relieve, and tenants who felt no traditional duty to
masters whom in their hearts they regarded as alien oppressors.

In Argyll, elements of *duthchas* still survived – among the
common people, if no longer among the chiefs and the profit-
oriented landowners who were rapidly replacing them. But
famine was there too. In Ireland, the potato blight had struck in
1845. It arrived in Scotland a year later. Famine was mainly
confined to the Highlands and Islands, where the potato had
become the mainstay diet of families driven or resettled from
their traditional lands to make way for sheep. It was never as
severe as in Ireland. There was no mass starvation, and – as
Tom Devine explains in his book *Clanship to Crofters' War* –
there were job opportunities in the Scottish industrial cities,
while the provision of relief by landowners was incomparably
better organized than in Ireland. Above all, most of Scotland
south and east of the Highlands was relatively unaffected. This
encouraged a powerful philanthropic relief effort by the rest of
the country.

But the impact of the blight on the fragile subsistence economy of the Highlands and Islands was none the less disastrous.
While there was no dying on the Irish scale, the death rate rose
steeply, assisted – as in Ireland – by typhus and other famine-
related diseases. Relief was efficient, but offered by the Central
Board of Management for Highland Relief on heartless and
humiliating terms. Those who passed the 1848 Destitution
Test received a pound of oatmeal for a day's labour; half a
pound was offered to the old and infirm, while children were to

be fed only on evidence that their school attendance was regular.

Sir Charles Trevelyan, assistant secretary to the Treasury, oversaw relief in Scotland on the free-market principles he had applied to such lethal effect in Ireland. In a letter to the Celtic historian William Skene, a member of the Central Board, Trevelyan wrote that 'the pound of meal and the task of at least eight hours' hard work is the best regime for this moral disease'. But, desperate as their situation was by 1848, four out of five people in Wester Ross and three-quarters of the people of Skye looked to their honour and refused to take the Destitution Test.

The most obvious result of the famine was that emigration from the Highlands and Islands reached levels never seen before or since. Many thousands left for Canada and Australia between 1846 and 1857; unknown thousands more chose 'internal emigration' and arrived on the rainy pavements of Scottish cities.

Some of this movement was voluntary, with 'assisted' passages wholly or partly paid for by the landlords. Some of it was coerced 'clearance'. As relief payments wound down and the famine receded, landowners feared that support for the destitute would now fall on their own shoulders; the rural poor had to be removed before they became a liability. The methods used combined carrot and stick in many different proportions. They ranged from benevolent offers of free passage to Canada (and in rare cases Highland lairds travelled with their people to ensure that they were safe and comfortable in their new homes) to the use of clubs and the firing of thatch to evict households unable or unwilling to pay increased rents. Alan Begg, a local historian at Kilmartin in Mid-Argyll, has written that 'the infamous Highland Clearances . . . didn't happen much in this part of Scotland, as the lairds used other ways to get their hands on the land . . . the lairds forced the rents up and up until eventually the

crofters had to give up. The other method was not to renew
leases, which was a regular practice.' In Argyll, the outcome of
either method was much the same. The emptied landscape
would be turned over to blackface 'Linton' sheep, the joint-
tenancy *bailtean* would be replaced by a single tenant farmer in
a slate-roofed house with chimneys, and bracken would grow
over the pastures once kept green by cattle.

In the decade after 1846, the population of many parishes
and even whole islands fell by between a third and a half. The
parish of North Knapdale around Arichonan held 2,170 persons in 1841. By 1851, in the third year of famine, the
population had fallen by about a quarter, to 1,666. By 1881, it
numbered only 927.

Mid-Argyll had experienced the dissolution of the clan
system and the development of a cash economy much earlier
than the northern and western Highlands. North Knapdale,
including Arichonan, had been bought by a speculating busi-
nessman in the 1790s, who sold it to the Malcolms in 1801. By
then, the Malcolms had already accumulated great wealth; in
the late eighteenth century their Jamaica estates and business
were returning the huge sum of £40,000 a year, and they began
to purchase territory in South Australia in 1839. They possessed
estates and country houses in England and bought a succession
of large town houses in London, one of them decorated with a
full-sized Michelangelo cartoon hanging on the wall. In their
new Argyll properties, they poured capital and energy into a
development programme which transformed the landscape and
the life of its inhabitants over the next fifty years; they invested
in the construction of the Crinan Canal, began the systematic
draining of the Crinan Moss bog with trenches eleven feet
deep, peeled the accumulated peat off the alluvial soils of
Kilmartin Glen and replaced traditional cottages with solid
houses of stone and slate.

They were efficient, paternalistic landlords. Unlike some of
the worst proprietors in the north and the isles, the Malcolms

tried to avoid the use of force and showed concern for the fate of their tenantry; Neill Malcolm III not only paid for passages to Canada and Australia but apparently provided ongoing grants to support Poltalloch tenants while they found their feet in Ontario.

None the less, the remnants of the old *baile* joint-tenancies, with their non-commercial subsistence agriculture and their inability to pay viable rents, stood in their way. Until the land could be worked by larger commercial farms, with the hills cleared for sheep, the estates stood no chance of returning a profit. The joint-tenancies had to go, and their inhabitants with them. The famine made the change seem even more urgent. The method which the Malcolms appear to have preferred was to increase rents on the tenancies and then to serve eviction notices for non-payment. There is no record of resistance or 'any discription of tumult' before 1848.

But at Arichonan, something went wrong. The rents were raised, and the people refused to pay. The eviction notices were twice served, and the people refused to leave. This was unusual. Something new was in the air in that rebellious year, not just in the hills but throughout the district.

Neill Malcolm was away, and in his absence the estate factor (manager) and the authorities panicked. A posse of nine police-men, with the Poltalloch factor, the Sheriff Officer and twenty-five estate workers, climbed up the track to Arichonan to serve the final eviction notice. One version of what happened, which I have heard, tells that the men of Arichonan had been drawn away from the houses by a ruse, and that the raiding party found themselves faced by a rank of defiant women. What is certain is that the posse met resistance. A large crowd, which soon grew to over three hundred as people ran up from nearby settlements, confronted them. The police seized a few men as hostages and the posse retreated downhill to Bellanoch on the Crinan Canal, pursued by the crowd which besieged them in the Bellanoch inn.

Two local men who had the people's trust, the innkeeper at
Crinan and the well-respected farmer at Ardifuar, George
Campbell, were brought in to mediate. The prisoners were
released, and the arrest party made its way back to the small
town of Lochgilphead, only to find the streets full of people
roaring their support for the families of Arichonan. The Sheriff
wrote to Edinburgh demanding the despatch of troops 'by the
quick steamer'. In Ireland, the troops would have been sent
and blood would have been shed. But the Edinburgh authorities, their own resources stretched by rioting and Chartist
demonstrations, decided that Mid-Argyll could clear up its own
mess. To borrow one of Elizabeth Grant's favourite sayings,
Argyll could 'give its ain fish guts to its ain sea mews'. They
sent no soldiers.

In the long run, the men and women of Arichonan could
not win. They surrendered, but may have won some assurance
of lenient treatment. As Michael Davis records in his study
Poltalloch and the Transformation of Mid-Argyll, they were later
persuaded to leave Arichonan 'after negotiations in Gaelic . . .
only five individuals were sentenced, and these lightly by the
standards of the day (eight months in Inveraray Jail)'. What
happened to them afterwards is unknown. Sheep were moved
onto their abandoned lands, and one cottage was rebuilt to
house a shepherd.

The Irish Famine was by far the greatest human catastrophe in
nineteenth-century Europe. Between 1845 and 1850, around a
million people died of hunger or of disease associated with
hunger (some historians put it higher, but there will never be
precise figures). The death toll and the pell-mell emigration
which followed reduced the population of Ireland from over
8 million to 6.5 million in only ten years. The whole course of
social and economic development in southern Ireland was
irrevocably changed. The famine's legacy of grief and anger to
Ireland and to the post-famine diaspora, above all in North

America, still shapes Irish political instincts in the twenty-first century.

The Highland Clearances were a lesser, slower tragedy. But as memory and myth they still provide a powerful component of Scottish political instincts, and not only in the Highlands. Just as Irish-Americans have sought to have the Famine accepted as part of the 'Holocaust Studies' curriculum at American universities, so a number of Scottish scholars and writers seek to understand the Clearances as a form of genocide, cultural rather than physical, which deliberately destroyed Gaelic society through a prolonged act of 'ethnic cleansing'.

In both cases, the motive is patriotic. These are attempts to hitch national experience onto universal bandwagons: most recently, to the victimologies of the twentieth century from Auschwitz to Bosnia. Several previous efforts were made to reinvent the Clearances in this way. The first began while the Clearances were still in progress, when they were represented by Victorian radicals as the inevitable consequence of aristocratic landlordism and privilege, an evil anachronism which was under attack by liberals and land reformers all over Europe. The second reinvention – and the most persuasive – arrived in the twentieth century. Socialists identified the cause of the Clearances as the impact of the cash economy and market forces on a traditional, collectivist society; clan chiefs used their authority to become aggressive capitalists for whom people and land became exchangeable commodities. Today, as a mild Land Reform programme is put through the Scottish Parliament, all three versions are in vigorous use – sometimes in the same speech. The Highland Clearance myth, employed as a sort of victim's ticket to board the world, remains an integral part of Scottish identity.

A 'myth' is not necessarily untrue. It means, as I use the term, a historical narrative which is used to support wider assumptions about moral worth or national identity. The Clearances happened, and they were a human disaster – at

times, an atrocity – on a grand scale. One of Europe's small
peoples, rich in its oral culture and its ingenious forms of
community, was uprooted, pauperized, not infrequently
terrorized and driven out of its own country. Living landscapes became dead, soggy wildernesses. A beautiful language
was treated as a shameful patois and pushed to the edge of
extinction.

Quantifying the Clearances is difficult and also misleading.
The population of Scotland by 1841 was about 2.6 million, of
which the Highlands and Islands accounted for less than
250,000. At the height of the Clearances, in the decade after
1847, some 16,000 people emigrated from the Highlands to
North America and Australia. The net Highland population loss
between 1855 and 1895 was only about 9 per cent – not much
more than the decline in many parts of the Lowlands. But this
conceals the difference between displacement and depopulation. Most of those evicted or rack-rented out of their homes did
not board the emigrant ships but were resettled within the
Highlands – generally on barren strips of coastline where the
only reliable crop was potatoes. In many cases, and above all
after the famine, their lives were materially worse than those of
the emigrants who had gone weeping to the boats but had
found fertile soil allotted to them in Ontario or South Australia.

Equally important, those who had been removed to the coast
were still the helpless tenants of landlords against whom they
had no legal protection whatever. But the emigrants, clearing
virgin forest off a Canadian homestead deep in snow, had the
consolation of knowing that at last they owned the land they
lived on. No laird, no rent-collector, no factor with an eviction
order would ever trouble them or their children again.

A component of the Clearances myth in Scotland has been
the dimly comforting illusion that the emigrants were
inconsolable in their exile. In the words of the 'Canadian Boat
Song':

From the lone shieling of the misty island
Mountains divide us, and the waste of seas –
Yet still the blood is strong, the heart is Highland,
*And we in dreams behold the Hebrides.**

But James Hunter, in his path-clearing book *A Dance Called America*, has shown how misleading this is. In Ontario, Manitoba and especially Cape Breton, the Gaelic-speaking settlers continued to treasure the culture they had brought with them. But they became and remained enthusiastic, grateful Canadians, citizens of a country they considered free and just in ways that Victorian Scotland could never be.

John Smith, leader of the Labour Party until his fatal heart attack in 1994, was a Mid-Argyll man. If he had lived, he and not Tony Blair would have led Labour back to power in 1997 and become prime minister.

When he died, there was an unexpected surge of grief across all Britain. He had seemed at first bustling, ambitious, lawyerly – much like the rest of them. But then his quality began to show through. It was seen that he was high-spirited, but also that he was angry about the selfishness and unfairness of his times, that he meant what he said. I went to his funeral, and stood outside the Cluny church in Edinburgh in the crowd, as they carried his coffin carefully down the steps to the hearse. A few people wiped their eyes; most remained impassive, their faces closed. Questioned, they said reluctantly that John Smith had been an honest man, not proud, a man who listened to ordinary folk and who should have led the country.

---

*The author of this masterly verse is still unknown. It has been attributed to the novelist John Galt or to Walter Scott, but it has qualities unlike the work of either man. The poem appeared anonymously in *Blackwood's Edinburgh Magazine* in 1829.

He loved Scotland extravagantly. His most important 'unfinished business', as he used to call it, was establishing a Scottish Parliament within the United Kingdom, the job which Tony Blair was to complete for him. The Parliament met for the first time on 12 May 1999, five years to the day after John Smith died. An ardent party man, he disapproved of the SNP and of nationalist rhetoric at the expense of the Union. If he had been alive that day, and if he had been warned what she was going to say, he might have tried to stop Winnie Ewing, the oldest member, opening the session with the words: 'The Scottish Parliament, adjourned on the twenty-fifth day of March 1707, is hereby reconvened!' But, knowing him, I know how deeply and uncontrollably those words would have stirred him.

They buried him on the isle of Iona, near the graves of Scotland's early kings. That saluted his romantic, Highland side. But it was also a statement. His Christian socialism arose from Argyll, whose ruined villages write a very simple message on the landscape about what the uncontrolled strong will do to the unprotected weak.

John Smith's father was the head teacher at Ardrishaig, a little town on Loch Fyne where the Glasgow mailboats used to end their run. But the family's roots lay a few miles further south, in a forgotten settlement called Allt Beithe in the hills beyond Tarbert. His cousin John Smith of Glendarroch has told the story of Allt Beithe's terrible end, and of the providence which allowed them both to be born.

In 1845, a year before the potato blight, the cholera plague reached Argyll. Perhaps a dozen people lived in the settlement then; it could be reached only over a long, rough track, and it was some days before friends in Tarbert noticed that nobody from Allt Beithe had been seen in the town for a while. A rescue party set out, and went first to the hamlet of Baldarroch, where they found only the dead lying in their houses. Climbing on, they reached Allt Beithe. There 'they found everyone dead or dying except for a baby, Archibald Leitch', a little boy of two.

He was carried back to Tarbert and brought up by relatives, and in time grew up to become a boat-builder and the great-grand-father of both John Smiths.

The houses at Allt Beithe were set alight in order to cleanse the place of infection, and only ruins remain. In the local anti-quarians' magazine *The Kist*, the Tarbert cousin has described how he found his way up there, one day when he was younger, and noticed flat slabs of stone still in place by the hearth of one of the houses. 'On lifting one, a few locks of reddish hair were found; they had obviously been placed deliberately, but why? We left them there, where they belonged.'

When I met John Smith, in Edinburgh or in his dark little MP's room at Westminster, we talked first about politics and then, when I had scribbled enough into my notebook, about memories of this landscape. The combative politician van-ished; whisky appeared; a disarmingly sentimental man explored his own childhood. Did he ever see the famous vagrant they called Old Tobermory? He did; he remembered; he was delighted.

Old Tobermory was known to us all, and yet unknown. His real name was a mystery; some said he was called John Maclean, and others that he was born Jock Lynch. Unknown, too, was the story of how he became a wanderer, although alco-holism may have been the cause of it. I remember him appearing from time to time in summer outside the houses at Crinan Harbour. He would knock on the doors and the inhab-itants would come out to watch as he performed his act, a trembling, shuffling dance followed by a whining, tuneless chant in what must once have been Gaelic. People gave him a little for it; something to eat, or small change. He was whiskery and ragged, and looked not long for the world. But there was respect as well as pity for him. Old Tobermory belonged to the trees and the rocks, to forgotten heights of land and unvisited shores; he was the last of a departed tribe.

In summer, the old man lived in caves. This coast has

thousands of them, on the mainland and the isles. Galleries of sea caverns face the Atlantic, noisy with gulls and ravens. Boulder caves on the hills are spaces between rock-masses tumbled downhill by the 'Lomondian' glaciers, in that fearsome period around 9000 BC when the ice suddenly ended its retreat and advanced once more to cover Argyll for a millennium. Rock shelters, overhangs which could protect a hunting band from the rain or hide a fugitive, are everywhere.

Most caves are close to the shore, tunnelled out by the sea at the end of the Ice Age when the land rose as the weight of glaciers was lifted from it. Then they were submerged as the melting ice brought the sea level up again. If human beings used the caves before then, all trace of them was washed away by the rising sea; if Palaeolithic groups ever reached Argyll – and they probably did not – nothing would be left of their presence or of their paintings on cavern walls. The first evidence of occupation – shell middens, flint-flaking waste, the odd bone point – was left when the sea had fallen again about seven thousand years ago.

A cave is a mneme, a damaged cell of memory preserved when all that existed in the open air – peoples, crafts, cults – has rotted away. In Scotland, the memory found in their damp, impacted floors or in the nettle-infested ground at their entrances is about fear: the fear of death by cold, of discovery by armed pursuers, of a world deaf to the voice of God, of the police looking for whisky-stills or of busybodies coming to drag an old man off to the poorhouse. Argyll's caves have been invoked against them all.

St Columba's Cave, near Ellary on the shore of Loch Caolisport, looks out over a peaceful and sheltered arm of the sea, with a level beach good for pulling up boats. It is famous for harbouring the saint, who is said to have landed and lived here for a time on his journey from Ireland to Iona; one version of history states that it was from Ellary that Columba walked or rode the seven miles to Dunadd, in order to announce his arrival to his kinsman, King Conall mac Comghail of Dalriada. In the cave's recesses there is a rough altar and three engraved crosses in the rock, the first two dated to around the seventh century. A stream of clean water rattles down the rocks near the entrance, which is overhung by scrub birch trees and rowans. Summer visitors are touched by the holy solitude of the place, but soon retire to their cars slapping their necks and wreathed in pale swarms of midges.

Marion Campbell excavated here some twenty years ago, and found evidence of many other occupations. Her finds were re-examined recently by Christopher Tolan-Smith, and his book *The Caves of Mid-Argyll* puts together a rough sequence. Early Neolithic and Bronze Age groups visited the place on for-aging expeditions along the shore, leaving scraps of pottery and a few worked flint or antler tools. Iron Age people used the cave as a workshop for leather and metal crafts, throwing away quantities of bone needles and awls, the joints of butchered cattle, goats, pigs and deer, and some fragments of imported Roman crockery. Then, in the Columban time, came Christian monks of the Celtic church – possibly the saint himself among them – who transformed the cave into a chapel.

The holy men were suddenly evicted around the ninth cen-tury, the time when Viking raiders sacked the Iona monastery and began to settle along the west coast and in the isles. The Norsemen, their boats probably dragged up on the grass above the high-tide mark, seem to have rested there for short intervals, mending their gear, cooking and dividing the loot between them. Marion Campbell found a folding 'balance' or scales made of copper alloy, an item for weighing out small quantities of precious metal which turns up at early Norse sites from Scandinavia to Ellesmere Island in the Canadian Arctic. A little later, when the Vikings were no longer raiders but had become a settled ruling aristocracy in their empire of the 'Sudreys' (the Southern Isles, as they named the Hebrides), local people ven-tured back and resumed metalworking at the cave mouth.

Around the twelfth century, the Church returned too. The cave once more became a shrine and a place of pilgrimage, and a small medieval cemetery was established immediately outside it. A new chapel was built between the cave and the shore.

For three or four centuries, there was peace, psalms, perhaps miracles. Then the Reformers came from the Lowlands, seeking idols to destroy. They tolerated no shrines or pilgrimages and dismissed the whole constellation of petty, half-forgotten Celtic saints beloved by the Gaelic population. Worship at Ellary was closed down. The cave was purged of Papist superstition and abandoned, or – as archaeologists say – 'returned to economic use'. By the nineteenth century, fishermen had built a stone wall with a wooden door across the entrance in order to use the interior for storing and drying nets.

But then Victorian piety and antiquarianism came into play. The laird at Ellary chased out the fishermen and had the cave floor partly shovelled out (an archaeological calamity), in order to 'restore' a suitable space for worship. Seventy years later, his successor – a clergyman – decided to rearrange the interior yet again. But before the work began, he was persuaded to let Marion Campbell excavate around the cave mouth and sift through the spoil heap of earth thrown out by the previous 'improver'.

Today the cave is visited by people looking for an assortment of different experiences. There are occasional pilgrimages, and a religious service is held there each year on St Columba's Day. Holidaying families wander into the dark recess and sometimes picnic there in foul weather. Archaeologists come with digital cameras and lights to illuminate the faintest of the crosses. Prim information panels provided by Historic Scotland stand in the grass, their words pearled over with raindrops.

This cave is a witness to the way that Scotland's cultural landscapes have always been used. In a country of slender resources, that human use is never single, except for brief intervals, but essentially multiple. Often the uses are contradictory;

these contradictions may be reconciled by sharing or negotiation, or by possessive, monopolizing violence. The new Ancient Landscape museum at Kilmartin is constructed around this philosophy of manifold ways of seeing and desiring and exploiting a single place, and Rachel Butter, one of the museum's founders, expressed it precisely when she described the raised-beach gravel terraces of Kilmartin Glen in her 'Introduction and Guide'.

Up to a few years ago, a museum curator would have confidently invoked the divine rights of science to justify the priority of archaeology over ground so densely used for prehistoric monuments and ritual. But Rachel Butter writes: 'This landscape has been valued in several opposing ways. The gravel terraces were attractive to people over four thousand years ago: here they buried their dead and perhaps enacted the ceremonies which gave meaning to their lives. Recently the same terrace has been valued by some people as a source of gravel for building and a commercial resource, and by others as a source of information on how people lived in the past.'

With these words, Rachel Butter transcends years of sometimes enraged contest between local contractors, the council which licensed them to extract gravel and destroy a unique early henge monument, the landowners, the museum's interest in conservation and the interests of contract archaeology companies tendering for a rescue excavation. Maybe Butter – as an archaeologist – ground her teeth as she wrote. But to prefer one use to all the others would be to betray the essential concept of a cultural landscape defined by multiple use.

Argyll, like all Scotland, is a palimpsest. Its surface is like a vellum manuscript repeatedly scraped down to allow new words to be written over the previous text. Caves are like the frayed fringes of those manuscripts, where the scraping process is not quite complete and where fragments of the older messages can be recovered and read.

*

Old Tobermory used many caves. His favourite was Uamh nam Bo Dubha, the Black Cow's Cave, an utterly remote hole at the tip of a peninsula looking southward down the Sound of Jura. He was not the first inhabitant; ancient limpet and periwinkle shells can be found in the earth floor, left by bands of hunter-gatherers who stopped in the place to cook and eat the food they had collected from the shore. But like his predecessors, Old Tobermory rearranged what he found in the cave in order to make himself comfortable. There is a wall of loose stones built halfway down the cave's throat, to keep out the wind and give him some privacy, and a platform which may have been his bed. Within the wall, ash still remains from his fires of drift-wood and peat. Some people think he wintered here; others believe that certain families in the hills offered him straw and the corner of a byre until the worst of the frosts and gales was over.

In summer, Old Tobermory would take to the roads. Wherever he went in Knapdale and Lorn, there were familiar caves to house him, used in living memory by other wandering solitaries. Sometimes they sheltered families of travelling tinker people who would stay for a few days to patch the ket-tles and cauldrons of local people. Their scraps of copper and tin waste and the ash of their fires would be left on the cave floor to join the slag dropped by other itinerant metalworkers over the last three or four thousand years. Most of these caves were selected for habitation because they were close to a road, and usually near a crossroads or track junction, so that the cave-dweller – silently watching from the inner darkness – could see who was approaching and keep an eye on the life of the dis-trict. Once or twice, as a child, I was terrified by peering into such caves and meeting the faint gleam of human eyes within.

The old man had a few companions. One of these was 'Lord Archibald', or the 'Lord of the Isles', who claimed descent from the earls and dukes of Argyll. The local historian Alan Begg remembers him as 'a rough-looking character. He always had good boots, but seldom had socks on, two coats but no shirt and an old felt hat. He had a big black bushy beard, looked fierce, but in fact was really quite a civil soul.' The pair of them would sometimes settle for a drinking sojourn in the majestic ruin of Carnasserie Castle, above Kilmartin, which the 'Lord of the Isles' claimed as an abode fit for a man with the blood of kings. They would light a fire of sticks in the huge stone fireplace of the castle hall, and passers-by would hear them singing warlike songs in Gaelic. What became of 'Lord Archibald', I do not know. But one winter some thirty years ago, Old Tobermory was found dead by the road which runs through the Pass of Brander.

The Scottish Land Court was in session on the island of Benbecula. It was 1957, and I had been sent to the Western Isles by the *Manchester Guardian* on my first reporting assignment.

The Cold War was at its height, and the Air Ministry had decided to establish a rocket-testing range in the Uists. The Ministry required land, but the acres of fertile machair they wanted were under crofting tenure, protected by the complex legislation of the 1886 Crofting Act and its amending successors. Only the Land Court, the body set up to adjudicate disputes under the Acts, could permit the 'resumption' of crofting land for non-agricultural purposes.

I had never been to the Outer Isles before. The skies were blue and a biting spring wind blew in from the Atlantic over the green levels of sandy machair, soon to be covered with flowers. My lodging was in a croft at Iochdar, in South Uist. Between court sessions, I sat in the kitchen talking to the crofter's two black-haired daughters or walking by the shore. This was a Catholic island, and a shrine to the Madonna stood on the sand-hills looking out over the ocean which had taken so many young lives from the Uists: 'Failte Reul na Mara' – Hail, Star of the Sea.

From the shrine, I could see most of the township. Its pattern of widely spaced houses, floating on the green turf like a fleet of trawlers at anchor, told me that this was a form of community I had never encountered. Each croft had its vegetable garden, and wobbly wire fences marked out the arable fields of the 'inbye' land. Inland lay the common grazing, of which the township allotted shares to each croft by ballot.

It was a community which defied normal definition. These were individual smallholders, but they were not a true peasantry: they did not own their land. They were tenants on an estate owned by somebody, but that somebody had no power to evict them or raise their rents without navigating through the formidable protective barriers of crofting legislation. Each croft had its own arable fields, and yet this was a tightly collective society in which no change could be made without the consent of neighbours.

The Court met in the community hall at Balivanish, on Benbecula. The chairman was Lord Gibson, a judge of powerful eccentricity in an old Scottish tradition. Advocates in Scotland tend to declare political allegiance as their careers advance, more as a sort of gamble on the party likely to hold power than as a statement of personal conviction, and Lord Gibson had long ago declared for Labour. For that reason, and because he was unpopular in the Faculty of Advocates, Gibson's career had not prospered, and his appointment to the Scottish Land Court had been regarded in Edinburgh as the equivalent of managing a power station at Krasnoyarsk, which in those days was the Soviet reward for Politburo veterans who had fallen out of favour.

Lord Gibson, however, took over the Land Court with relish. He would show them! Not short on vanity, he insisted that as Chairman of the Land Court he was entitled to a ceremonial mace, to be carried before him in procession. The Lord President of the Court of Session had a mace. Why not the President of the Land Court? Attempts to dissuade him failed; he persisted and grew aggrieved. The exasperated Faculty consulted the Lord Lyon King at Arms, Scotland's chief Herald, who at that time was Sir Thomas Innes of Learney.

A resourceful Lyon, Sir Thomas went to his toolbox and made a mace out of his kitchen rolling-pin. He turned it and carved it into pretty contours, then applied varnish and polish. Finally, he tipped it with a gleaming gold point which was one of Lady Innes's old lipsticks. This mace was borne before Lord Gibson on great occasions, but whether he ever took a closer look at it is not recorded.

The hall on Benbecula was packed with crofters, missile experts, military officers in uniform and Edinburgh advocates in wigs. One morning, Lord Gibson announced that he had come to a decision. In a long, strange speech, he lectured the hall about the decline of the Gaelic language, and deplored the fact that Gaelic was not a medium of instruction in local schools. This was a consequence of the repressions which had followed the 'Forty-Five' Jacobite rebellion, he explained. But now, exactly 210 years after the Heritable Jurisdictions Act had abolished the courts of feudal lords and clan chiefs, the Land Court was going to redress the balance and strike a blow for the preservation of Gaelic culture.

He would grant the resumption of crofting land required by the Air Ministry, but only on conditions. These were that the range should be operated by a regiment speaking exclusively Gaelic, and that the regiment should wear a special uniform with tartan trews which would be designed by a friend of his in Lochboisdale. 'This time,' announced Lord Gibson, 'we can make the Western Isles the Gaelic-speaking area that it was in Bruce's time.'

There was a moment of stunned silence. It was broken only by suppressed grunts. Glancing at the front rows, I saw that a young advocate with whom I had travelled on the boat from Oban had turned puce and stuffed a handkerchief into his mouth. (He is now a Lord of Session, and two years ago played a leading part in the Lockerbie trial in the Netherlands.)

The Court was suspended, and the officers and lawyers stood around in the wind outside, some incoherent with rage and others leaning against the wall to sob with laughter. I had my story, but only for a day. That night, some anonymous gentlemen called on Lord Gibson for a little talk about NATO and 'interests of state'. Next morning, he reappeared, pale and dejected, to announce that he had reconsidered his remarks and concluded that the government's decision to establish a guided missile range was an Act of State not open to question in any court of law. 'Accordingly, I withdraw my remarks of yesterday unreservedly.'

The range was built, and its staff and its demands still dominate the economy of South Uist. Its tracking station on the hill ('Space City') dominates the landscape. Gaelic is now a medium of instruction in the schools of the Western Isles, although not for the English military families of the base.

We mocked old Lord Gibson at the time. Today I feel differently about him, for two reasons. In the first place, the presence of this block of monoglot English-speakers in South Uist was one of the motives which provoked the new Isles local government, Comhairle nan Eilean, to encourage Gaelic pre-school playgroups and Gaelic-medium and bilingual primary schools, a crucial stage in the revival of the language which is now spoken by some 65,000 people. But, secondly, Gibson's humiliation unmasked for a moment the true nature of the unreformed British State. It revealed the executive absolutism, unrestrained by any constitution, which sets the will of Parliament and Cabinet above the law.

Perhaps Lord Gibson's speech that morning in 1957 was absurd. But the events of that night, when officers and security men bullied a judge into withdrawing his judgement, were a disgrace to democracy.

12

Who possesses this landscape? –
The man who bought it or
I who am possessed by it?

Or has it come to this,
that this dying landscape belongs
to the dead, the crofters and fighters
and fishermen whose larochs*
sink into the bracken
by Loch Assynt and Loch Crocach? –
to men trampled under the hoofs of sheep
and driven by deer to
the ends of the earth – to men whose loyalty
was so great it accepted their own betrayal
by their own chiefs and whose descendants now
are kept in their place
by English businessmen and the indifference
of a remote and ignorant government.

Norman MacCaig, 'A Man in Assynt'

Arichonan was a *baile* – an ancient nuclear community whose form may well have evolved from settlement patterns in the Iron Age. Iochdar in South Uist is a crofting township, a relatively modern invention. Crofting, as it is known today, originated as a system devised by landlords and improvers in

*laroch/larach = the foundations of an old building

the late eighteenth century which spread all over the Highlands and Islands in the ensuing hundred years.

Crofting began as the clan system fell apart, and as the traditional leaders of Gaelic society entered the expensive, cash-driven economy of the rest of Britain. Their search for new sources of revenue began with two commodities: kelp and sheep. (Kelp is a term for the broad-leaved seaweeds, mostly *Laminaria*, which grow around low-tide mark and which could be dried and burned down into a rich alkaline ash, a raw material for the manufacture of soap, glass and other chemical products.) Clearing the population from their subsistence-patch farming in the hills and resettling them along the shore served two purposes. It freed huge inland tracts for large-scale sheep grazing, and it provided the landlords with a local labour force to carry out the heavy work of harvesting, burning and processing the kelp.

But there was another crucial point to the introduction of crofting, and it was to cause much of the suffering, destitution and conflict of the nineteenth-century Highlands. Crofting was designed to reduce or destroy the independence of the tenantry. The new 'crofts', usually laid out on acid, stony soil, were seldom productive enough to feed a family, even with the widespread introduction of the potato to replace grain crops. In order to survive, men and women were obliged to take up inshore fishing or to work for wages at the kelp or as estate labourers. Most of them did all three.

At this period, roughly up to 1820, Clearance aimed at displacement and uprooting rather than emigration. The landlords needed their tenants as a labour force, but also – given that ancient attitudes were often slow to dissolve in new realities – as evidence of prestige; some chiefly families still felt feudal pride in the sheer numbers of their followers. The kelp industry went into an enormous, artificial boom during the Napoleonic Wars, when Spanish supplies of alkaline ash were blocked; the price of kelp soared from £3 a ton in the 1780s to

£20 by about 1801. But voluntary emigration was in full swing by the late eighteenth century, and in those years the landlords fought desperately to discourage it.

This was the first phase of the Clearances, the 'Dance called America'. When James Boswell and Dr Johnson visited the Highlands and Islands in 1773, they found the chiefs struggling to hold back a wave of enthusiasm to leave the country. At Armadale, in Skye, the two visitors joined 'with much activity' in a brisk new reel named 'America'. As Boswell described it, 'the first couple begin, and each sets to one – then each to another – then as they set to the next couple, the second and third couples are setting; and so it goes on till all are set a-going, setting and wheeling round each other . . . It shows how emigration catches till all are set afloat.' It was an allegory of what Dr Johnson called the 'epidemical fury of emigration', or, as a Sutherland estate manager complained at about the same time, 'a sort of madness among the common people'.

At this stage, emigration was often – perhaps usually – an organized, hopeful undertaking. The parties heading for the Americas were usually led and selected by 'tacksmen' (the class of tenants-in-chief who ranked directly under the chieftain). It was the tacksmen and their agents who chartered ships, raised money and made efforts to ensure that plots of land in a coherent settlement scheme were ready on the other side of the Atlantic. This was anything but the forced flight of helpless paupers. Instead, it was a kind of rebellion by men of substance and their steadiest followers.

This phase of voluntary emigration, from about the 1740s to the end of the Napoleonic War, has been called 'the People's Clearance'. It involved people who were no longer prepared to live in a land where they were rack-rented by increasingly greedy landlords and humiliated by the suppression of Highland culture which had followed the 1745 Jacobite rebellion. Many of the tacksmen had fought at Culloden for 'Bonny Prince' Charles Edward and the Stuart cause. Once in America, however, they developed a startling loyalty to the Hanoverian dynasty, and all but a handful took up arms against the American Revolution. (For all their courage, the only rebellious thing about the Jacobites was that they rebelled. In its social attitudes as well as its religious outlook, Jacobitism was a deeply conservative creed preoccupied with authority and rank, and any crown was to be preferred to a republic.)

But the poor – the small crofters and the landless cottars – remained behind, envious of an escape they could not afford. And emigration almost ceased during the wars against France, until the temporary Peace of Amiens in 1801 incited a new rush to leave. Alarmed, the landlords campaigned to secure the 1803 Passenger Vessels Act, which blocked the outflow by prescribing impossibly high living conditions on ships making the crossing. As the factor of one Hebridean magnate wrote, 'If emigration from Uist took place to a great extent, it would prove most harmful to the interests of Clanranald as thereby the kelp would remain unmanufactured.'

Everything changed with the end of the war in 1815. World trade resumed, and the Highland kelp market collapsed. A new and much grimmer phase of the Clearances now began. The landlords returned with fresh intensity to the replacing of people by sheep; a fresh torrent of displaced families arrived on the coasts, at a time when the crofting settlements were already facing hunger as the kelp industry withered. Meanwhile the population was rising steeply, mainly in the Isles; croft holdings were subdivided into impossibly small patches and – as on the micro-holdings of Ireland – only the potato crop prevented general starvation.

The proprietors, once so eager to keep the people on their estates, now reversed their policy. Crofters and cottars had become a liability, and they must go. In 1817, the same pressure groups which had promoted the Passenger Vessels Act successfully lobbied for its repeal. The 'surplus' tenantry, struggling to feed itself on what the historian James Hunter has called 'deliberately unviable crofts', had no money for emigration, and the landlords petitioned the government to subsidize free passages. The government refused, and many proprietors were obliged to pay shipowners and agents to get rid of their own tenants, often on leaky, dangerous timber ships making the return voyage to the Canadian forests.

Paying for emigration was still a good bargain for landlords. James Hunter notes that the owner of the Isle of Rum paid £5 a head to get the entire population transported to Nova Scotia. They had produced an annual total of £300 in rent, but a single sheep farmer now took over the empty island and paid the landlord £900 a year.

This second phase of the Highland Clearances lasted until the 1880s. It combined the older policy of displacing people from land which could be turned over to sheep with a determined drive towards emigration. It reached its peak in the decade after the Potato Famine of the 1840s. But the worst brutalities had already been prefigured in the Sutherland Clearances between 1807 and 1821. Thousands of families living in the inland valleys of the Countess of Sutherland's estates were driven from their homes by ferocious eviction squads, who did not hesitate to club people into submission and burn their houses over their heads. The Countess's factor, the notorious Patrick Sellar, considered that a population he regarded as degenerate primitives should be deported wholesale to Canada: 'they are just in the state of society for a savage country'.

If the phrase 'ethnic cleansing' had been current in 1820, Patrick Sellar would have accepted it as an excellent description of what he was trying to achieve. He regarded Highlanders as a failed race; a dirty, improvident leftover from the distant past who bred like flies and obstructed good modern practice in farming. At the time, news of what was going on in Sutherland reached London and shocked liberal opinion. Today, however, in a period when market forces are worshipped and revision is the fashion in history, Sellar is sometimes pictured as a much misunderstood reformer. The best comment on this line is to be found in the anonymous entry on Sellar in John and Julia Keay's *Collins Encyclopaedia of Scotland*. After listing some of his deeds and his subsequent trial for arson (at which he was acquitted), the entry concludes: 'As some are still pleased to point out, there are two sides to this story, one of them purveyed by people whose contempt for the Gaelic evidence is equalled by their ignorance of that language.'

Not long ago, I met somebody who witnessed a remarkable scene in an Easter Ross churchyard. A Canadian family was visiting the place, probably in search of ancestors. They came across a tomb which seemed to surprise them. The head of the family, a middle-aged man in a baseball cap, urged his wife and daughters to walk away. When they were out of sight, he glanced around, unzipped his trousers and pissed at length on the grave of Patrick Sellar.

The revolt at Arichonan was not a completely isolated event. About fifty cases in which the people fought back against eviction and sheep-farming have so far been unearthed from the archives, for the period between 1780 and 1855, and the historian Tom Devine assumes that more will come to light. But these were sparks which never came together into any lasting conflagration. Effective, planned resistance did not begin until the 1880s, some forty years after the Famine, when the Clearances were long past their peak. Even then, it was external factors which encouraged Highlanders to defend themselves. One was the 'Great Depression' of 1873–96; the fall in grain prices actually benefited the crofters, who by now were buying in much of their food rather than growing it, and reduced the paralysing weight of poverty. Much more important, though, was the example of Ireland where Michael Davitt's 'Land League', founded in 1879, was fomenting a new wave of agrarian rebellion.

In 1880, William Gladstone became prime minister for the second time, and launched his heroic attempt to solve 'the Irish Problem'. The following year, the Liberal government drove the Irish Land Act through Parliament, granting to the Irish tenantry security of tenure and the fixing of 'fair' rents by arbitration.

By now, effective contact had been established between the Scottish Gaeltacht and the Irish land-reform campaigners. Fishermen from Skye, especially, had used their calls in Irish harbours to meet Land League supporters, and the most prominent journalist committed to the crofters' cause, John Murdoch, had spent years in Ireland before editing the *Highlander* in Inverness. Studying the astonishing concessions of the Land Act, the crofters sensed that their own moment for action had arrived.

Violent protest finally broke out in the Highlands and Islands at the 'Battle of the Braes' in Skye, in 1882. Crowds of women with sticks and stones led the fighting against an arrest squad supported by fifty Glasgow policemen. It was not in itself a big affair – nobody was killed, and not many were hurt – but Scottish and English journalists gave it wide publicity. Its immediate cause shows that confident militancy had been building up for some time; the Braes crofters had been con-ducting a rent strike against Lord Macdonald in order to force him to return common grazing lands seized nearly twenty years before. News of the 'Battle' touched off unrest all over the north-west of Scotland and the isles, with rent strikes, land occupations and raids on deer forests and sheep farms.

This was alarming enough to the authorities. But the move-ment went on to acquire coherent political leadership. The Highland Land Law Reform Association, modelled on Davitt's Land League, gathered many thousands of supporters and announced that it was forming a 'Crofters' Party' to campaign for parliamentary seats. The London papers began to use head-lines about 'The Crofters' War'. Gladstone realized that he must act before the Highlands became uncontrollable, and he decided to take the risk of applying 'Irish' solutions to a part of mainland Britain. In Ireland, the Land Act had been accompanied by 'coercion', harsher measures against rural violence. In Scotland, he hoped that land-tenure reforms would be enough.

The Napier Commission began taking evidence (in Gaelic and English) in 1883, 'to inquire into the condition of the crofters and cottars in the Highlands and Islands'. Its report, given urgency by the election of four 'Crofters' Party' MPs, produced the Crofters Act of 1886. The Act granted the crofters much the same rights given to Irish tenants in the Land Act: above all, security of tenure against the landlord and 'fair rent' to be settled by an impartial tribunal. The Crofters Commission, set up under the Act, began to slash rents by up to a third, and carried out a wholesale cancellation of rent arrears.

In British terms, the Crofters Act was revolutionary. It violated the sacredness of private property rights, smashed the sovereignty of Highland landlords and – in one part of Britain – established an entrenched class of smallholder tenants with a legal right to remain on their land. The crofters did not become outright owners; a croft was still in theory a tenancy on some proprietor's estate. But this was the nearest Britain ever came to creating an independent peasantry, on the model of France, Poland or most other European nations in the late nineteenth century.

The Act was far from perfect. In the decade after its passage, there were more violent conflicts than before. Gladstone's Liberal government was defeated in its attempt to secure Irish Home Rule, and the Tory administration which followed sent warships with troops and marines against land rebels in Skye and the Outer Hebrides. The Act made no provision for the landless cottars, the poorest of the poor, and mass emigration continued well into the next century. More generally, the Crofters Act and its successors have been criticized for stranding the crofters in an economic limbo. They had gained security of tenure. But the restrictions on enlarging a holding or on realizing the value of the land and its improvements through sale locked them into powerlessness, and often into poverty.

For all that, the Crofters Act was a surge into liberty: one of the great emancipations of nineteenth-century Britain. Its most dramatic impact was not in the Hebrides but in Shetland, where inherited debts had squeezed many crofters into a condition close to serfdom. Shetland tenants were forced to pay rents in kind (fish or knitwear); starved out of the cash economy, they were made to exchange their produce for goods in stores owned by the hated 'Scots lairds'. To this day, Shetlanders look back to 1886 with joy, as the descendants of slaves look back to Abolition. It remains their defining moment of freedom, their Liberation Day.

But the legacy of the Crofters Act is about more than crofting. It was to have slow-working but profound effects on political attitudes throughout Scotland. At first, most Scots understood it as a recognition that the Highlands and Islands were 'different', or as a mere relief measure which made a compassionate exception to general rules of property. But by the later twentieth century, as the movement for self-government began to crystallize and debate practical reform, new questions were being asked.

How 'different' had the sufferings endured by the common people of the Gaeltacht really been, and had not rural landlords done just as much damage in the Lowlands? Was not the underlying problem the transplanting into Scotland of the English tradition of property, the doctrine – unique in Europe – of a totally free and uncontrolled market in land? (Sir Frederick Pollock, one of the great historians of common law, had written in the 1880s that 'the English law of real property is the most unmitigated nonsense ever put together by the perverted ingenuity of man'.) Surely, the real implication of the Crofters Act was that Scotland – and not just one distressed part of it – was 'different' too, a small European nation which must devise its own legal balance between the rights of the individual and the collective. Thoughts like these lie behind today's Land Reform debates in the revived Scottish Parliament.

When the women of the Highlands began to throw stones in 1882, and when their men began to tear down fences and kill the landlord's deer, things had changed. Ever since the Clearances began, outsiders had asked why there was so little resistance to the evictions, and why it took at least a century before the crofters and cottars felt confident enough to fight. As the potato famine began, Hugh Miller wrote in his Free Church paper *The Witness*: 'They [the Irish] are buying guns and will be bye-and-bye shooting magistrates and clergymen by the score; and Parliament will in consequence do a great deal for them. But the poor Highlanders will shoot no one . . . and so they will be left to perish unregarded in their hovels.'

John Stuart Blackie, the Gaelic enthusiast who founded the first chair in Celtic at Edinburgh University, said the same thing but more prosily in his 1885 book *The Scottish Highlanders and the Land Laws*. After describing 'some splendid specimens of the untrousered, strong-legged Celt', he commented that Highlanders 'might have been better treated if they had at an earlier period, and with greater observance, applied to a Government accustomed to act only on compulsion from below the highly stimulant recalcitration of a Kenmare or Killarney squatter'.

But, with a few exceptions, they did not resist. It was with resignation that they suffered hunger, intimidation and some-times violent eviction ('the bailiffs putting out the fire with the basins of milk', as one Skye woman recalled for the writer David Craig). One of the most-quoted witnesses is the geologist Archibald Geikie, who was visiting Skye when the people were 'put out' from their homes at Suishnish in about 1850:

As I was returning from my ramble, a strange wailing sound reached my ears at intervals on the breeze from the west . . . I could see a long and motley procession winding along the road . . . There were old men and women, too feeble to walk, who were placed in carts; the younger members of the community on foot were carrying their bundles of clothes and household effects, while the children, with looks of alarm, walked alongside . . . When they set forth once more, a cry of grief went up to heaven, the long, plaintive wail, like a funeral coronach, was resumed, and after the last of the emigrants had disappeared behind the hill, the sound seemed to re-echo through the whole wide valley of Strath in one prolonged note of desolation. The people were on their way to be shipped to Canada.

There is no shortage of explanations: the submissive element in the ethic of *duthchas*; the preaching of Presbyterian ministers who warned their flocks not to resist what must be the will of the Lord; the failure to develop any alternative leadership when the clan hierarchy abandoned its duty of protection; above all, perhaps, the hopelessness of resistance when the consequences would probably be mass arrests of the men and separation from their women and children who would be packed off to Canada on their own. Blackie, even though he thought that organized 'recalcitration' might have been effective, felt that there was a special dignity, even 'a manly independence of character', in the way that these people accepted their fate.

But the incorporation of the Highlands into the new national myth of Scotland has made that passivity hard to accept. Scots are supposed to fight for their 'fredome', not to bow before their persecutors with the grace of martyrs. On a much slighter scale, there are echoes here of the moral agony inflicted on the post-Holocaust Jewish generations by the fact that most Jewish communities in Nazi-occupied eastern Europe went quietly to the slaughter, urged by their own leaders to board the trains and lorries without a struggle. Israel is about a different, militant image of Jewishness; the imagined new Scotland is about vigorous, 'Touch Not the Cat' Scots who are quick to fight for their rights. And yet both Clearances and Holocaust are now part of national narratives. Discords have to be orchestrated down, so that they do not challenge the main theme.

Both countries have rearranged history in much the same way. In Israel, the sacrificial ghetto risings in Warsaw or Vilnius are given a central emphasis which upstages the stoicism of most victims. In Scotland, media treatments of the Clearances usually form a crescendo leading up to the Battle of the Braes, the Park deer raid in Lewis, the 1948 land raid of the Seven Men of Knoydart and other acts of defiance. Plenty of those acts took place, especially in the decade after 1881, and in themselves they deserve to be legendary. But they were exceptional, and the true *leitmotif* of the Clearances was submission – Geikie's 'long, plaintive wail'.

Early theories of race were also used to explain the failure of a traditionally warlike people to defend itself. In Walter Scott's time, the Highlanders were identified as a species of 'noble savage', embodying simple natural virtues lost to the sophisticated. Perhaps, some people speculated, such noble-savage races were culturally static, lacking the dynamic capacity to adapt to external change. John Stuart Blackie, writing in the 1880s, clearly thought of Scottish Gaelic culture as a capsule which was bound to deflate when pierced by outside contacts. The Highlanders' character, he noted, survived 'so long as they were allowed to grow up freely out of their own roots, and to wave their branches in the breezy atmosphere of the clan life in the glens, forming for many centuries a world of their own, full of natural self-formative forces, and unaffected by uncongenial influences intruded from without'.

This was a quite perverse view of history. The early medieval kings of Dalriada, the Lords of the Isles and many of the clan leaders had been aggressively outgoing. The Gaeltacht, with its network of sea communications, remained open to Scandinavian, Irish or Continental influences as well as to cultural and economic changes in the rest of Scotland. Indeed, one of the main problems of the old Kingdom of Scotland had been holding the Gaeltacht back, rather than finding ways to draw it into the world.

Blackie, a high Victorian, was insistent about the physical splendour of his untrousered Celts, which he attributed to 'the inherent virtue of the race, grown strong by the stimulus of a healthy air and the exercise of a hardy life . . . [they] presented a type of physical manhood equalled only by Roman senators and Venetian doges in their best days'. Patrick Sellar, a highly intelligent man for all his brutal reputation, took a quite different view. Writing some sixty years before Blackie, he defined the Highlanders as racial degenerates. Blackie thought isolation had preserved their culture. Sellar, in contrast, had argued that isolation had led to a process of negative evolution. A warrior race, once vigorous enough to beat off the Romans, had decayed to the point at which outside contact could only break down its ethical structure. Sellar presented the Highlanders as ignoble savages, and he did not hesitate to compare them to the 'aborigines of America'. The population of the Highlands and Islands, he wrote, were 'with relation to the enlightened nations of Europe in a position not very different from that between the American colonists and the aborigines of that country':

The one are the aborigines of Britain shut out from any general stream of knowledge flowing in upon the Commonwealth of Europe from the remotest fountain of antiquity. The other are the aborigines of America equally shut out from this stream; both live in turf cabins in common with the brutes; both are singular for patience, courage, cunning and address. Both are most virtuous when least in

contact with men in a civilized State, and both are fast sinking under the baneful effects of ardent spirits.

As the rest of the nineteenth century was to show, to term a
population 'aboriginal' was to suggest that they had no legal
rights to their land. In Manitoba, the Dakotas or Australia, possession based on unwritten community memory had no force
against the title deeds of white settlers. Sellar wanted
Sutherland to be understood as an East Atlantic colony, in
which the duty of government was to support the civilized
colonists as they advanced their farming frontier into tribal territory.

At the time, many Lowland Scots probably agreed with
Sellar. It was not opinion in Edinburgh and Glasgow which
stood up for the crofters' rights and prepared the way for the
Napier Commission. The *Scotsman*, for example, became hys-
terical in defence of law, order and the landlord. Apart from the
tenantry on the ground, the effective reform forces were three:
a tiny group of Highland intellectuals which included John
Murdoch, Alexander McKenzie and John Stuart Blackie; the
London journalists who reported the Clearances in metropolitan newspapers; and British politicians – not all of them
Liberals – who came to see the arbitrary power of Highland
landlords as both morally scandalous and a threat to public
order. With a few exceptions, the only Scots entitled to the
glory of having forced the passing of the Crofters Act were the
crofters themselves.

As the nineteenth century passed, 'Highlandism' took a firm
grip on Scottish identity. Tartan and bagpipes became national
symbols as the Scots proclaimed, in effect, that 'we are all aboriginals now'. Sellar's dismissive racialism went out of fashion.
And yet there are those today who look at the crofting counties,
those communities which have been confirmed in the tenure of
what is so often the worst land, and wonder if they are not
looking at 'Indian' or Aboriginal Reservations under another

name. As long as the rich soils of Scotland remain a speculator's free-fire zone while the barrens are reserved for one specific community, the ghost of Patrick Sellar will never be laid.

Who should be blamed for the Highland Clearances? This battle is still being fought, in books and newspaper articles. There are two sides, whose responses are predictable.

There is 'Clearance Denial' and 'Clearance Memory' (which is the orthodoxy). The deniers and revisionists usually make two points: that uncontrolled population growth in the Highlands and Islands made emigration the only humane solution, and that instances of violent eviction were the exception and not the rule. The deniers, who are usually right-wing in ideology, insist that state intervention would only have made the situation worse. Many of them even deplore the Crofters Act as a disastrous interference with the free play of market forces. The landlords, they say, were only the agents of inevitable change, and most of them tried to soften the impact of that change on their dependants.

The 'Memory' camp retort with the recollections of those who were cleared: heartbreaking testimony from all over the Highlands and Islands from those who were forced out of their homes. As most of the commemorators can read Gaelic and most of the deniers cannot, orthodoxy usually wins this round. This is not always fair; as with money, bad landlords drive out the reputations of good ones, and there were many responsible chiefs and tacksmen who ruined themselves in vain efforts to improve their estates without coercing those who lived on them.

The orthodox victors also attack one of the sturdiest 'denial' arguments: that Clearance was the only possible response to the population explosion between about 1780 and 1840. They say that the 'explosion' is largely a myth. This is contestable. It is true that the increase in the Highlands as a whole was modest. But it varied wildly from place to place. On the north-west coast and in the Isles, the population growth between

1801 and 1841 was 53 per cent, and in certain islands it was faster still. In such places, holdings were being subdivided into hopelessly tiny patches and only the potato stood between the crofter and starvation.

Was emigration the only solution in the first half of the nine-teenth century? Only to the insular British mind. In other parts of Europe, rural overpopulation was building up too, but gov-ernments there were more imaginative about what could be done. As a rule, they did not try to prevent voluntary emigra-tion to America or the absorption of surplus rural population by new industrial cities. But they carried out drastic domestic reforms as well, intended to break down feudalism in the coun-tryside and create a class of owner-occupier peasants. The Danes brought this about by carefully planned change, begin-ning in the 1780s. The French Revolution drove through the same transition with radical speed and violence, and spread the doctrine of a free peasantry into the countries conquered by France in the decades after 1789.

Britain, however, had long ago abolished its peasant class, above all in England where the 'enclosure' process had turned smallholders into landless agricultural labourers. In a country politically dominated by aristocratic estate-owners, the idea of reversing this process – expropriating landlords and giving their tenants full possession of their land – was unthinkable. Even in the 1880s, when Gladstone was driven to try desperate Continental solutions for Ireland and then for the Highlands, he dared not go that far. And yet in Scotland, given the poli-tical will, the 'free peasant' solution was always possible. In the context of Land Reform, a good case can be made for it even today – throughout Scotland – if the new legislation gives all tenants the right to buy their farms out. As large-scale com-mercial farming goes into terminal decline, the creation of a 'Scottish peasantry' dealing in specialized agriculture and land conservation makes a great deal of sense.

In the end, the argument about 'blame' grows dull and

repetitive. The 'Clearance Denial' case is certainly the weaker. The oral and written evidence of brutality is too damning and too widespread to be dismissed, and historians who beseech their readers to 'lay aside emotion' are unreliable historians.

But perhaps the most solid point is this. By establishing the crofting system in order to make their tenantry dependent, the landlords created for themselves the social problems which they tried to solve by the Clearances. This was an avoidable tragedy, whose causes were stupidity and improvidence as much as greed for cash.

13

How We Love Our Highland Playground

cover headline for *Harpers* special issue on 'Greater England', 1992

What is it to be, a preserved green paradise for the recreation of the descendants of Dr Johnson, Charles St John [an English sportsman famous for shooting ospreys] and the Victorian trippers? Or a reserve for a Gaelic and crofting way of life? Or a region like any other, there to be exploited for money and jobs by those who care to remain within it?

T. C. Smout and Sydney Wood, eds, *Scottish Voices: 1745–1960*

Near the ruin of the big house at Poltalloch, built by the Malcolms at the height of their fortunes, there is a group of cup-and-ring marks engraved on a dark, smooth slab of rock at the edge of a field. Most of the marks are concentric circles pecked into the rock around a central 'cup'. There are a few cups without rings, a 'star', and something resembling a star with a ring around it.

The cup-and-ring marks were cut between 5,500 and 4,500 years ago, in the Neolithic and Early Bronze Age. They are found in several parts of Scotland, but Argyll is particularly rich in them. Kilmartin Glen, the valley in which the Poltalloch ruins stand, and the surrounding countryside have something like a dozen known groups, done over a period lasting at least a thousand years in a stylistic 'family' of assorted designs. Many more must lie hidden under turf or moss.

Some circles are large, some small. Some have three rings

and some two. Almost all have a gutter-groove running down-hill from the centre like a radius line. Nobody knows what the gutter was for, although liquid could have drained down it – water, beer, blood? But nobody knows what the cup-and-ring marks were 'for', either. They occur almost invariably on slop-ing, whaleback sheets of living rock, seldom higher than a few hundred feet above sea level, often in places with a long view. Most of the clusters I know in Mid-Argyll are open to the south or west.

Cup-and-ring marks are 'rock art'. They were cut by people who knew how to grow crops and make pottery. But they belong in the same family as the rock art of hunter-gatherers – the paintings and engravings in the caves of Lascaux or Altamira, in the mountains of the Sahara, in Namibia or Queensland or New Mexico.

I often visit the Poltalloch carvings. But these days, I try to look at them in a new way, which may also be the rediscovery of a very old way. This rediscovery is the notion of 'cultural landscape', related to the wider notion of 'Total Ecology'. It involves abandoning the anthropocentric perspective of the modern West, and returning to the vision of human beings who understood themselves and their imagination as components of the natural world.

When archaeologists and anthropologists first became inter-ested in rock art, they treated it as art on rock. In other words, they approached it much as they approached a painting in the Louvre or a fresco in an Italian church. They looked at what was painted or engraved, at the forms composed of pigment or delineated by pecking with stone tools. They also saw the rock, but what of it? The rock was just the equivalent of El Greco's canvas or Leonardo's white plaster wall. What mattered was 'the art' which the canvas or the wall supported.

Only now do scientists begin to see their mistake. The 'art in a frame' approach is in fact an eccentric, very recent way of appreciating and marketing visual culture. It embodies the

Western habit of chopping things up into separate segments in order to study them more closely. But for most human beings, over most of time, the distinction between art and frame has meant little or nothing. Why should the pigment carefully applied to the rock face be inherently more magical or intriguing than the cracks, stains and crevices of the rock itself? It was in Australia, through talking to Aboriginals still involved with the spirituality and usefulness of decorated rock shelters, that it dawned on archaeologists that by separating the art from the rock they were missing the point.

They are a single context. At the start of this chapter, I introduced the Poltalloch site in a typically Western way, offering a description of the incised markings and ('some have three rings, some have two') beginning to divide them into museum-case categories. But to reach back towards the way this place was perceived by Neolithic people, I would have done better to include the colour of the stone, the glacial striations running across it in parallel lines, perhaps the concentric grey-green circles formed on it by lichen, perhaps the hollows at the top of the slope which invite a child to squat down and look out over the carvings into the distance.

And even that would be incomplete. The context is not just the sheet of rock, but the landscape itself. In the journal *Antiquity* (September 2001), Mairi Ross writes: 'Let us acknowledge where the rock is located, near what landscape feature, in relationship to what body of water, in what relationship to the sky.' She is thinking about hunter-gatherers in Australia and North America, who incorporate landscape features into their cosmology and who 'used rock art as a navigational device which cognitively represented the environment as a network of places'.

Much of that also applies to the Neolithic inhabitants of Mid-Argyll. They may have had small patches of grain and herds of goats, but much of their food would have come from hunting, fishing, collecting berries or foraging on the shore between tide-marks. The climate was warmer and drier than it is now, so that the hunters went jogging after their game through open elm and oak forests, among thickets of hazel. Like the Aboriginals, they probably had a phenomenal knowledge of long-distance paths, and the most interesting guess about cup-and-ring marks associates them with places where paths intersect. Here people may have stopped to meet other people, casually or by convocation, and camped for days and nights to gossip and do ritual business.

The fact that these places often had 'a long view' may be important. These were people who had a sense of themselves within a landscape, neither as owners nor as distant specks traversing a hostile space but as partners in this cosmos spread out around them. The sensitivity of Neolithic and Bronze Age populations to landscape and place is now accepted among archaeologists. But it has always been obvious to local people that many burial cairns are 'tombs with a view' carefully placed to command a vista of sea and hills, or that the positioning of henge monuments or circles of uprights can allude to the shape of a valley or the glimpse of a distant peak. A generation ago, isolated standing stones were bullied to confess that they were astronomical markers, foresights aligned on some distant skyline notch where the sun or moon might set at the equinox. These days, scholars are more inclined to put away their compasses and consider the landscape as a composition; which converging arms of the sea, or which symmetrical pattern of mountain crests, was this stone positioned to celebrate?

In the same way, the Heritage Industry, official and unofficial, has broadened its criteria for scheduling and adopting sites. It is no longer the single castle or megalith which is to be conserved, but a 'cultural landscape' – the whole context of the monument as well. This is a late conversion, but a great one. In Scotland, especially, it allows many revelations.

Scotland, as the photographer Patricia MacDonald knows, is a poor woman with little flesh between her skin and her bones.

Everything done on that thin, stony ground from the beginning – from the retreat of the ice to the advance of the motorway – leaves its scar or its pock on the surface. A cultural landscape is very much what Scotland is: something showing marks from all periods and land-uses of all kinds, an artefact whose art is human and inhuman at once, a picture which is paint, frame and National Gallery together.

This implies the acceptance of constant change in the cultural landscape's aspect. But it also calls for wariness about whether human or natural agency caused the changes. Take an example of transformation in which humans played no part. In Kilmartin Glen, the climate began to change at about the time when people stopped using the cup-and-ring places. It rained more, and became stormier. Birch replaced the big oaks; the soil turned more acid, and as the valleys grew waterlogged a thick blanket of peat began to unroll itself across what had once been a firm, fertile land surface. One consequence was change in the human part of the landscape. Food grew scarcer; the building of big sacred monuments almost ceased; society seems to have disintegrated into smaller, more insecure and combative units.

In another example, physical alteration has been human-driven. A very old man, a centenarian dozing in a council retiral home in Ardrishaig, might have seen the coastal hills above the Sound of Jura redecorated four times. As a child, he could have still known the communal 'lazy-beds', the ridges – each a long sandwich of rotted seaweed and piled turfs – into which the potatoes and oats were planted. Alexander Fraser, a minister in Knapdale, recorded that 'as ships sailed up the Sound of Jura, the seafarers said that the fields under the run-rig system looked like so many striped petticoats spread out on the hills'.

A few years later, as the people of the hills were expelled, the coloured stripes faded into the light green of sheep pasture, reddened in autumn by bracken which invaded the grassland no longer kept healthy by grazing cattle. Later again – around the mid-twentieth century, as big estates foundered under death duties and the loss of heirs in war – the white dots of sheep vanished and the landscape turned a dark, monotonous blue-green. A spiky mantle of Sitka spruce, planted by brigades of needy students or unemployed shipyard workers, had been cast over it by the Forestry Commission, its new owners.

And now the aspect has changed once more. The forest reached maturity and was felled; the hillsides re-emerged, but smeared brown with the raw litter of stumps and mud. The crofters and the shepherds and the forestry labourers have all come and all gone. But a network of new tracks left by the Forestry is encouraging incomers to build holiday homes, in places where nobody has lived for a hundred years.

When I was a boy, there were two occasions in Argyll when my parents pointed to somebody and said; 'Look! Do you know who that is?'

The first occasion was outside the Crinan Hotel. The weather was shocking. But on the end of the hotel jetty a gaunt, bareheaded old man in a black oilskin was standing by himself, leaning into the freezing blast of sleet coming at him from the north-west. We watched this extraordinary sight for a while. I saw the man raise his streaming face towards the sky, eyes shut as if he were in ecstasy. My mother said to me, 'That's Lord Reith!'

The other occasion was on a steamer making its way from the Isle of Coll towards the shelter of the Sound of Mull. It was raining and darkness was coming on, but a big man in an ankle-length raincoat, a scarf round his neck, was standing on deck talking loudly to a companion. My parents consulted among themselves: could it really be? Then my father pointed to the big man and said to me in a quiet voice, 'That's Fraser Darling.'

I had not known who Lord Reith was, and the fact that he was the founder and head of the BBC had to be explained to me later. But I knew about Fraser Darling. He was the great naturalist. He had written *Island Years* and *Island Farm* and *Natural History in the Highlands and Islands*. He knew all about Atlantic seals and red deer, and had lived on uninhabited islands to study fulmars and cormorants. And he, I had heard people say, was working on a post-war plan to save the birds and animals and rescue the Highlands and Islands from neglect and poverty.

Frank Fraser Darling permanently changed Scottish attitudes to landscape. Since his death in 1979, his reputation has been harshly fought over. But one achievement is not contestable. He forced his readers, his audiences and his colleagues to accept that the landscape of the West Highlands was not 'natural' but an artefact. Fraser Darling would not have used the term 'cultural landscape'. But he was the first influential thinker in Scotland to insist on a holistic approach to human settlement and its physical environment of land and living creatures.

Even now, tourism authorities and promoters still occasionally refer to the Highlands as 'our last natural wilderness'. But before Fraser Darling, that cliché was universal. Fraser Darling's message, put simply, was that the immense, stirring bareness of the hills and glens, the treeless slopes rising from peatbogs up to spires of rock at the summit, were not ancient and natural at all. Instead, they were the record of a recent and gigantic crime.

This crime was deforestation, by human agency. Once almost the whole mountain area from the eastern Grampians to the sea-lochs of the Atlantic had been covered by forest. Some of the trees had been deciduous oak and elm, but most of them were the Scots pines of the ancient Caledonian Forest, the 'Great Wood of Caledon'. The forest had been badly reduced by war – burnings to destroy cover for outlaws or clan enemies – and by the sale of timber for ship-building or for charcoal to fuel the iron industry. But the real culprit, according to Darling, was the sheep.

Fraser Darling insisted that sheep, in contrast to cattle, were destructive grazers addicted to the seedlings of trees. The wholesale invasion of the Highlands by sheep-farmers had killed the forests by preventing their regeneration. A few decades later, the creation of vast sporting estates had led to reckless overstocking of red deer, almost equally lethal to woodlands. In consequence, the forest perished and the soil once gripped by its roots leached away downhill. The slopes were denuded by headlong erosion, and good grass pasture – once conserved by the presence of human beings and their cattle – turned to sterile bracken and peatbog.

In the final pages of *Natural History in the Highlands and Islands*, Darling wrote: 'We are apt to view with pleasure a rugged Highland landscape and think we are here away from the works of the mind and hand of man, that here is wild nature. But more often than not we are looking at a man-made desert . . . the bare hillside, kept bare by burning and the grazing of an artificially large stock of sheep [is] not wild nature.'

He may have exaggerated, in order to make his point. The 'Great Wood' certainly did not blanket the whole of the Highlands below the treeline. The forests appeared after the last invasion by glaciers some ten thousand years ago. Oak and elm spread from the south and east, but the Scots pine, strangely, came from the opposite direction. It seems to have originated in the far north-west, and then marched southwards with its bottle-green foliage and red trunk until Rannoch Moor and the glens of the Central Highlands were covered by huge but probably fairly open pine forests. The uplands and more exposed areas would have always been open moorland, and the pines never dominated the wooded slopes of the west coast or the isles. And climate change, the wetter, stormier times which set in about four thousand years ago, was at first more damaging to the forests than the human species.

But these are minor complaints. Fraser Darling's recognition of a 'man-made desert' did not only transform Scottish perception of the Highlands. It was one of the first statements in Britain that the environment was not a 'natural' but a political terrain. It is true that Darling was not original in his sense that it was absurd to reform human conditions in isolation, as if they were not an integral part of a wider ecology. He probably studied the work of Patrick Geddes, Scotland's pioneer of holistic regional and urban development. More obviously, he was influenced by the classic age of mammoth integrated planning in which he grew up. Darling was certainly inspired by the Tennessee Valley Authority in the United States, the grandest project of the New Deal, and he had watched the Soviet Five-Year Plans combine social, civil and electrical engineering in colossal transformations of landscape. Whatever its sources, Fraser Darling's imaginative energy appealed to Tom Johnston, the most ambitious of all Secretaries of State for Scotland, who conscripted him in 1942 to work on planning the future of the crofting areas. This task culminated in his six-year *West Highland Survey*, finally published in 1955.

Fraser Darling acquired many disciples, but also enemies. He was a trying personality to work with. A massive Yorkshireman, he insisted without much evidence that he was biologically a Scot: 'in no other race are found at the same time such power for successful action and such nullifying defeatism'. His intolerance of critics and the tremendous power of his descriptive writing concealed the fact that his scientific credentials were actually minimal. He believed in observation and intuition rather than systematic analysis, and many of his theories about bird or mammal behaviour, gathered with much personal hardship during fieldwork spent camping on uninhabited islands, are now dismissed as amateurish. His claims to have established personal empathy with individual seals enchanted the readers of his books, but dismayed the professionals.

His mission from Tom Johnston, as he understood it, was to design a simultaneous regeneration of the natural environment, the economy and the population of the West Highlands. This would be carried through by comprehensive planning backed by the government. He intended to transform the living standards and opportunities of the crofters with a mixture of farming improvements, tree planting, better roads opening the region to tourism and the creation of small industries driven by power from the new hydro-electric schemes.

The ideas were excellent. Unfortunately, Darling did not really like the crofters. Neither, after an initial honeymoon, did they like him. Fraser Darling never accepted that the crofters' 'inertia' was in reality an almost fanatical determination to defend their independence on the stony land they loved. They well remembered the last time that they had been the objects of social experiment, also accompanied by big talk about 'improvement'. The outcome of that had been the Clearances. The crofters appreciated state protection and subsidies, but otherwise they asked to be left alone to find their own solutions in their own time.

Fraser Darling complained that the crofting community was 'defeatist' (a favourite word of his, which in the wartime and post-war years carried a special sting). He criticized the people of the Highlands and Islands for their diet, and even for their aesthetic taste. They had 'an excessive dependence on oatmeal'. In *The Story of Scotland*, he wrote that the townships formed 'a relatively primitive population . . . reduced from a state of simple self-sufficiency to one of dependence on manufactured goods', which included the import of 'processed foods, of cheap dressy clothes, of bijou furniture . . .' There was something to this. I remember well the revolting Glasgow bread, gas-bleached in a plant bakery, which was often three or four days old by the time the steamer delivered it to the Isles. But Fraser Darling's language could be outrageously colonial. He might have been a District Commissioner exasperated at tribal backwardness in Northern Rhodesia.

At times, he could sound almost racist, using the nickname

'Donald' for the stereotype Gael as 'Fritz' or 'Mick' were used
to slight the Germans or the Irish: 'Donald is indifferent on the
whole, not consciously indifferent, but unconscious of ultimate
consequences, and he always desires to please.' The crofters
recognized this tone, and resented it. The 'defeatist' remark, in
particular, was never forgotten by a community which had lost
an appalling toll of its sons on land and at sea during the two
World Wars.

But his weaknesses – arrogance and insensitivity – do not
diminish the force of his vision. Fraser Darling was certainly
authoritarian, and the methods he recommended for the transformation of the Highlands and Islands could be called
'bureaucratic'. But his diagnosis of what was wrong, like his
target-list for change, was imaginative and well-chosen.

The *Survey* demanded a radical change in land use. Sheep
numbers were to be reduced to a fraction of their current numbers, to let the land rest for an 'atonement' period of at least a
century. Red deer numbers should be halved, and there should
be a fresh programme of afforestation. 'Total ecology' was the
only possible approach; to provide hydro-electricity or roads
without linking them to a general solution of socio-economic
problems would be futile. Darling looked forward to a future
for the Highlands as 'continuing productive wild land in which
perhaps twice as many people could live than are there at present'.

There were also prophetic elements in the *Survey* which
baffled Darling's contemporaries but which are now at the core
of any discussion of British farming. He warned that in the
next hundred years attitudes to land use would change. The
commandment to 'grow more food' would be replaced by pleas
to produce less. Subsidies to encourage food production on
marginal land should stop; instead, there should be less land
under agriculture but it should be better farmed and integrated
with forestry. Only correct land use could reverse depopulation.
'Devastation has not quite reached its uttermost lengths, but it

is quite certain that present trends in land use will lead to it, and the country will then be rather less productive than Baffin Land.'

To drive through this plan, Fraser Darling proposed a towering command structure on the model of the Tennessee Valley Authority, an independent board with full executive powers. But the *West Highland Survey* came to nothing. It was neither Fraser Darling's awkward personality nor crofter opposition which defeated it. It was civil service hostility, above all from the Scottish Department of Agriculture. The Department was committed to increasing production on marginal lands, and to raising sheep numbers. It was unwilling to abandon the old subsidy system. Above all, it would fight to the death rather than surrender most of its control of the Highlands to a new and impregnable power centre.

Change did come in the second half of the twentieth century, but it came piecemeal and often wastefully. Roads were widened and the air and sea connections to the Isles were improved, bringing a flow of summer tourism into the whole region. Grand industrial projects were planted – the Invergordon aluminium smelter, the Corpach pulp mill, the Dounreay nuclear reactor , the 'fabrication yards' building huge semi-submersible concrete platforms for the oil industry – but they tended to wither after a few years' activity. The Highlands and Islands Development Board, established by a Labour government in 1965, possessed nothing like the powers which Fraser Darling had demanded for his *Survey* board; intimidated by the Department of Agriculture, the HIDB wasted time on empty dreams about industrial 'growth centres' and in its first ten years paid little attention to crofting.

Crofting, none the less, has revived. The apparently unstoppable drain of people away from the land has halted and even reversed. Inevitably, crofting remains a part-time occupation, its income supplemented by renting caravans, work in the North Sea oilfields or fish-farm employment. There is still poverty, above all among old men and women whose income is so low that they cannot qualify for improvement loans. But today there are long waiting lists for crofts when they fall vacant, for the first time in many generations.

The reason for the revival is not government or European support, although the Common Agricultural Policy has begun to shift its focus towards the needs of smallholders. It is crofter self-help: the coming of a younger generation with technical experience and the will to take lessons from the practice of small farming throughout Europe. In 1986, just a century after the Crofters Act, the new Scottish Crofters' Union was founded in a surge of enthusiasm rising from the townships.

Since then, this fresh confidence has moved crofters to buy out several large, neglected Highland estates and run them through community trusts. The British government and the Scottish Executive now support this approach as a solution to the plague of the absentee or irresponsible landowner, and the coming Land Reform in Scotland is expected to entrench the right of a local community to purchase its land at 'a fair price'.

There are, however, some absentee landlords who cannot be touched. One of Fraser Darling's legacies to Scotland was his enthusiasm for taking large swathes of landscape into public trusteeship in order to conserve their wild life and ecology. By the end of the twentieth century the National Trust for Scotland, the Scottish Wildlife Trust, the John Muir Trust and the Royal Society for the Protection of Birds had acquired vast properties in the Highlands and Islands. These are not arms of the State, but 'conservation charities' which claim to adminis-ter their properties in the public interest.

This claim was furiously challenged by Ian Mitchell in his recent book *Isles of the West*. Mitchell's polemic against a 'new lairdism' which was secretive, authoritarian and tilted against the interests of crofting and local communities was often well-founded. He accused the charities of remoteness, being managed from Edinburgh or even from the south of England,

and he asked why so many of the charity administrators on the spot were young and inexperienced English science graduates with little or no knowledge of crofter society, Highland history or the Gaelic language.

Mitchell found the John Muir Trust the least objectionable, 'solicitous of local opinion about its management policies'. He reserved his most scathing criticism for the Royal Society for the Protection of Birds, based in Bedfordshire, and for the restrictions it imposed on farming in the isles of Coll and Canna in the interests of nurturing the corncrake. Mitchell objected that the humble corncrake was not really a 'globally endangered species' at all, given its flourishing numbers in eastern Europe. He quoted local opinion that the RSPB was autocratic, unapproachable and committed to putting the supposed interests of birds above those of the human inhabitants of its properties.

There has always been a danger inherent in reviving visions of 'total ecology' or 'living landscape'. This danger, which seems to tempt white European Protestants especially, is impatience with the human corner of the picture. I remember, when Kenya was still a British colony, the white administrators who would exclaim at the end of a hard day: 'God, I must drive out to the game park! What I need is an hour's worth of lions and grass and no bloody human beings.'

Too often, the undemanding majesty of the wild is set against the squalor of Homo Petens, Nagging Man with his insignificant little concerns. Fraser Darling was not quite immune to this attitude, and wrote (in *Island Years*) that 'I find truth in wilderness . . . In my view, humanity spoils when it packs, and I find myself moving to the fringe.' But he at least worked hard to ensure that the human inhabitants of his planned new world should grow in numbers, and would not be pushed out for the sake of seals, sheep, deer or heather.

Other holistic prophets were less tolerant about their own species. Ian Mitchell cites John Muir, the Scottish environ-

mental missionary who launched the National Park movement in the United States and who regarded 'man as the
only unclean animal', rejoicing when his view from a mountain
peak was free of 'human impurity and filthiness'. Max
Nicholson, director of the Nature Conservancy between 1952
and 1966 and the most powerful committee-man in the British
'conservation industry', wrote about 'our degenerate and self-
disgusted, materialist, power-drunk and sex-crazed civilization'
which required 'a return in some form to the wilderness . . .
Modern man cannot hope without some serious preparation
and training to be anything other than a misfit and a blot on the
wilderness scene.'

The slab of stone at Poltalloch, engraved with its swirling
symbols, looks out on a landscape of sea and hills, on fields
which carry cattle and sheep and, in winter, clamorous hordes
of greylag geese from the Arctic. Standing beside the cup-and-
ring marks, I can see the rock of Dunadd and the peak above
the silent ruins of Arichonan and smoke rising from the houses
of hardworking people I know well. Human beings are not a
misfit in this half-wild territory which they have changed so vis-
ibly, and which has been changing them for over eight
thousand years.

In writing about self-disgust, Nicholson displayed it. Could
there be greater self-hatred than to imagine Eden, and then to
carry out a Clearance which would evict all men and women
from the garden in the name of serpent conservation?

14

Tory values are in tune with everything that is finest in the Scottish character. Scottish values are Tory values.

Margaret Thatcher, 1988

Impress this on the minds of your young cousins . . . [that] I can never consent to assist idle and dissipated characters however nearly connected to me, but am prepared to go to any reasonable extent in supporting such of my relatives as conduct themselves prudently and industriously.

William Jardine, co-founder of the 'princely hong' of Jardine Matheson, the greatest of all Scottish trading houses in China, in a letter of 1830 to a nephew seeking a post in the firm

I was eighteen years old when I was conscripted into the Royal Marines to do my National Service. Less than a year later, in 1951, I disembarked from a septic old troopship called the *Empire Pride* at Singapore. Our duty was to combat the Communist insurgents in the Malayan jungle, the Malayan People's Liberation Army, who had taken up arms three years before to free the peninsula from British imperialism. A few thousand ill-armed guerrillas, mostly Chinese, were contriving to hold down some 50,000 British, Commonwealth and Gurkha troops, and they continued to do so for many years after I had finished my term of military service and returned home.

We were defending the British Empire. I was not sure what this would look like, nor whether it was worth defending. But I had been told that Malaya, in particular, contained a great many Scots who might find me a prosperous career if I conducted myself prudently and industriously.

From Scotland, I brought two pieces of paper in my black tin trunk. One was a copy of the Scottish Covenant. This was the petition for a Scottish parliament, launched by John MacCormick and his 'Scottish Convention' movement in 1949 and signed by something like two million people. 'We, the people of Scotland . . .' it began. In my innocence, I assumed that far-flung colonial Scots would be proud to sign it, if not in blood then at least in a gush of sentimental patriotism.

Our camp in the state of Perak was close to the metal-roofed bungalow of an Aberdonian tin-mine manager, Mr Johnston Mather. He was the bit of Empire we were to protect, and he rewarded us with invitations to drink whisky – the large half-and-half glass known as a *stengah* – or occasionally to Sunday curry tiffin at the Ipoh Club. One evening when I was alone with him in the bungalow, I shyly unfolded the Covenant and asked him if he would like to sign.

Johnston Mather was a small man with hard yellow knees. He sat in his cane chair and looked at me for a long time. When he seemed about to speak, we were interrupted by a flying beetle the size of a small crow which droned across the room and crashed into one wall after another. Presently it fell behind the drinks cabinet, where its drone changed to a shrill scream of fear. Mather's Highland terrier got up and strolled over to the cabinet. There was a crunching noise and the screaming stopped. Mather continued to stare at me. Then he said: 'Laddie, if you know what's good for you, you'll just put that piece of nonsense away and we'll hear no more of it!'

The other piece of paper was a letter of introduction. The summer before, on leave at Crinan in Argyll, I had met a nice dark-haired girl from the West End of Glasgow who was staying in the hotel with her mother. I was definitely interested in Diana, who seemed impatient for real life to begin. For non-romantic reasons, her mother was definitely interested in me.

'Well, fancy you going to Malaya!' she said one afternoon. 'I know somebody out there – well, he's a relative of my husband's, actually – who might be very helpful to you. I don't say anything would come of it, but Lofty might just think you were his sort of young fellow.'

'Lofty' Grant, it turned out, was a senior partner in Guthrie's, the most powerful of the Scottish partnerships which had dominated the Malayan economy for a century and a half. The colony of Singapore had been founded in 1819, and twelve of the first seventeen trading partnerships set up there were Scottish. Guthrie's arrived in 1821, set up by young Alexander Guthrie from Brechin and run by family members for the ensuing hundred years. At first it dealt in existing South Asian produce: sugar and spices, vegetable oil, coffee and some minerals. Soon it branched out into banking and insurance: the financing of colonial enterprise. But in 1896, with the first success of rubber planting in Malaya, Guthrie's invested massively in the new plantations, offering management services and capital on a scale no other company could rival. Huge fortunes were made in the rubber boom, and then lost again in the slump of the 1930s, but Guthrie's was so big and so diversified that it survived to profit from the renewed demand for rubber on the eve of war and – after the Japanese occupation – during the Cold War which followed.

Nothing came of my introduction. Lofty Grant, tall and taciturn, was kind to me in Singapore but probably sensed that I was deficient in prudence and industriousness. He took me to the Tanglin Club where I sat awkwardly beside the pool in my itchy new khaki drill uniform, conscious of my acne and uncertain of what was expected of me. I did not hear from him again. But I had been given a taste of the Scottish colonial network which I never forgot. Guthrie's, although bigger and richer than most, was absolutely typical of 'the Scottish Empire'. It was a private partnership which remained patriarchal: firmly in family hands. Its recruitment, still mainly from the north-east of

Scotland which Alexander Guthrie had left more than a hundred years before, was operated through a network of friends and relations back in Scotland who recommended likely lads on the basis of intelligence and moral character. While retiring partners and employees might return to Scotland with substantial personal fortunes, profits were almost entirely re-invested in Asia and very seldom repatriated to finance ventures at home.

Above all, these Scottish private partnerships were interested in trade, not territory. The idea of an expanding empire which directly governed alien continents left outfits like Guthrie's indifferent. Doing business was what mattered, and as long as their access to markets in Africa, Asia or the Americas was not blocked by tariffs or the hostility of native rulers, they did not much care which colour the territory was painted on the atlas or whether the local rajah, emperor or paramount chief had sworn allegiance to Queen Victoria.

The historian Michael Fry, in his book *The Scottish Empire*, argues that a definable difference existed between the 'Scottish' and 'English' Empires. The latter was about conquest and the creation of new political structures; the former was about the pragmatic business of settling emigrants in new territory and making money. It was English minds that cooked up the late-Victorian vision of a global empire of loyal English-speaking colonists gathered under the Union Jack. Significantly, the book which did most to promote this vision was entitled *The Expansion of England*.

Sir John Seeley's lectures on imperial history, first published in 1883, assume a mother-country referred to as 'England' and a future 'Greater Britain' of English-speaking settler dominions united with the motherland in a federated global superstate. Seeley refers to Scotland only as an example of how the existence of non-English and aboriginal minorities need not obstruct an essential Englishness. 'If in these islands we feel ourselves for all purposes one nation, though in Wales, in

Scotland and in Ireland there is Celtic blood and Celtic languages utterly unintelligible to us are still spoken, so in the
empire a good many French and Dutch and a good many
Caffres and Maories may be admitted without marring the eth-
nological unity of the whole.'

Seeley was writing before the 'scramble for Africa' landed
Britain with immense new tropical possessions, many of them
unsuitable for permanent European settlement and all inhabited by tens of millions of 'Caffres'. Less excusable is his
treatment of emigration as an orderly, voluntary process of
'Teutonic' expansion into empty continents; he mentions neither the Highland Clearances nor the greatest European
emigration of the century, the flight of a large part of Ireland's
population after the Famine.

British India was for Seeley the grand exception and problem, an empire ruling 255 million non-Europeans which had
developed 'partly it may be out of an empty ambition of conquest and partly out of a philanthropic desire to put an end to
enormous evils'. He tugged and teased at the Indian question,
but found no coherent way to fit India into his basically 'eth-
nological' prophecy of a Greater Britain. Seeley admitted
India's huge commercial importance to Britain, and he also
firmly supported the new policy of coercing India into 'civilization'. Since 1858, when the Indian Mutiny was crushed,
'the Government is now as sincerely paternal as any
Government can be, and . . . it has abandoned the affectation of
not imparting the superior enlightenment we know ourselves
to possess on the grounds that the Hindus do not want it'.

That 'affectation' was exactly what marked off the Scottish
approach to India from that of the English. Up to the Mutiny,
Scottish administrators and the Scots who effectively ran the
East India Company had broadly taken the view that Indian
society and culture should be allowed to develop along their
own lines. As Fry recalls, several of them (Lord Minto,
Governor-General from 1806 to 1811, and Thomas Munro who

became Governor of Madras in 1819) were enthusiastic 'orientalists' who tried to promote Hindu intellectual life and to control the inroads of Christian missionaries. Such men were often aware of this contrast between arrogant English instincts and their own more liberal approach to India. Munro observed that 'Englishmen are as great fanatics in politics as Mahomedans in religion. They suppose that no country can be ruled without English institutions.' As early as 1821, he confessed his fear of 'some downright Englishman who will insist on making Anglo-Saxons out of Hindoos'. But the Mutiny fatally undermined the case for tolerance, and when the killing was over, the 'downright Englishmen' were able to set about the forcible Westernization of India without fear of criticism.

Was there an element of hypocrisy in this Scottish disdain for imperial regimes imposed by bayonets? Great trading houses like Guthrie's or Jardine Matheson liked to imply that they could do business under any flag. But the reality was that their own position ultimately depended on the use or threatened use of force. If British and other European armies had not been prepared to invade the realm of the Manchu emperors in the late nineteenth century, Jardine Matheson's grip on the opium trade through Canton and Hong Kong would have been broken. If British eighteenth-century armies had not defeated France at Quebec, little would have been heard of the North West Company – an almost exclusively Scottish enterprise – or even of the Hudson's Bay Company, also dominated by Scots. And if my little section of Marines and I had not been laying ambushes in the mountain jungle, Johnston Mather would have abandoned his tin mine and Guthrie's would have lost control of several dozen rubber estates. And, of course, the soldiers and their generals who conquered a third of the world for the Crown and the Union Jack were as likely as not to be Scots themselves.

In this sense, the 'Scottish Empire' in the 200 years between 1760 and 1960 has been described as parasitical. Here is one way of looking at it: the English, with their self-consciously Roman sense of assimilating mission and their equally Roman understanding of an empire as a set of institutions, erected a solid framework. Then the sinewy vine of Scottish energy, ambition and adaptability swarmed up it and bore its own fruit. Another saying turns that relationship round, claiming that without the Scots the British Empire could never have existed. All that can be said is that without Scottish administrators (an absurdly high proportion of those who governed that bargain-basement of Dominions and Crown Colonies and Protectorates), without Scottish settlers and managers and, above all, without Scottish finance, the growth of Empire would have been much slower and far more vulnerable to war and economic disaster.

But 'parasitical' is the wrong word. 'Symbiotic' is better. Scottish colonialism already had an identity of its own by the time of the 1707 Union, and could exist without the support of a territorial imperium. None the less, the conditions offered by partnership in the expanding British Empire were a luscious opportunity for Scotland's established trading methods and for its already ancient tradition of emigration. Although these methods originated in late-medieval and then mercantile Europe, they flourished under the unrepeatable conditions of the Victorian century, when a free-trading Britain dominated world export markets. They sickened but survived during the mid-twentieth century, as state regulation limited the opportunities and dangers of industry and commerce. Now they have finally disintegrated, as free trade roars back in the form of a globalized market which has torn open almost all remaining private companies and numbed the creative nerve of British capitalism.

But some traits of the Scottish Empire did not change, and they were recognizable in the late sixteenth-century Baltic and recognizable in Hong Kong in the 1950s. Lofty Grant in Singapore and Diana's mother in Glasgow had also lived in

Gdańsk and Aberdeen when Zygmunt III was King of Poland and James VI was King of Scotland. One day in Malaya, my patrol emerged into a remote clearing and found five Scottish families living in wooden houses near an open-cast tin mine. Almost all of the men came from Angus, Aberdeenshire or Moray; several had been at school together; several were related directly or by marriage to the family which owned the mine; all could remember who had recommended them, and who had interviewed them in Kuala Lumpur with letters from Scotland on his desk. But I would have found the same patriarchal pattern if I had entered the offices of a Calcutta bank in the 1840s, or ridden into a village on the Cape Fear River in North Carolina in the 1760s.

In May 1988, Mrs Thatcher made a notorious speech to the General Assembly of the Church of Scotland. One thing that lady did not lack was courage carried to the point of impudence. In this 'Sermon on the Mound' (nicknamed after the Edinburgh site of the General Assembly), the prime minister decided to remind the Scots of what she considered to be their true character. She had once said that 'the Scots invented Thatcherism long before I was heard of'. Now she announced that the real Scottish virtue was rugged individualism, the entrepreneurial spark which made a Scot sally out into the world armed only with a gift for money-making and a conviction that he could succeed on his own.

The Kirk was appalled when she quoted the New Testament to support her belief that wealth-creation mattered more than neighbourliness. But her grasp of history was as weak as her borrowing of the Gospel was outrageous. With a few exceptions, Scottish enterprise has never been individualistic. On the contrary, it has been a matter of small, authoritarian oligarchies, tightly controlling their own recruitment and run as disciplined collectives for the benefit of a group – usually a family, sometimes a particular district, and often both. The internal principles on which these private partnerships were run had little to do with open competition. Advancement was founded on nepotism and maintained by obedience. Everybody hoped to become rich. But personal initiative, especially in a young probationer, was often growled down as disloyalty.

Scottish involvement in the worlds beyond the sea started in the Middle Ages. Perhaps it began even earlier. The Norsemen who colonized Iceland seem to have taken Gaelic-speakers with them from their empire in the Hebrides. By the time of the Wars of Independence, beginning in the late thirteenth century, small merchant ships were sailing regularly between eastern Scotland, Scandinavia and the Hanseatic cities on the North Sea and the Baltic. That was why William Wallace had written to the Senate of Lübeck in 1297, announcing that the English had been beaten off and that the Scots were ready to resume trading.

Scots went overseas in several different guises. One was soldiering abroad for money or glory. This was a tradition which began in Gaelic society with generations of young swordsmen who sailed to Ireland in search of action, at first in clan wars and later against the English. By the seventeenth century, Scottish mercenary soldiers were serving in almost every north European army from France to Russia, draining the land of young men and perceptibly affecting the birth rate by their absence. The battlefields of the Thirty Years' War, which ended in 1648, were heaped with dead Scotsmen who had fought as individuals or in whole regiments. Between 1625 and 1642, Scotland's Privy Council licensed over 47,000 men to enlist in foreign armies – out of a population of well under a million. A single military dynasty, the Munro lineage from Easter Ross, is said to have had three generals, eight colonels, five lieutenant-colonels and thirty captains – to say nothing of subalterns and private soldiers – in the army of King Gustavus Adolphus of Sweden. (One of them, Colonel Robert Munro, wrote an unsparing journal of his campaigns in Germany and

Poland which is still horrifying to read. He published it, he told the reader, so that 'at least thou shalt see my thankfullness to my Camerades and Country, and examples of frequent mortality, to make thy use of'.)

A second type of emigration was the trading colony. This was to become the matrix for many other forms of Scottish presence abroad: the settled group in a foreign port, closely disciplined and carefully recruited through family networks, dependent on rights granted by the local ruler. Out of these colonies developed the private partnerships, banks and trading houses which, after the Union, were to dominate the commerce of the British Empire, above all in southern Asia, Canada and Australia. Later still came the phase of mass emigration, the movement of population from the Highlands and Lowlands which carried whole families out to settle 'empty' territory in the Americas and Australasia.

In contrast to the chaotic rush to the ships which followed the Irish Famine, much of the Scottish emigration – even during the Clearances – was planned and financed in advance. This was often arranged by partnerships based in Glasgow or Greenock; they raised funds to pay for passages and (sometimes) the bridging costs required to cover the grim interval between establishing an agricultural colony in virgin lands and getting enough of a harvest to avoid starvation. In return, they took a stake in the colony's future fortunes and hoped to recover their investment.

When Scots talk about 'Scottish colonies' set up when their country was still independent, they are thinking above all about the disaster of the Darien scheme in 1699. This was the last, fatal effort by Scotland to establish a colony which would survive competition from the English and the Dutch. Three thousand Scots went out to settle on a swampy promontory in what is now Panama; they took with them something like a quarter of the nation's capital, intending to found a great trading emporium open to the merchants of the world. Only a fraction came home. Disease, hunger, boycott by England and finally a Spanish force sent to evict them brought the plan to rapid ruin. The consequences led to the heaviest decision in Scotland's history. Darien's revelation of the nation's weakness, the catastrophic financial loss and the demoralization of the Scottish middle class persuaded Scotland's leaders that independence had failed to meet the test of changing times. If the nation were to survive at all, some sort of Union with England must come – and the sooner the better.

And yet the obsession with Darien is misleading. It was a final gamble, in which Scotland staked all its resources and lost. But a long history of Scottish colonial enterprise lay behind Darien, and much of it was a history of success. The mystery is why Scots so seldom mention it, and in particular are so silent about the first great rural emigration and the first constellation of trading colonies.

The rural settlement was the Plantation, establishing tens of thousands of mostly Lowland Scots in Ireland, above all in Ulster, from the late sixteenth century onwards. Politics, or at least political correctness in the modern context of the Troubles, help to explain that reticence. But the other silence covers Scotland's most ambitious, long-lived and profitable foreign venture in all the centuries before the Union. This was the Scottish colonization of Poland, which reached its peak of prosperity in the early seventeenth century.

William Lithgow had no ears. That was why they called him 'Lugless Will'. As a young fellow in Lanark in the late sixteenth century, he had been caught in bed with a girl by her two brothers, who cut his ears off. He became a writer of fourth-rate poetry and first-rate journals, and spent much of his life as what we would now call an 'explorer'. In the book he eventually wrote about his travels, *A Total Discourse of the Rare Adventures and Painfull Peregrinations of Long Nineteen Yeares*, published in 1632, there are many woodcuts of him strutting about Troy or Judaea in the magnificent Turkish costume he designed for himself. The turban covered where his ears had been.

Lugless Will travelled on foot. He took a ship when he came to water, but otherwise he walked. In the early decades of the seventeenth century, he walked though England, Ireland, France, Spain, Switzerland, Germany, the Low Countries, Bohemia, Hungary and Poland. He walked over much of the Near East as well, marching far into the Sahara, tramping round the ruins of Troy and shuffling in the disguise of a Catholic pilgrim across Lebanon and Palestine to Jerusalem.

He was more than slightly daft. Will Lithgow was 'gallus', a Scots word meaning 'wild, unmanageable, bold; impish, mischievous, cheeky'. He was boastful, prurient and bigoted. Pages are covered by praise of his own exploits, stories about sex in strange lands and frantic mockery of Papism. He drank tremendously, and sucked up to grandees shamelessly. He could be crazily generous, but nursed slights for years. Physically, the sheer toughness of this young man was incredible. All around him, others died of fever, from cannon-balls fired by Moorish pirates or from the scimitar-slashes of brigands. Lugless Will bandaged his wounds and kept walking, until tortures in a Spanish Inquisition dungeon permanently crippled him and he was obliged to come home. But why he kept walking he never explained.

All across Europe and the Levant, he ran into fellow-Scots. The year 1616 found him in Podolia, in what is now Ukraine, vainly seeking a guide to take him into Tartary. He gave up and turned north, striding over the Carpathian hills into the territories of the Polish Commonwealth until he came to Kraków. 'Being Arrived in Crocko or Crocavia, the capitall City of Polland (though but of small importance) I met with diverse Scotish Merchants, who were wonderfull glade of mine arrival there, especially the two brothers Dicksones, men of singular note for honesty and Wealth'. Later he travelled on to Lublin, on the way to Warsaw. 'Here I found abundance of gallant rich Merchants my Countrey-men, who were all very kind to me, and so were they by the way in every place where I came, the conclusion being ever sealed with deepe draughts, and God be with you.'

From Warsaw, he hitched a ride on a wagon bound for Gdańsk 'with a Generous young Merchant William Bailey my cliddisdale [Clydesdale] Countrey man'. At Gdańsk, the main Scottish settlement in Poland, he fell ill and nearly died, 'insomuch that my Grave and Tombe was prepared by my Countrey-men there'. But three weeks later, indestructible Will was fit enough to take ship for Denmark.

He was impressed by the vigour of the Poles. He described 'a large and mighty Kingdome, puissant in Horse-men, and populous of strangers; being charged with a proud Nobility, a

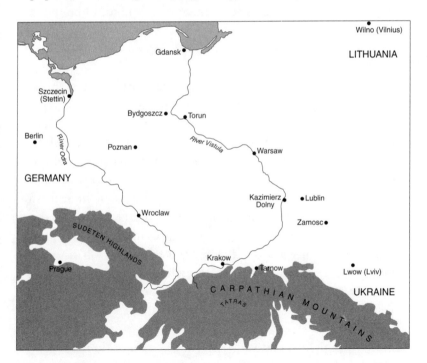

POLAND: SCOTTISH SETTLEMENTS ON THE VISTULA

familiar and manly Gentry, and a ruvidous [rude, rugged] vulgarity. They are all, for the most part, of square and thicke
bodies, having Bull-necks, great thighes and legs, grim and
broad faces, and commonly their shaven heads are finely covered with overthwarting strokes of crooked shables [sabres] . . .'

But Lithgow was above all amazed by the Scottish penetra-
tion of Poland.

> For auspiciousness I may rather term [Poland] a Mother and
> Nurse, for the youth and younglings of Scotland, who are
> yearly sent hither in great numbers, than a proper Dame for
> her owne birth [progeny]; in cloathing, feeding and inriching
> them with the fatness of her best things; beside thirty thou-
> sand Scots families that live incorporate in her bowells. And
> certainely Polland may be tearmed in this kind, to be the
> mother of our Commons, and the first commencement of all
> our best Merchants wealth, or at the least, most part of them.

Scottish historians know this passage well. Brief as it is, this is
one of the very few first-hand accounts of the Scottish colony in
Poland which still exist. For no good reason except the lack of
sources, the colony was almost forgotten in later centuries,
mentioned in history books only in passing if at all. And yet this
was one of the most remarkable colonial migrations in early
modern Europe, and a massively important episode in Scottish
economic and social history. Studies in the last few decades
have produced further tantalizing glimpses of the Scottish presence. But nobody has yet attacked the enormous job of sifting
the surviving Polish and Scottish archives to write a comprehensive survey of the Scottish settlements which lined the
Vistula river and its tributaries from the Baltic to the
Carpathians.

One problem is that Lugless Will was a bumptious exagger-
ator. His figure of 30,000 Scottish families, not counting the
'youth and younglings' apparently shipped out on their own, is

hard to take seriously. If an average settler family numbered even as few as three, then this would amount to something like a tenth of the entire population of Scotland at the time. Will Lithgow was just guessing. But there are other contemporary guesses which put the total population of the Scottish colonies at about 50,000 – probably including the large number of wandering Scottish pedlars, men who travelled through the villages of Prussia and Poland with packhorses but who did not belong to any of the organized settlements. All that can be said is that a substantial percentage of Scotland's people left for the Vistula. Given that most of them came from the east coast, between Edinburgh and Inverness, and adding into the sum the outflow of young men heading for the Baltic as mercenary soldiers, most of them from the same areas, it follows that whole tracts of Aberdeenshire and Angus must have become a demographic wasteland inhabited by women, children and the old – a countryside worked by grandparents.

The first Scots to settle arrived in Gdańsk in about 1380, and established themselves in a suburb outside the wall which was later called Stary Szkoty – Old Scotland. A Scottish factor handled the colony's interest and negotiated with the city's authorities. At the time, Gdańsk or Danzig was a self-governing merchant city under the control of the Teutonic Knights, who had won it from the Poles in 1343. But the port at the mouth of the Vistula was still open for trade, and in 1454 Poland's recovery of Gdańsk and its Baltic coast reunified the whole Vistula basin, a network of navigable waterways reaching more than four hundred miles inland. The Scots brought in cloth goods, iron and tinware, salted fish and later coal. But their central business was the Vistula grain trade.

It was the right business at the right moment. Western Europe, soon to be enriched by wealth from the Americas and the East Indies, was entering an economic boom period, above all in the textile industries of the Low Countries. The population, reduced by something like a third by the Black Death in the 1340s, began a rapid rise in the fifteenth century. But the countryside, where much agricultural land had fallen out of cultivation after the Black Death, was failing to meet the food demands of the cities, and enterprising merchants – the Dutch, above all – travelled eastwards to find new and cheaper supplies. Along the Vistula and its tributaries, the Polish nobility gradually turned over their vast estates to the production of wheat and rye. The grain was taken by wagon down to river ports; there it was sold and loaded onto rafts, which made their way downstream to the sea at Gdańsk.

The Scots infiltrated this trade at every point. At their main base at Gdańsk, they were in tough competition with the Dutch. But in the sixteenth century they were able to spread a chain of small settlements upriver, buying bulk grain from the producers and running many of the riverboats. Profits were often used to finance the needs of the up-country wheat magnates and develop the trade, an early example of the backwoods banking which was to be the main instrument of Scottish colonialism in the centuries to come. By the early seventeenth century, the peak of the grain trade's prosperity, there were over four hundred large or small Scottish settlements in Poland and along the Prussian coast.

In the 1620s, the average profit on a cargo of rye or wheat sold in western Europe was almost 30 per cent. Serious wealth was amassed. In 1651, during the Civil Wars in Britain, King Charles II appealed to the Scots in Poland for funds and they collected the enormous sum of £10,000; when most of it was embezzled by the courier, they subscribed all over again. Scots were soon entrenched in many other branches of Polish foreign commerce, including the monopoly of Hungarian wine imports, while the uncounted flock of Scottish pedlars, some on foot with backpacks and others with a horse, became familiar figures in the villages of north-central Europe.

For the aristocracy and the Polish Crown, the Scottish colonies were an indispensable source of wealth. The travelling packmen, on the other hand, paid no taxes and upset the Polish retail guilds by undercutting prices (their memory lives on in Polish sayings such as '*skąpy jak Szkot*' – mean as a Scot – or in German shops which advertise stock clearances at '*Schottenpreise*' – Scottish prices). Polish kings tried without much success to outlaw the pedlars, by restricting trading licences to organized settlements which paid tax. Otherwise the Polish Commonwealth was remarkably tolerant to communities which, after the mid-sixteenth century Reformation, were mainly Calvinist. There were occasional outbursts of intolerance: attempts at forced conversion, or the Kraków riot in 1647, when students tried to storm the house of a Scottish family. But many Scots rose to positions of power, among them the Davidsons of Zamość, the Akenhiffs from Tarnów, the great banker Piotr (Peter) Fergusson-Tepper and the Ross clan, one of whom became the king's secretary and notary. Alexander Chalmer (Czamer), born at Standing Stones near Dyce, outside Aberdeen, was a textile merchant who was four times Mayor of Warsaw in the late seventeenth and early eighteenth centuries.

The colonies were strictly run as small, self-governing communities in which all members were expected to contribute to common funds and charities. The main settlements were grouped into at least twelve 'Scottish Brotherhoods', each headed by an annually elected committee of 'Elders' with a board of judges entitled to impose fines, and there was a general meeting of all the Brotherhoods each year at the city of Toruń on the Vistula.

Few emigrants seem to have arrived as family groups, but – after the first few years – the Scots established a natural preference for marrying one another's widows or daughters. Recruitment, however, was difficult to control. The procedure, especially at Gdańsk, was to accept only young men who had already been inspected and approved by friends or relations in Scotland (another pattern which was to endure). But the pull of rumoured wealth and the push of Scottish poverty, especially after a series of 'dearth years' bringing semi-famine at the end of the sixteenth century, meant that boys and girls, sometimes little more than children, were being crowded into ships at Aberdeen or Dundee and unloaded on the waterfront at Gdańsk with no provision for food or shelter. Patrick Gordon, consul at Gdańsk in the early seventeenth century, wrote home to complain of 'boys incapable of service and destitute of means of living . . . dying in the streets'. The presence of these starving waifs embarrassed the Scottish merchants, who begged King James VI to ban the emigration of all youths who had no relations in Poland or less than a year's upkeep money in their bags.

Keeping contact with Scotland was often hard. Some colonists either returned home when they had made their pile ('Polland . . . the first commencement of all our best Merchants wealth') or sent money back to Scotland for family use or for the public good. The Scots in Poland made a collective donation to the restoration of Aberdeen's Marischal College, for example, and Robert Gordon, a rich Gdańsk merchant, endowed Robert Gordon's College at Aberdeen. But most charitable spending – like most investment – stayed in Poland and went into setting up scholarship schemes, schools, hospitals and Protestant churches. These were not only for Scots. The immigrants seem always to have worked for the improvement of the Polish 'ruvidous vulgarity' around them, sometimes by 'correcting' their religion but more often through education and the relief of poverty. The merchant Alexander Cockburn founded an art gallery and a technical college at Gdańsk; many other Scots endowed orphanages, trusts for the local poor and bursaries for Polish students studying Protestant theology.

The disinclination to send capital home, the preference for ploughing it back into the local economy and society, is one of the ways in which the Polish colonies prefigure Scottish behaviour in future empires. It recurred throughout the nineteenth and early twentieth centuries from Vancouver to Melbourne to Hong Kong. It was not invariable. After the invention of the steamship, big taipans from the China coast or Bengal often retired with personal fortunes to build draughty Scots-Baronial castles in Argyll or buy a bankrupt chieftain's estate in the Hebrides. But the serious money, as it showed up on a balance sheet, was rapidly put back to work as loan finance for a Polish linen factory, an Australian sheep station or a Burmese railway. And the Polish episode also shows another enduring business trait: a penchant for hazardous lending at low interest. The banker William Hewson, like Fergusson-Tepper, often had up to three-quarters of his capital out on loan.

A second precedent set by the Polish venture was assimilation. By the late seventeenth century, many Scots of the second or third generation were marrying Polish women and sometimes converting to Catholicism. The sea voyage home was long and perilous, Scotland was poor, and it would seem that many colonists arrived intending to remain. Sending children home to Scotland to be educated was not a very attractive option. Most families, or at least the male members active in commerce, seem to have been expected to speak Polish and probably German. Their integration into the political and commercial world created a growing loyalty to the Polish Commonwealth, and by the late eighteenth century, when the grain trade was long past its peak, the remaining Scots were well Polonized. In the catastrophe which began with the Partitions and the destruction of the Polish state in 1795, many Poles with Scottish names and dual identity fought in the insurrections of 1794, 1830 and 1863 to regain the independence of their adopted nation.

In the nineteenth century, a fresh but smaller emigration began, as enlightened Polish magnates invited Scottish engineers and agricultural experts to settle and start industries or improve their farms. Mona McLeod's book *Agents of Change* tells the story of her own Garvie family who took over the linen mill at Żyrardów, near Warsaw, and expanded it into one of the most successful textile firms in the old Russian Empire. Other ancestors of hers settled on the farming estates of General Ludwik Pac, at Dowspuda in north-eastern Poland. Again, the Scots stayed put for generations, and were drifting from bilingualism to using Polish as a first language when the outbreak of the First World War in 1914 forced tragic choices on the community. The Russian government of the Tsar's Polish provinces offered them either Russian naturalization or expulsion. Many of the leading families left. After the war, as Mona McLeod writes, 'there was no place for divided loyalties' in the new and independent Poland. 'The Scots who stayed on became Poles.'

This talent for assimilation was typical for the future. Although the Scots in the British Empire did not intermarry with non-European populations, they merged rapidly with other settler communities and found little difficulty – much less than English colonists – in acquiring new patriotisms. In a very few places, above all in Gaelic-speaking Cape Breton in Nova Scotia, a particular Scottish culture has maintained itself, based on language, music and transmitted memories of the old country. Elsewhere the Scottish diaspora across the world easily lost its sense of involvement with 'actually-existing' Scotland, beyond a stylized attachment to Burns Suppers, to Highland Games and – in some places – to anti-Catholic bigotry.

Nowhere was integration more rapid than in the United States. As in the case of the Polish colonies, Scottish historical memory is erratic; the emigration to Canada between 1815 and 1914 is fondly remembered, but little is said about the far larger numbers – well over a million – who settled in the United States in the same period. This is a startling feat of amnesia. Its explanation may be that these Scots moved largely as individuals or as families, rather than in transplanted communities which were slow to dissolve, and also that they entered a relatively developed economy where urban and industrial jobs were waiting for them. Both factors made for easy absorption. American Scots, one of the most successful of all the immigrant nationalities, soon had little reason to think about Scotland except in terms of a comfortable nostalgia.

The Irish diaspora is acutely interested in Ireland; the world Polish community ('Polonia') is still reasonably well-informed about events in contemporary Poland; Basques and Albanians in the United States follow politics and football in Bilbao and Tirana. But Americans, Canadians or Australians of Scottish descent who visit the old country are interested almost to exclusion in the past. They visit the chieftain holding a garden party for his 'clansmen' on the castle lawn, or search for ancestors in the archives of New Register House and in country graveyards. The restoration of a Scottish Parliament, the debate around Scotland's place in the European Union or the unforgivable poverty still to be found in Scottish cities are topics which they avoid, sensing an invitation to some uncomfortable commitment.

Perhaps this is just as well. Some recent attempts to inject political awareness into Americans of Scottish descent have been ominous. In the summer of 2000, a vitriolic controversy broke out in the normally sober pages of the journal *Scottish Affairs* when a contributor claimed that the introduction of a 'Confederate Tartan' in Alabama was part of a move by ultra-right hate groups to infiltrate the Scottish-American community and recruit its members for neo-Confederate ideology and the doctrine of white supremacy. Some of those groups, wrote Edward H. Sebesta, were inspired by the film *Braveheart*, seething – in their view – with their own 'Celtic' spirit of anti-State violence.

A furious retort came from the Tennessee anthropologist Celeste Ray, a student of 'Scottish Heritage Southern Style', who called Sebesta 'befuddled' and accused him of gross exaggeration. But her own account showed how the American fashion for 'roots' and ethnic heritage has begun to re-process notions of Scottishness. 'A newly invented "tradition" at several Highland Games in America involves members of clan societies gathering . . . and forming a St Andrew's Cross on the games field. Participants toss a torch onto a central bonfire as they announce the clans at the gathering and the places in Scotland from which their ancestors emigrated.' Far from being racially exclusive, Ray went on, the clan members at the Games included Afro-Americans, Native Americans in plaids and Mexicans in kilts and sombreros. As she says, 'heritage is a rhapsody on history. We strike the chords we wish to hear.'

The Scottish colonization of Ireland, above all in the province of Ulster, is far better known than the emigrations to Poland and elsewhere around the Baltic. The Ulster 'Scots-Irish' are still there, and the descendants of the 'plantations' of the sixteenth and seventeenth centuries remain the backbone of the Protestant 'Loyalist' community. Ulster Scots, still spoken, is undergoing a cultural revival, to some extent as a riposte to the Gaelic-Irish culture and language fostered in the schools of the Catholic and Nationalist population. But in several ways the settlement in Ulster was untypical, and its influence on the later patterns of Scottish behaviour in the British Empire has been slight.

In the early seventeenth century, when the planned settlement in Ulster began to take root, there were two Scottish presences in Ireland. The first was ancient, reaching back to the common Gaelic world which united Ulster with the Highlands and Islands in the time of the Dalriada kingdom. The almost independent Lordship of the Isles, which reached the peak of its splendour in the fifteenth century under the MacDonald lineage, was powerful on both sides of the Irish Channel; its leaders moved easily between Ireland and Argyll, raising armies or taking refuge in bad times. Its centre was on an islet in a loch at Finlaggan, in the island of Islay. Here the Lord of the Isles was inaugurated in the old Dunadd style, placing his foot in a stone footprint, carrying a white rod and his forefathers' sword and wearing a white tunic to prove his 'innocence and integrity of heart'; bards chanted his genealogy and the feasting lasted for a week. Although the Lordship had fallen in 1493, elements of this common Gaelic world survived powerfully into the seventeenth century. A branch of the MacDonalds or MacDonnells had settled in the Glens of Antrim, still to this day a Catholic and Republican stronghold. Great figures like Randal MacDonnell, Earl of Antrim, moved between Ireland and Gaelic Scotland as they played their tortuous part in the civil wars which devastated the three kingdoms of the British Isles in the 1640s. Alasdair Mor MacDonald, an ambidextrous giant with a sword in each hand, was the son of Alasdair Coll Ciotach ('Colkitto') from the Scottish island of Colonsay. But he brought an army from Ireland in 1644 to help Montrose's rebellion against the Roundheads and to take vengeance on the Campbells of Argyll who had broken the Lordship and seized MacDonald lands.

In 1603, James VI of Scotland had become James I of England and Ireland. He brought to this Union of Crowns a pitiless hatred of Gaeldom on both sides of the water. James had already planned an onslaught on the Western Isles which would expel their people and replace them with a Lowland Protestant settlement: 'rooting out or transporting the barbarous or stubborne sort, and planting ciuility in their roomes'. This scheme fortunately came to nothing. But the new king of 'Great Britain' found it easy to adopt the existing English policy of forcibly planting English and Scottish immigrants in Munster and above all in Ulster.

Until James's accession, Ulster had remained the most Gaelic and defiant region of Ireland. But in 1603 a rebellion led by Hugh O'Neill, head of northern Ireland's greatest family, surrendered to the English. Four years later Tyrone and Tyrconnel, the last traditional Gaelic chieftains in the north, despaired of their cause and went into exile on the Continent.

This 'flight of the earls' left Ulster defenceless against further plans for colonization, and a fresh 'plantation' was launched in 1610. Settlers were recruited from England and from the western lowlands of Scotland. By 1622, something like 12,000 British settlers, of whom slightly over half were Scots, had taken over land in Ulster from its Irish inhabitants.

But James at the outset took control of the Scottish emigration away from the Scottish Privy Council in Edinburgh. London was in charge now, and the English planners of the scheme maintained tight central management of the colonists, who were deployed over the landscape in a uniform pattern. Each farming estate was a hierarchical structure of tenants, small lease-holders and craftsmen centred around a landowner in a fortified brick or stone house. All must be Protestants; the Irish occupiers of the land were to be evicted. There was no room here for the self-governing colonies cooperating with the 'natives', which had been the Scottish pattern in Poland.

The inevitable rebellion broke out in 1641. On the face of it, there was no reason why Sir Phelim O'Neill, leader of the rising in the north, should have drawn a distinction between the oppressors. Lowland Scots had been no less willing than Englishmen to profit from the 'ethnic cleansing' of the Plantations. And yet Phelim O'Neill commanded his men to spare the Scottish settlers; they 'should have nothing to do with any Scottish man, but only with the English'.

Why he took that line remains a mystery. Possibly it was no more than a device to split the settlers. More probably, it was a political gamble on the influence of fateful events in Scotland. The historian Nicholas Canny has pointed out in his book *Making Ireland British* that – paradoxically – the Irish Catholic rebels were inspired by Scotland's Presbyterian revolution of 1638, the signing of the 'Covenant' which defied royal authority over church governance. But, whatever its calculations, the tactic was at first effective. All over Ulster, the Scots either argued for negotiation with the rebels rather than resistance or declined to stand up for English settlers whose houses were being seized and burned. As an English witness stated, 'the Scots did not partake with nor assist the English, but suffered them to be robbed, stripped and slain in their presence'.

Some Scots went further. In the first stage of the 1641 rising, a number of Scots joined the rebels, especially in County Fermanagh. At Newtown Butler, where English settlers had barricaded themselves inside a church, one witness saw 'David Little of Balle Balfour, piper, who played upon his pipes before the said Irish rebels when they took the church at Newtown from the English Protestants'. There were many such incidents. Afterwards, the English survivors said bitterly that the Scots were simply covetous for a share of the loot from sacked English houses. That was occasionally fair comment, but the evidence suggests that the Scots – perhaps in spite of themselves – discovered some genuine residual fellow-feeling for the Irish. It can hardly have been an inherited Dalriadic nostalgia for the Gaelic world. Most of these settlers were Scots-speaking Protestants from the Lowlands, brought up to despise the culture of their own Gaeltacht as '*barbare*'. But rebellion was in the air of the 1640s, and this was a tempting chance to strike a blow at the 'auld enemy' and at the patronizing English who treated the Scots as inferior partners in Ulster.

The impulse soon died away. Phelim O'Neill's insurrection broadened into a war of bloody battles and rebel massacres of helpless civilians. His order to spare Scottish settlers lost all effect, and Scots also became victims. Within a few months, volunteers to fight the rebellion were being recruited in Edinburgh and in 1642 Major-General Robert Monro (the journal-writer and veteran of the Thirty Years' War) landed at Carrickfergus with a Scottish army of 10,000 men. But the time for independent Scottish action in Ireland was over. Within a few years, the Ulster Scots had been subdued by Cromwell's brutal and complete conquest of both Ireland and Scotland. The hostility between English and Scottish colonists was replaced by common loathing of the 'Papist' Irish, and a much larger Scottish inrush took place in the second half of the seventeenth century. Some were Presbyterian fundamentalists avoiding persecution. Most, however, were economic migrants fleeing the renewed succession of 'dearth years' which hit Scotland in the 1690s. Between 60,000 and 100,000 Scots crossed the Irish Channel and settled in Ulster in the years from 1650 to 1700.

And yet Protestant Ulster, Scottish as its majority became, has never been consciously a Scottish colony. Instead, it has insisted, from before the 1707 Union until this day, on its 'Britishness'. This is an old-fashioned use of the term. Here is an identity founded not on language or descent but on three essentially political conditions: the supremacy of the Protestant faith, the control of the Six Counties by Protestants and loyalty to a Protestant dynasty across the water. The last Britons are to be found in County Antrim or County Down. But the words they use to proclaim their Britishness are often Scots.

As the British Empire spread across the globe in the eighteenth and nineteenth centuries, the distinction between English and Scottish patterns of colonialism survived. The English approach was imperial in the classic sense, concerned primarily with political and military power and territorial possession and less focused on the details of settlement or trade. English emigrants did settle in huge numbers in all the continents where the climate allowed it, and English (or at least London-based) capital flowed into investments in both temperate and tropical colonies. But this was a loose, diffuse process compared to the purposeful and tightly organized operations of the Scots.

Michael Fry quotes the impressions of the English politician Charles Dilke, after his visit to Bombay in the 1860s. 'For every Englishman who has worked himself up to wealth from small beginnings without external aid, you find ten Scotsmen.' The English explained this by supposed national characteristics:

Scots were thrifty, independent by nature and grimly industrious. But the truth was much more interesting. The Scots tradition of emigration in pursuit of trade or soldiers' wages was older and stronger than that of the English, and rooted in a much wider class base. The idea of living abroad – for years or perhaps permanently – was a familiar option for at least two centuries before the Union.

As on the Vistula in the seventeenth century, the nineteenth-century Scots in Asia, Australia and North America ran a dual business. They went into entrepôt trading – export-import business – and they used the profits for grass-roots banking, financing local enterprises on the ground – especially if they were run by other Scots. Sometimes this dual activity succeeded on a colossal scale; out of one small, hard-fisted family outfit on the South China coast grew the Jardine Matheson trading empire and the Hongkong & Shanghai Bank. But the typical Scottish unit was small: the 'private partnership' which used the special provisions of Scots law to set up a predecessor of the limited company.

At first, these tiny 'colonies', scattered by the hundred not only across India and the Far East but in the 'settler' territories of North America and Australasia, had to accumulate most of their capital on the spot. But by the late nineteenth century, the success of industry at home – iron and steel, shipbuilding, heavy engineering – was transforming Scotland into a small country with a large surplus of capital. The private partnerships tapped into this. Groups of solicitors, above all in Edinburgh, were formed to act as agents for the partnerships, borrowing money from thousands of mostly small investors whose cash was pumped out to fuel the firms overseas. The results were spectacular, especially after the Scottish banker Robert Fleming devised the general investment trust in the 1870s.

In the 1880s, it was said that three-quarters of British companies founded for overseas investment were of Scottish origin.

In the last decades of the century, the capital equivalent of something like 10 per cent of Scotland's net national product was being exported – again, a figure far above the English proportion. Scottish private partnerships advanced speculative loans, often to risky projects which conventional banks rejected. These loans made possible, to take a few examples, the development of tea planting in Ceylon and Assam, the construction of roads and railways in the Canadian West and the spread of sheep-farming in Australia. Nearly half of all Australian borrowing in the late nineteenth century came from Scottish sources, and Eric Richards, writing in *The Scots Abroad*, suggests that 'more than a third of all Australian pastoral, mortgage and investment company securities were owed to Scotland'.

Other such partnerships founded most of the great shipping lines – Peninsula & Orient, British India, Elder-Dempster, Anchor Line and the rest – which held the British Empire together at its apogee. But the central achievement of the Scots was to provide supplies of cheap risk finance to an Empire which, in spite of its majestic outlines, was chronically starving for capital.

Under the revolving fans in the counting houses, rows of young Scots in white suits sat at their account books, invigilated by men who knew their fathers. In bungalows set among scorching tea-slopes or rubber estates, planters born in Aberdeenshire farm-bothies or over a grocer's shop in Dundee swallowed cold drinks made by Fraser & Neave and wrote encouraging letters home to brothers about to leave school and board a steamer for the East. The climate was different, but the human and economic architecture of these countless Scottish colonies was the same as it had been in Gdańsk or Zamość nearly three hundred years before. Outsiders called them 'clannish', but that was the secret of the private partnerships' strength; a disciplined family business can hold down its running costs or take chances with creditors in ways which no public company would dare to attempt. But it was also, in the end, their doom.

The world changed. In the twentieth century, free trade faltered, protectionism returned and the Empire itself began to disintegrate. The partnerships withered; they were run by people qualified only by family connections or hard supervisory work in the field, and very few of them had any formal business or managerial training. Many of the big agency and trading houses failed, or amalgamated, or retreated into banking based now on the City of London. The return of global free-market capitalism at the end of the century completed their ruin. In a last effort to raise capital, many of the Scottish firms became public companies, only to be taken over and swallowed by bigger multinational players.

Today, Scots are scarcely aware of this dense web of trading settlements which once covered much of the world. Still less can they imagine a Scotland with a capital surplus big enough to finance much of the industry, commercial agriculture and transport infrastructure of distant continents. 'We are a small European nation,' people say hopefully, as if Scotland had never dared to be an actor in the outside world before.

This loss of memory is not hard to understand. Where, after all, did the money go which was amassed in those phenomenal generations? What does modern Scotland have to show for it, apart from dank pseudo-baronial castles built out of fortunes from Bengal or Manitoba which are no longer even considered fit to be used as mental hospitals? Other imperial states grew wealthy on empire, for a while at least. But Scotland in the 1960s, as the British Empire fell apart, had no vault of accumulated private capital to prevent its housing degenerating into the worst slums in Europe, or to save its industries from being taken over by outsiders who soon closed them and threw their workers on the street.

Scotland today is moving away from the despair of the late twentieth century, and putting hope – at least in its public rhetoric – in self-help and a home-based 'knowledge economy'. But the mystery remains. Within the oldest living memories, Scotland was a country with a domestic capital base strong enough to finance not only its own industrialization but a fair part of the planet's development. And yet within half a century it had become a place where 'attracting inward investment' seemed to be the only formula for prosperity. Part of the reason was complacency: the failure of Scotland's industrialists to move out of heavy engineering and defence contracts, and to diversify before it was too late. But this does not explain the loss of Scotland's power to generate capital for its own needs.

Where did all that money go? In one sense, the answer is straightforward. The money is still out there. It became the fixed capital – the railroads, plantations, ranches and banks – of a score of countries in Asia, the Americas, Australasia and much of eastern and southern Africa. As property, it now belongs to governments, local companies or multinational corporations based anywhere from the United States to Japan. But, with very few exceptions, it no longer belongs to the Scots.

The real question is why those groups which were so aware of their national identity, and so 'clannishly' exclusive, felt no urge to improve their own country. Here and there, individuals such as Robert Gordon of Gdańsk brought back their personal fortunes and spent them on the common good of their fellow-Scots. Andrew Carnegie used his American steel profits to give Scotland a chain of public libraries. The Malcolms of Poltalloch transferred profits from Jamaica and Australia into the London stock market, and used the proceeds to finance their great land improvement schemes in Mid-Argyll. But most Scottish tycoons spent their wealth on themselves, on steam yachts, granite palaces or Highland sporting estates (James Matheson used his immense opium-trade profits to buy the island of Lewis, where he became a notoriously brutal clearing landlord).

The notion of redirecting their business towards investing in the Scottish economy would have puzzled such men. The governors of the private partnerships often came from poor rural backgrounds, and their image of Scotland – which became utterly anachronistic in the Victorian decades of industrial upsurge – was of a hard, stony land without prospects of its own. They were patriots in their sentimental fashion. But they were also prisoners of an ancient emigrant tradition which had begun when famine was frequent and hunger – for food or for land – was endemic. Their best service to Scotland, they might have said, was to help the deserving young to leave it.

15

The Chaplain of the United States Senate told his guests what they had to do. First, they were to yell out 'Tartan!' Then they were to yell out 'Freedom!'

It was 6 April 2001, National Tartan Day in the United States. On the steps of the Capitol in Washington stood three Scotsmen, taking their orders from the Chaplain. Obediently, they all shouted, and yet each felt differently about the words they had to shout.

For Sir Sean Connery, a steadfast and emotional Nationalist, it was simple: he meant what he said. For Henry McLeish, who had become First Minister of Scotland after the death of Donald Dewar, the feelings were more mixed. Normally he would leave *Braveheart* exhibitionism to the SNP. But McLeish was an experienced Labour politician who was in America to sell Scotland. Tartan Day came at the end of a week of relentless export promotion: Scotch whisky, Scottish woollens, Scottish tourism. For these, it was his duty to make a clown of himself; he only hoped that not too many Scottish journalists were watching.

The third man was John Swinney, leader of the Scottish National Party. It was hardest for him. Like McLeish, this serious, clerkly man was in Washington to help Scotland's trade and promote its image. But which image? 'Fredome' wrested from a rampart of English corpses, or 'Independence within the European Union' respectably gained by votes, majorities and parliamentary resolutions? The hot blood of William Wallace, or the chilly bottles of 'Highland Spring' mineral water waiting around a negotiating table?

It had taken three generations for the SNP to become a sober, credible party, a possible party of government. John Swinney was the trustee of that hard-won sobriety. On the SNP benches in the Scottish Parliament, the only splash of tartan is the plaid around Winnie Ewing's shoulders. But he knew what his duty was that day, although everyone could see his embarrassment. 'Tartan!' said John Swinney, loudly and without clearing his throat. And then 'Freedom!'

This comedy on the Capitol steps already had its own history. It was in 1997 that Senator Trent Lott of Mississippi, a man who likes to wear a Buchanan tartan kilt and who holds the William Wallace Award of the American Scottish Foundation, introduced Senate Resolution 155. This bill, which became law in March 1998, declared that 6 April – the date of the 1320 Declaration of Arbroath – would be National Tartan Day in the United States for all time coming, 'to recognize the outstanding achievements and contributions made by Scottish Americans to the United States'.

Senator Lott is a right-wing Republican from the south. His campaign for Resolution 155 had been aimed at the moderate end of that same constituency which invented the 'Confederate Tartan' – the movement for 'Scottish Heritage Southern Style'. But in order to mediate this stroke of ethnic vote-hustling to the United States as a whole, he invented for the Senate's benefit a remarkable interpretation of history. The 1776 American Declaration of Independence, according to

Resolution 155, was 'modelled on that inspirational document' the Declaration of Arbroath.

In his speech introducing the motion, Senator Lott went into more detail. 'On a hot steamy day, a group of men stood in a building in the British colony of Pennsylvania . . . debating and then signing their own declaration of independence. They used the Arbroath Declaration as the template for their own thoughts, their own words.' In another speech following the Resolution's adoption, Senator Lott explained that 'National Tartan Day is about liberty. It is about the demand of citizens for their freedom from an oppressive government . . . by honouring April 6, Americans will annually celebrate the true beginning of the quest for liberty and freedom . . . Arbroath and the declaration for liberty.' The historian Euan Hague, who wrote a mordant account of the whole affair in the Winter 2002 issue of *Scottish Affairs*, noted that Lott used the word 'liberty' eleven times in the first speech and seven times in the second.

> The Scottish clansmen who met on that cold day and declared their independence were our clansmen, no matter what nation we hail from. They were our brothers.

All this is pure fiction. If nothing else, it is a fine example of the forgery which goes into the 'forging of nations'. It is not just that the signatories at Arbroath were neither citizens nor 'clansmen'. It is not just that their document could not be a declaration of independence because the Kingdom of Scotland in 1320 had never been anything other than independent. It is because, as Euan Hague put it, 'the Declaration of Arbroath is conspicuous only by its total absence from historical assessments of the concepts enshrined in the Declaration of Independence'.

In other words, there is not a scrap of evidence that any of the Americans gathered on that 'steamy' Pennsylvania day gave a moment's thought to the Declaration of Arbroath. Few of them would even have heard of it. Neither their discussions nor the language they chose for the Declaration show any allusion, conscious or unconscious, to fourteenth-century Scotland.

Thomas Jefferson himself, claimed by Senator Lott as a Scotsman although his Caledonian ancestry was remote, had an ambiguous view of Scotland. His mind had been largely trained by Scottish ideas and teachers, and he venerated Edinburgh University. But he knew that 'loyal' Scottish opinion was hostile to American independence, and he was alarmed that American Scots were being mobilized to suppress the revolution. James Witherspoon, one of the two Scottish-born signatories of the Declaration, persuaded him to drop a phrase attacking 'Scotch and other mercenaries'.

Neither Witherspoon nor his compatriot John Wilson is known to have spoken or written a word about Arbroath in their lives. This is not to say that the 1776 Declaration owes nothing to Scottish political ideas. Witherspoon, a beetle-browed, vehement Presbyterian minister who had preached in Paisley before emigrating to become the President of Princeton, had taught his pupils the Scottish Enlightenment principles of reason, economic liberty and free enquiry as the natural human condition. That irresistible phrase about 'the pursuit of happiness' is usually attributed to the ideas of the Glasgow philosopher Francis Hutcheson and his influence on Jefferson, but it could well have been contributed by Witherspoon. It was certainly a notion familiar to eighteenth-century Scottish thinkers. But none of those thinkers had anchored his ideas in Scotland's medieval past, a period which polished intellectuals of the day dismissed as half-barbaric. The Declaration of Independence certainly did owe an unquantifiable something to Scotland – but to Hanoverian Edinburgh and Glasgow, rather than to Arbroath in the time of Robert the Bruce.

And yet the matter of 'Fredome' remains. Is it possible that Senator Lott and his allies are right for all the wrong reasons –

that a certain idea of liberty did come early to Scotland, and that this idea recurred throughout the centuries which separate the time of Bruce and Wallace from the restoration of Scottish autonomy in 1999? Many Scots like to believe this. The fashion in history has been dismissive about such national continuities. All the same, it would not be the first time that an 'invented tradition' turned out to be perched on subterranean foundations of truth.

The Declaration of Arbroath is not so much a proclamation as a letter, addressed to the Pope. The Vatican text is lost, and only the copy kept by the Scots survives. A single sheet of badly worn parchment, it is written in Latin and dangles the seals of eight earls and thirty-one barons. It is now thought that few if any of them were actually present on 6 April 1320, and that the document was drafted by Bernard of Linton, Abbot of Arbroath, who was Bruce's chancellor and adviser.

The letter's purpose is diplomatic propaganda. It is intended to convince the Pope of Scotland's legitimate and ancient existence as a kingdom, and to persuade him to drop his support for Edward II of England. To back its case, the letter retails a myth of Scottish royal continuity, through an unbroken lineage of 113 kings beginning with the arrival of the Scots as voyagers from 'Greater Scythia' and culminating with Robert I ('and no man foreign has been among them'). One passage emphasizes the nation's pious devotion to the Apostle Andrew; another gives a list of English atrocities committed by Edward I and Edward II during their recent attempts to conquer Scotland.

The magnificent part, which is also the most angrily disputed part, is quite short.

By the Providence of God, the right of succession, those laws and customs which we are resolved to defend even with our lives, and by our own just consent, he [Robert] is our King . . . Yet Robert himself, should he turn aside from the

task that he has begun and yield Scotland or us to the
English King and people, we should cast out as the enemy of
us all, as subverter of our rights and of his own, and should
choose another king to defend our freedom: for so long as a
hundred of us are left alive, we will yield in no least way to
English dominion. We fight not for glory nor for wealth nor
honours; but only and alone we fight for freedom [*libertas*]
which no good man surrenders but with his life.

Until recently, these words were taken at their face value – or,
more accurately, at their twentieth-century face value. Here was
a miraculously early statement of popular sovereignty, contractual
government and the national right of self-determination.
The oppressed subjects of dictators, or the leaders of liberation
movements in colonial territories, could claim a fourteenth-
century ancestry for their feelings. But then the revisionist
historians moved in.

Their motives were mixed. Some were exasperated by the
crudity of Scottish nationalist interpretations, which were
essentialist: Scots were presented as democrats by nature, and
Scotland's history was simplified into an endless struggle to
defend or regain independence. Others saw that the language
of that passage was a threat to the new academic school of
nationalist theory. For example, Ernest Gellner had proposed
that nationalism was a manifestation of modernity and industrialization; this meant that the creature could scarcely have
evolved before about 1750. Benedict Anderson's classic
Imagined Communities, published in 1983, pushed the limit back;
he related the origins of nationalism to the 'print-capitalist revolution' which took off in the sixteenth century. But both these
scholars, and most of their rivals too, agreed that modernization
was a necessary condition for the emergence of recognizable
nationalist ideas. And they all deplored the 'primordialists', the
critics of 'modernization theory' who suggested that nations
and the emotions connected with them might have existed

many centuries before books were printed in Mainz or fly-shuttles ran in the mills of Lancashire.

Three assumptions about the Declaration irritated the 'modernization' scholars. First of all (they complained), the notion that a fourteenth-century king was on contract – that he could be 'cast out' by his subjects if he failed to fulfil his duty to oppose the English – was unreal. Abbot Linton must have been trying to play up King Robert's power and authority by exaggerating his solidarity with his followers. Secondly, it was hopelessly anachronistic to take the wording about "the people" literally. The list of noble petitioners ends: '. . . and the other Barons and the freeholders and all the Commons of the Kingdom of Scotland [*tota Communitas Regni Scocie*]'. The historians suggested that this expression had nothing to do with the 'folk' of Scotland, the mainly peasant mass which was not considered to be part of the political community at all in late medieval Europe. Instead, it was a familiar 'baron-speak' used by feudal grandees who considered themselves 'virtual representatives'.

Lastly, the words about freedom. The text of the Declaration assumes a direct link between personal liberty and national independence, the normal association most people make today. If my country is invaded and occupied, or if I am the native of a colony, then I can no longer live the life of a free man or woman.

But then comes the double-take. The revisionist historian exclaims: I cannot be reading this! Surely such a link – the connecting-rod of modern nationalism's dynamic – was not even thought of until centuries later. It is almost as if the barons had left their e-mail addresses on the back of the parchment, and I admit that when I first read those sentences, it crossed my mind that the Declaration of Arbroath might be a nineteenth-century romantic forgery. Europe, especially east-central Europe and Russia, produced plenty of patriotic fakes (epic poetry, treaties, testaments) in that period.

The parchment, however, is 'real'. Its pedigree back to 1320 is verifiable. In short, it is the deconstructors, not the Declaration, who have a credibility problem. The 'primordialists' may overstate their case about the antiquity of nationalism, but it is difficult to deny that recognizable ideas about a relationship between national and individual liberty were around in medieval Scotland. Was this a freakishly 'precocious' understanding of freedom? The answer is that it was only precocious if medieval England or France are taken as the norm. Too many British historians still unconsciously see Scotland in this period through an English lens.

But Scotland, poor and small as it was, managed to follow its own distinct development with striking success. It was not conquered by the Normans, as England, Wales and Ireland were after 1066, because the Scottish kings cleverly domesticated the Norman threat; they invited Anglo-Norman nobles to settle on Scottish lands on Scottish terms, and took full advantage of their military skills. This eventually produced a new 'Scottish-Norman' nobility, alongside the old Gaelic and Scots elites, which saw no automatic reason to take the English side in disputes between the two kingdoms. But many held lands on both sides of the border, owing feudal allegiance to both kings, which made them easy to manipulate; the Scottish-Norman Bruces, and Robert himself in his early years, were among the families which frequently changed sides under English pressure. Only after the Scottish victory in 1314 at Bannockburn, as the English claim to sovereignty over the northern kingdom slackened, did their loyalty to the Scottish crown become more reliable.

The English saw Scotland as a country where the kings were weak and local warlords followed their own interests. This was misleading. Unlike England and France, medieval Scotland avoided expensive foreign wars and taxed the nobility only lightly; this allowed the kingdom to be governed by a loose but quite stable consensus between the Crown and the territorial magnates. It was a contrast to Norman and Plantagenet

England, where the royal need for money led to forced centralization and constant armed power struggles.

When the Wars of Independence began in 1296 (they were
to last intermittently for almost sixty years), these factors gave
the Kingdom of Scotland the resilience to hold together against
enormous odds, and to survive. There was a battle factor, too.
In the time of Robert the Bruce, infantry was making a
European comeback against the power of armoured knightly
cavalry. Bruce understood this change before his opponents,
Edward I and Edward II of England, and it was his combination of skill in exploiting ground and his use of the 'schiltron' –
the tight mass of pikemen which could break a cavalry assault –
which gave him his devastating victory at Bannockburn. The
battle was not decisive, in the medium term, and the English
later won some crushing victories over the Scots. But – as
Marshal Piłsudski used to say five hundred years later as he
defended Poland's independence – 'to be beaten and not to
give way is victory'. England was unable to conquer Scotland,
and the outcome of the Wars left an independent Scotland battered but triumphant.

The long struggle had begun with Edward I's invasion in
1296 when he seized the Stone of Destiny, followed the next
year by William Wallace's uprising. It was a moment when
Scotland had no formal leadership; the king, John Balliol, was a
prisoner in the Tower of London and Edward was setting up a
military administration to transform Scotland into an English
colony.

Wallace himself may have had Norman ancestry. But he was
only a minor noble from Renfrewshire, a huge and pugnacious
young man closer to the Scottish peasantry than to the great
barons with their complex intrigues and mixed motives. Little
is known about him for certain. He killed an Englishman in a
street quarrel at Dundee and became an aggressive outlaw. An
attempt to arrest him at Lanark miscarried, but his wife was
murdered in reprisal. Wallace attacked and slaughtered the

town's English garrison and its Sheriff. From a popular brigand harrying the foreigner, Wallace now became a famous guerrilla commander, gathering an armed following strong enough to attack English strongholds throughout the Lowlands. His triumph came in 1297, when he broke a much larger English army at the battle of Stirling Bridge. But his rule as 'Guardian' of a liberated Scotland was brief. Less than a year later, Edward I of England defeated him at the battle of Falkirk.

Wallace resigned his leadership and went abroad to seek support for Scotland's independence and the restoration of John Balliol as king, but by the time he returned in about 1302, the struggle was over and Edward was once more in control of Scotland. Although Wallace seems to have resumed guerrilla war, he was now a fugitive whom few dared to support. In 1305, he was betrayed to the English, brought to London and put to death in public with hideous cruelty.

But the Scottish people could not forget him. He became one of Scotland's 'precious few heroes', and his cult was genuine, widespread and long-lasting. Blind Harry's fifteenth-century epic 'Wallace', translated out of medieval Scots into stilted English by Hamilton of Gilbertfield, was – next to the Bible – the book most frequently found in Victorian households.

Wallace's image blurred and spread into myth. Every parish seems to have a stone where he stood or a cave in which he hid. His gigantic sword, kept in the Wallace Monument at Stirling, is mythic too: impossible to date, it seems to be 'my grandfather's sword' whose blade and hilt have often been replaced through the centuries. But he comes sharply into focus in the way that he defined his office during those few months of power. Even before Wallace's time, the Scots had evolved their own 'ideology of state', a very early ('precocious') concept of a national polity which had an abstract existence of its own, whether or not a king was ruling. When he had driven the English armies back, Wallace governed the land in the absence of a king as a 'Guardian', first as a member of a self-constituted junta acting in the name of the ambiguous *Communitas Regni* and later on his own.

A few years later, when the English besiegers challenged the garrison of Stirling to admit that they were defending the castle without royal authority, the defenders replied that they 'held it of the Lion'. They meant the red Lion Rampant, the heraldic beast of Scotland. But here, as with the Guardianship, is the idea of an 'essential' national community which persists in the dimension of time and which does not necessarily require a king or a set of feudal obligations to give it authority. 'Primordial' theorists usually explain early nations as communities united around ethnic identity. But the paradox of medieval Scotland is that the kingdom was able to behave in a 'nationalist' way precisely because it was an ethnic hybrid.

The term 'Scotland' was used long before anyone spoke of a single 'Scottish people'. For its diverse, often widely separated peoples, Scotland in that period was a loose alliance, a shelter-kingdom against outside predators. Such a kingdom could only be run by consent between its parts, and that consent – or informal contract – required an imaginative loyalty to something less personal and more symbolic than a dynasty.

In Wallace's time, the country was inhabited by Gaelic and originally Anglian societies, both lineage-based but speaking quite different languages. There were elements of Norse culture in the far north and the isles, while Norman feudalism – the unifying hierarchical structure in England – was weak and superficial, sometimes no more than the renaming of older Celtic land-tenure arrangements. Authority was simple and usually kin-based; obedience to higher orders from a 'centre' was far from automatic. The men commanded by Wallace at Stirling Bridge or by Bruce at Bannockburn were often unpaid volunteers rather than unwilling feudal levies or mercenaries. The common people fought from a sense of necessity; the ferocity and destructiveness of the English wars often faced them and their families with the desperate alternatives of resistance or death.

As subsistence peasants or village craftsmen, they were not socially 'free' in any modern sense. Many were unfree, living in 'foule thyrldome' or feudal servitude. But the burned and plundered landscapes of Lowland and central Scotland enforced a simple association of ideas. Only if their country was independent and free of invaders could its people live free of the fear of massacre, rape and looting. The choices in their normal lives were small but many: to renew the thatch this year or next, to decide how much grain to eat in winter and how much to save for seed, to let children play in a meadow out of sight of the cottage or to keep them in for fear of armed marauders. If Scotland lost its power to protect its people, even those freedoms would be lost too.

Why spell out the obvious? Small countries with dangerous neighbours have always concluded that personal freedom and national independence hang together. If Sparta had managed to beat off the Macedonians, its women would not have been driven off into slavery. That is what the Declaration of Arbroath is saying. Unfortunately, this simple point undermines the blinkered argument that national and personal freedoms were only fused in recent times by the propaganda of modern nation-states. Perhaps the problem is that theories about small countries are often composed in large, safe countries with bad consciences about their imperial past. They prefer not to imagine what it feels like to see foreign troops riding down the street.

There is something wrong with academic studies of nationalism. They define the subject too tightly and force it into Procrustean categories. Ernest Gellner's brilliant understanding of how 'modernity' transformed nationalism into a state doctrine of popular sovereignty is valid, but the 'primordialists' are not entirely wrong either. The fact is that the emergence of a concept of the nation was an untidy development, ill-suited to cramming into exclusive 'stages'. Arbroath shows that quite 'un-modern' communities could invent an abstract terminology of nationhood when they needed to do so, and that the identification of personal and national independence could happen in very different times and places.

Some of the wording of the 1320 Declaration relates to medieval concepts, for which there are no easy equivalents. But when the Scots barons (or Bernard de Linton) wrote about the 'freedom which no good man surrenders but with his life', they were not talking about their own feudal privileges. They were expressing something broader: the *liberté* or *wolność* for which the French or Polish resistance fought the Nazi occupation. Robert Burns, in 'Robert Bruce's March to Bannockburn', pulled out all the romantic organ-stops to dramatize this fusion of free man and free nation. But he was probably right about fourteenth-century Scotland:

> . . . *See approach proud Edward's power,*
> *Chains and Slaverie. –*
> *Wha will be a traitor-knave?*
> *Wha can fill a coward's grave?*
> *Wha sae base as be a Slave?*
> *– Let him turn and flie . . .*

16

'HERE LYETH ROBERT GRIERSON WHO WAS SHOT TO DEATH BY
COMMAND OF COLANEL JAMES DOUGLASE AT INGLES TOUN IN
THE PAROCH OF GLENCAIRN ANNO 1685.

This Monument to Passengers shall cry
That goodly Grierson under it doth ly
Betrayd by knavish Watson to his foes
Which made this Martyrs days by Murther close.
If ye would knou the Nature of his Crime
Then read the story of that Killing Time
When Babels brats with Hellish plots conceald
Designed to make our South their Hunting Field.
Here's one of five at once were laid in Dust
To gratify Rome's execrable Lust.
If Carabines with molten Bullets could
Have reached their souls these mighty Nimrods woud
Them have cut off; for there could no Request
Three minutes get to pray for Futur Rest.

Inscription on a tombstone at Balmaclellan in Galloway,
quoted in Thorbjörn Campbell, *Standing Witnesses*

We were indeed amazed to see a poor commonalty so capable to
argue upon points of government, and on the bounds to be set
to the power of princes in matters of religion: upon all these
topicks they had texts of scripture at hand; and were ready with
their answer to any thing that was said to them. This measure of
knowledge was spread even among the meanest of them, their
cottagers, and their servants. They were, indeed, vain of their
knowledge, much conceited of themselves, and were full of
a most entangled scrupulosity; so that they found, or made,
difficulties in every thing that could be laid before them.

Gilbert Burnet, on the failure of his 1669 mission to calm religious
zealotry in south-western Scotland

I don't remember the name of the woman who opened for me
the book of the Covenanters. I was nine years old, and it was
the summer of 1942. My family, in one of our many wartime
moves, was spending a few weeks as paying guests in a large
house near Glencorse. The house stood at the foot of the
Pentland hills, and its neglected grounds had become a purple
jungle of rose-bay willowherb as tall as I was.

The woman seems to me now to have worked in the house.
I feel her behind me, standing above me, as I recall sitting on
the steps at the back door and looking through the illustrations
in the book she had lent to me. I remember that sometimes she
spoke a little, guiding me among the martyrs.

The death which upset me most was the fate of young
Margaret Wilson, tied to a stake in Wigtown Bay on 11 May
1685, and left to drown as the incoming tide rose over her.
When the water was at her face, they pulled her up and gave
her a last chance to sign the Abjuration Oath. She refused, and
they pushed her head down again.

Children have a way of grasping essentials, a talent for
absorbing the mnemonic qualities of a myth without knowing
anything of 'what actually happened'. It was many years before
the tangled religious and civil conflicts of seventeenth-century
Scotland made any sense to me. But the house stood less than
a mile from Rullion Green, the battlefield in the lap of the
Pentlands where in 1666 a tiny army of 'Saints' was slaughtered
before they could reach Edinburgh. I often ran over the turf
among the Covenanters' memorials which stood on the moor.
Nearby was a haunted house at a place called 'Martyr's Cross',
where a woman was reported to tread loudly across the gravel at
night, weeping for the dead men. When I was shown the book,
I was ready for it.

There were several strands in the Covenanting myth which
a child could grasp. One was the sense of what is now called
'cultural landscape': human beings acting in nature. Men,
women and children had done their singing, journeying or

dying in these hills, in this same obstinate wind with its scents of heather and bog-myrtle and its lapwing cries. The Covenanters were usually small farmers and their families, most of them living in Galloway and Ayrshire in south-western Scotland, and the belt of Lowland hills between the Irish Sea and the outskirts of Edinburgh was their home, their refuge and the route of their insurrections.

Another strand plain to a child's imagination was loneliness or scatteredness. There is no 'centralization of memory' in the case of the Covenanters. Apart from a monument in Greyfriars Churchyard at Edinburgh and a modern cross in Nithsdale, there has been no attempt to erect a single 'national' shrine which would incorporate the movement into Scotland's official memory. Instead, the graves of the martyrs are dispersed. Some are in remote country churchyards. But others – this is the iconic image of the Covenanters – are stones of solitude: semi-legible graves in a fold of the hills or by the ruins of an upland farmhouse, places where men faced their executioners. Many are nearly impossible to find, or to reach without heavy-duty walking gear. In his wonderful book *Standing Witnesses*, the retired teacher Thorbjörn Campbell records how he visited these stones over many years of pilgrimage, copied their inscriptions and listed their map references.

This quality of scatteredness has many elements. At one level, the Covenanting memory was not suitable to be centralized and appropriated, to be the subject of a statue in an Edinburgh square or an obelisk outside Glasgow's City Chambers. It could never fit into the 'modernizing narrative' of the new Scotland. The problem was not just that the insurgent Covenanters never numbered more than a few thousands. It was the movement itself, a league of fundamentalist Calvinists whose programme for a godly Scotland was theocratic and ferociously intolerant. Even the term 'Covenanters' is misleading. They were the tiny minority who refused to admit that Scotland's Covenants had become a dead letter, in new times when most Scottish Protestants recognized – reluctantly enough – that they belonged to history.

There were two great Covenants in seventeenth-century Scotland. The first, in 1638, was a genuine national declaration; signed in ink or sometimes blood on a tomb-slab in Greyfriars Churchyard at Edinburgh, it committed independent Scotland to defend the Presbyterian faith against all intrusions of Episcopacy and Popery. The second, the Solemn League and Covenant of 1643, was essentially a treaty between Scotland and the English Parliament against royal power. Never honoured, it made Scottish support for the English rebels against King Charles I conditional on the entrenchment of the Presbyterian religion in England and Ireland as well as Scotland.

For twelve years after 1638, Scotland was ruled by supporters of the Covenant. But relations with the English Parliamentarians turned sour. The Scots, suspicious of Cromwell's ambitions and alarmed by the execution of Charles I in 1649, laid plans to restore his successor, Charles II. In 1650, Oliver Cromwell invaded Scotland, smashed the Covenanting regime and enforced a temporary Union with England under the Commonwealth. In 1660, the monarchy was restored and the Stuart kings, Charles II and his son James VII and II, set out to impose Episcopal church government on Scotland, purging the land of ministers faithful to the old Presbyterian vision of a church independent of royal authority whose only head was Jesus Christ.

Why popular resistance to the new regime had its core in south-western Scotland has never been fully explained. But Ayrshire, Dumfriesshire and Galloway had been ultra-Calvinist territory well before the Restoration. In 1648, the 'Whiggamore Raid' had ridden out of the West and captured Edinburgh, installing a populist clerical dictatorship (the 'Rule of Saints'). The policies of the 'Saints' were a strange combination of social revolution and fanatical repression; they purged church and state of all 'malignants' and moderates, made local parishes responsible for the relief of the poor and sick, established schools in every parish, made church attendance compulsory and encouraged a return to witch-hunting. But their rule was brief, ended by Cromwell's conquest only two years later.

In 1666, as the religious purges of Charles II began to bite, the Saints tried to repeat their success, and a small army of ill-armed farmers and ministers set off once again from Ayrshire across the hills towards Edinburgh. But within sight of the city, at Rullion Green, they were defeated and massacred by troops commanded by Major-General Tam Dalyell of the Binns. (Dalyell, a bearded veteran who had served in the armies of the Russian Tsar, was unfairly demonized for his atrocities as 'Bluidy Dalyell'. He was a hard man in battle, but he despised cold-blooded cruelty and protested, vainly, against the mass hanging of Rullion Green prisoners by the Edinburgh authorities.)

Ten years of intermittent persecution followed. The Covenanters (the 'Society People' as they called themselves) worshipped at illegal conventicles, services held in isolated farm buildings or outdoors in the high hills. Mounted sentries watched for the approach of government troops (another image which has become a Scottish icon), while outlawed preachers spoke 'the word of God and the Covenanted Work of Reformation' against Popish idolatry and 'bloodie Prelacy'.

Their doctrines, which survive in many 'free churches' today, were a logical distillation of Calvinism. They believed that the 'natural' human being was utterly corrupt, but that God, in an act of predestination before the Fall of Man, had chosen a minority to be saved and redeemed through the entry of divine grace to transform their 'carnal' natures. This body of the Elect would ascend to heaven; the rest – the 'reprobates' – must burn in hell, no matter how virtuous their outer lives and deeds appeared to be. For the Covenanters in seventeenth-century Scotland, these beliefs implied that only the

Elect, in their local 'kirk sessions', were entitled to choose their ministers or to guide the daily lives of the people. Bishops were 'hellish prelates' and emissaries of Satan. Earthly rulers were almost certainly reprobate, and could only govern justly when they obeyed the Elect's advice. Above all, no prince, monarch or Privy Council was entitled to interfere in the life and rights of God's church. As a tombstone at Dumfries reads, 'Here Lyes William Welsh, Pentland Martyr for his Adhering to the Word of God and Appearing for Christs Kingly Government in His House'. For a state confronted with beliefs like this, there could ultimately be no compromise.

Fighting broke out once more in 1679, after Presbyterian fanatics pulled Archbishop Sharp of St Andrews out of his coach at Magus Muir and slashed him to death. A month later, in June 1679, a force of dragoons sent out to arrest Covenanters and led by John Graham of Claverhouse ran across an armed conventicle at Drumclog, near Kilmarnock. The preacher, warned by the sentries, had time to send away the women and children and to finish his sermon with the words: 'Ye have got the theory: now for the practice!'

Claverhouse was badly beaten in the fight which followed, losing thirty-six men. But this was the last Covenanting victory. A few weeks later, a large rebel army was overwhelmed by government troops at Bothwell Brig near Glasgow and Claverhouse chased the survivors back to Ayrshire.

From now on, the struggle became a rural guerrilla war. Claverhouse's troops occupied the countryside, while dragoon patrols raided houses for weapons and fugitives. The government, without great success, tried to isolate waverers from the hard core of resistance by issuing 'indulgences' to cooperative Presbyterian ministers. The resistance itself was led by a handful of legendary preachers and fighting men who moved from one safe house to another, issuing proclamations which amounted to declarations of war against the Stuart Kings and maintaining an effective underground communications network which reached as far as the Presbyterian exile communities in the Netherlands.

Richard Cameron came back from Holland to lead the movement in 1679, only to be killed in battle at Airds Moss the following year. Donald Cargill proclaimed the King excommunicated, but was caught and hanged in 1681. Alexander Peden, whose shamanic disguise-mask can still be seen in the Museum of Scotland, was famous for his supernatural powers, above all for his gift of prophesying the future; he died, probably of exposure, in a dug-out hiding pit in 1686. James Renwick, aged only twenty, went to Holland for doctrinal training in 1682 and returned secretly the next year to become the most famous of all these armed prophets. His father claimed that James had prayed in the cradle as a baby, but his conversion seems to go back to the day when, as an Edinburgh student, he watched the execution of Donald Cargill in the Grassmarket. Renwick was young and vigorous, and survived for over four years as a hunted man and outlaw, travelling disguised all over Lowland Scotland and baptizing some six hundred children. He was eventually arrested in Edinburgh, and executed in 1688 – a few months before the 'Glorious Revolution' overthrew the Stuart dynasty and ended the persecutions for ever.

The 'Killing Time' reached its peak in 1685, after an escalation of daring raids and ambushes against Claverhouse and the government troops. Alongside the preachers, a cadre of hardened guerrilla leaders was beginning to emerge; Black James McMichael, James 'Long Gun' Harkness and his brother Thomas 'White Hose' Harkness all became heroes among the Society People. In retaliation, the authorities brought in the compulsory Abjuration Oath. Carried from farm to farm by the dragoons, the oath was a solemn disowning of those who proclaimed rebellion against Royal authority. The penalty for refusing it was immediate execution, usually by shooting.

Many did refuse and were shot in front of their families, like John Brown of Priesthill. Claverhouse led that patrol in person.

Finding his men reluctant to kill a father in the presence of his wife and children, he took the carbine himself. 'I caused shoot him dead, which he suffered very inconcernedly.' Turning to Brown's wife, Isabel, he asked, 'What thinkest thou of thy husband now, woman?' She replied, 'As much now as ever.'

The 'Killing Time' took some 90 lives in the course of that year. In all the years of insurrection and persecution, the Covenanting dead probably amounted to something like a thousand, two hundred of them drowned when a ship carrying prisoners to Barbados sank off Orkney in 1679. By modern standards of brutality, it was a small affair. But it took root in Scottish memory. Later generations, who understood little or nothing about Calvinist fundamentalism and would have been repelled by it if they had understood, were touched by these men and women who preferred to die rather than to deny their faith.

The graves of the martyrs were lonely and scattered because the martyrs themselves had embraced their own loneliness. They were the faithful few, the 'savoury remnant' of the Lord's people in an evil world opening its jaws to devour them. A nation taught by Psalm 124 to see itself as a bird escaped from the fowler's snare ('when cruel men against us furiously Rose up in wrath to make of us their prey') could not deny the Covenanters a place in its heart.

In following centuries, commemoration dressed the Covenanting memory in many guises. Much piety was devoted to the scattered stones themselves, to identifying them and re-cutting their worn inscriptions, sometimes to replacing them with more modern and ornate memorials or erecting a new gravestone on the site of a previously unmarked martyrdom. Robert Paterson (1715–1801) was the pioneer of this kind of commemoration, and the original for Walter Scott's 'Old Mortality'. A farm labourer from the Borders, he abandoned his wife and children to spend forty years walking across Scotland with a bag of mason's tools, restoring and re-erecting the gravestones of the Cameronians (the Covenanting followers of the outlawed preacher Robert Cameron). 'Old Mortality', himself a convert to Cameronian doctrines, made no attempt to adapt the Covenanting myth to his own times. But the French Revolution, and the surge of radical unrest at the end of the Napoleonic Wars, brought the first re-interpretations.

On 13 June 1815, a crowd of several thousand people marched to the battlefield of Drumclog from the nearby town of Strathaven. Many of them were weavers, a declining trade which was to provide the core of revolutionary conspiracies in the West of Scotland in the next few years. Wary of the ruthless sedition trials against radicals who had voiced support for the French Revolution and the doctrine of the Rights of Man, the organizers said only that they wanted to celebrate 'the victory gained by the Covenanters over the King's troops'. But the local Sheriff, William Aiten, interpreted this as a call to republican rebellion, and he was not entirely wrong. The demonstration was held a few days before the battle of Waterloo, and its real motive seems to have been to rejoice over Napoleon's escape from Elba. When a toast to the 'Allied Sovereigns' (the anti-French coalition) was proposed that night in a Strathaven pub, it was shouted down by the demonstration committee who called on the band to play the air 'We'll up and war them a''.

Twenty years later, after the victorious campaign which culminated in the 1832 Reform Act, an obelisk and a school were erected on the Drumclog battlefield honouring 'those Christian Heroes, who on Sabbath the 1st of June 1679, nobly fought in defence of Civil and Religious Liberty'. No echo of the French Revolution here. This time, the commemorators used a new political language to suggest that the Covenanters had been proto-Liberals who had sacrificed their lives for toleration and democracy – hardly a description which the Whiggamore Raiders or James Renwick would have recognized.

Much later still, in the twentieth century, the Covenanters

were appropriated as forerunners of the working-class struggle for socialism and equality. In 1926, the year of the General Strike, a group of Ayrshire miners decided to erect a monument to the little-known martyr James Smith of Wee Threepwood, allegedly shot on his own doorstep for offering food to Covenanter fugitives. The Communist Party was strong in the South Ayrshire pits at the time. Union leaders could justifiably point to the early class consciousness of the Covenanters, to their hatred of landowners and aristocrats and their search for a collective society based on equality and mutual support. On a hill overlooking the site of Smith's house, the miners raised what Thorbjörn Campbell calls 'a large marker . . . incorporating pieces of glass to reflect the sun's rays'.

Curiously, Scottish Nationalism is the only major movement which has made no bid for the Covenanting memory. If the Society People could be constructed into proto-Jacobins, proto-Liberals or proto-socialists, where was the problem in guising them as patriots fighting – in their own way – to defend Scottish independence? Just possibly, respect for historical truth explains the omission. A search through the famous hagiographies written at the time or soon afterwards – the anonymous *A Cloud of Witnesses*, Howie's *Scots Worthies*, Wodrow's *Analecta* or Kirkton's *Secret and True History of the Church of Scotland* – reveals not a single coherent statement about Scotland the political nation, or about Scottish independence.

The Covenanters simply did not think in those categories. If in their struggles they worried at all about foreign or English domination, it was from their own narrow point of view: the fate of the one true faith under any new regime. They proclaimed the old image of the Scots – or at least the Lord's elected Scots – as new children of Israel toiling through a wilderness towards their salvation. But they imagined or personified Scotland as a community defined by its moral behaviour rather than by its history. One gravestone at Fenwick, in Ayrshire, records how a Covenanter's head was cut off and used as a football by a dragoon, 'by birth a Tyger rather than a Scot'. And Robert Renwick, on the scaffold, took leave of life with those mysterious words which are about inner strength rather than outer freedom: 'Scotland must be rid of Scotland before the delivery come!'

Where do the Covenanters – the movement as it really was, without all the later reinventions – fit into Scotland's pursuit of 'fredome'? For some Scots, they have no place in it at all. There is a popular argument that Scotland would have been better off without the whole Calvinist tradition of which they were the extreme manifestation. Not only Catholics and nostalgic Jacobites but also intellectuals raised in old-fashioned Presbyterian communities have argued that this particular Reformation brought Scottish culture to the edge of extinction. The music, the plays and most of the poetry fell silent; both the Gaelic and Scots languages were irreparably damaged; a strong and joyful popular culture of festivals and fairs was terrorized into grey conformity by the fear of hell. Alexander Peden, the preacher who hid behind that sinister mask and lived in an earthen burrow, was a saint to his brethren. But in his poem 'Scotland 1941' the poet Edwin Muir saw him and his theology as destroyers of an older, harmonious world:

> *The busy cornfields and the haunted holms,*
> *The green road winding up the ferny brae.*
> *But Knox and Melville clapped their preaching palms*
> *And bundled all the harvesters away,*
> *Hoodicrow Peden in the blighted corn*
> *Hacked with his rusty beak the starving haulms.*
> *Out of that desolation we were born.*

Truths about history are hidden in those fearsome lines. The 'starving haulms' (stalks) can stand for the devastating famine years which afflicted Scotland as the 'Killing Time' ended, a disaster which gave Scotland's ruling class another reason to argue that the Union with England was inevitable if the nation were to survive at all. But if modern Scotland and the 1707 Union were 'born of that desolation', then Knox, Melville and Peden ensured that it was a nation whose identity would be preserved by its religious distinctness.

If Presbyterianism had failed, Scotland today would be little more than an item of British regional geography. The Scottish Reformation would have almost certainly decayed into a variant of state-run Anglicanism, sooner or later merging with its more powerful sister church south of the Border. After the Union, the landed gentry remained overwhelmingly Episcopalian, and in the nineteenth century they became heavily Anglicized, adopting southern accents and manners and sending their sons to English public schools. Assimilation, cultural and political, could only reinforce their position as a class.

But the Covenanters, indifferent as they were to 'patriotism', ensured that this would not happen. Their long struggle against Episcopacy and against the right of local landowners to impose their own nominees as parish ministers invented a new sense of plebeian Scottish identity. Theological in its origins, this identity counterposed a common people entitled to run its own spiritual life to a privileged elite which was instinctively disloyal to 'Scotland's Covenanted Reformation' and thus to the nation itself. Authentic 'Scottishness' acquired a democratic component, as the fight to defend the right of individual kirk sessions (parish elders) to choose their own ministers continued down the generations. A fresh crisis broke in 1843, after a renewed Tory campaign to legalize the 'intrusion' of landlord nominees to vacant parishes. In the 'Disruption' of that year, a formidable section of the established Church of Scotland broke away and marched out of the General Assembly of the Kirk to found its own 'Free Church', independent of state subsidies and wealthy patrons. Once again, Scottishness had been associated with an ideology of equality and popular rights, defying forces of hereditary privilege which sought to enforce a more submissive social order imported from England.

Calvinist cultural repression, none the less, was real enough. Almost anything brightly coloured, ornamental or joyful – plays, fairs, fashionable clothes, the 'lewdness' of sexuality – was suspect. Alexander Brodie was one of the young men who in 1640 had gutted and smashed the decorated interior of Elgin cathedral in the name of the Lord. A few years later, Satan came to him disguised as a warm summer day. Brodie wrote in his journal that 'in going about the fields, I found the heart apt to rise with carnal delight in fields, grass, wood etc. This I desired the Lord to guard me against, that such decaying, corruptible poor comforts steal not away my heart.' Guilt – formless, unassuageable, darkening all pleasures with dread of what was to follow – entered the Scottish psyche.

And yet the legend of a 'merrie Scotland' murdered by the Reformation is showing signs of wear. Scotland's social life did change between 1550 and 1650, in some important ways for the worse, but the causes of that change are about more than the opinions of John Knox. At least as important, in the decline of the arts and of vernacular literature, was the abrupt end of royal patronage in 1603, when James VI inherited the crown of England and the Court, with all its pensions and subsidies, moved south to London. Neither is it fair to accuse the Kirk of a general hatred for culture or a suspicion of intellectualism. On the contrary, the Reformation in Scotland venerated both the Book and books.

John Calvin himself had been an omnivorous scholar, a reformer who armed himself in libraries in order to storm the fortresses of Satan. Scotland's parish schools created a nation more literate than most European societies of the time, and they spread that literacy much further down the social pyramid. The Covenanting story demonstrates the outcome: small farmers in the later seventeenth century who were accustomed to argue closely and logically on the basis of a written text.

Bishop Burnet's 'poor commonalty so capable to argue upon points of government' had found that reading and writing were incomparable defensive weapons, even more effective than pikes and pistols against powerful men out to rob them of their rights. Their 'most entangled scrupulosity' was precisely an entanglement of words designed to halt, trip and bring down an advancing persecutor. The skilled use of words and texts became the new instrument of 'fredome', at a time when a peasantry stood no chance in battle against the disciplined fire-power of Royal armies.

This was never forgotten. Twenty years after the Killing Time came the 1707 Treaty of Union with England. The Scottish Parliament was abolished; political authority was removed to London. The sectaries and their 'true work of Reformation' were pushed thankfully to the margins by Scottish Protestants, exhausted by half a century of religious violence and terror. But the 'scrupulosity', the reaching for the written word as if for a gun in a holster, endured.

In the eighteenth century, this militant literacy spread far beyond the pockets of post-Cameronians and 'savoury remnants' who continued to uphold Covenanting purity. By the end of that century, the habit of 'autodidact' learning – theological, scientific, philosophical – had become part of Scotland. Informal scholarship was sometimes self-taught, and sometimes supported by academics such as John Anderson (1726–96), whose applied-science courses for working men were to crystallize into the Andersonian Institute (now the University of Strathclyde). In the nineteenth century, this hunger for self-improvement was given its richest diet by the Chambers' publishing empire in Edinburgh, ceaselessly pumping out cheap and excellent popular science books, encyclopaedias, journals and miscellanies of instructive general knowledge. Later still, the Labour movement in Scotland was carried forward by men and women who had left school at thirteen but who, by kitchen-table lamplight or at Socialist Sunday Schools, had become combative discussants of the works of Marx and Engels, Proudhon and Kropotkin.

English Victorian visitors sniggered at 'Scotch learning'. In England the lower orders were suitably ignorant and deferential, but up here in Scotshire, a mere road-mender or grimy furnace-stoker might interrupt a gentleman and challenge him to back his views with written authority. The southern visitor saw only pedantry and a comical solemnity. But learning won in this way is too valuable to be worn lightly. It is certainly too precious to be casually diluted in order to keep the peace and avoid a row. After Bothwell Brig, the victors asked a dying Covenanter on the ground how he felt: 'Fully assured,' he managed to answer, 'fully assured.'

In talking about 'freedom' in the century after the Union, two unlike species are being given one name. There was this defensive, disputatious, word-slinging freedom ('they . . . made difficulties in everything that could be laid before them'), descending through the Covenanters from the dogmatic rhetoric of the Scottish Reformation. But there was also the serene intellectual freedom of the Enlightenment, which could only flourish when that rhetoric lost its grip on Scottish society.

A long hangover followed the convulsions of the seventeenth century. The 'Moderate' faction – more urban, less distrustful of worldly ambitions and pleasures – took control of the Kirk; Calvinist fundamentalism retreated to islands and backwoods, where its followers continued to split and secede on fine points of doctrine in relative obscurity. The new climate allowed a fresh generation of Scottish intellectuals (most of them sons of minor landowners) to speculate in peace. Building on research in mathematics, law and medicine begun in the previous century, the 'Literati' explored the nature of human society, the basis of cognition, the origins of the earth and the workings of the economic process. As Professor David Daiches has written, 'the seed-bed of much of the later thought of the western world is to be found in this little northern country'.

With a few 'sceptic' exceptions, David Hume above all, the thinkers of the Scottish Enlightenment were not atheists or agnostics. Even the Moderate notion of the Last Judgement continued to frighten these independent minds. Fear and loathing of 'Popery' persisted. And yet in spite of two Jacobite rebellions supported by Spain or France, in 1715 and 1745, the sense of Catholicism as the ideology of imminent foreign invasion diminished. The Europe familiar to David Hume and his contemporaries included Paris and Rome, not only the safely Protestant cities of the Netherlands or Scandinavia.

But of these two approaches to freedom, the popular version – the aggressive use of argument to defend rights and enhance group solidarity – has turned out to be the stronger and the more enduring. The Enlightenment, in contrast, is no more than a beautiful memory. In spite of all the energy put into commemorating the Scottish Enlightenment, evidence of its influence on living Scotland is pretty well invisible. The Enlightenment is statues, street names, public buildings. Almost its only institutional survival is a certain spirit in Scottish universities: the remnants of a resistance to over-specialization which goes back to the old *philosophe* belief in the wholeness of knowledge. But the bookshelf of a Scottish graduate in the early twenty-first century is more likely to hold Bourdieu, Lacan, Robert Putnam or Amitai Etzioni, plus a paperback about 'Celtic Civilization' and a video of *Braveheart*, than Adam Ferguson, Francis Hutcheson or Patrick Geddes.

'Scrupulosity', logic used as an ambush and words shooting to kill, prevailed in Scottish political life. Freedom understood as tolerance, the duty to seek compromise between hostile camps, was not highly rated in twentieth-century public discourse. 'We would not soil our hands with the likes of them' was more the style. In politics, party boundaries were defended with frantic loyalty. As late as the 1990s, politicians who made speeches about Scotland's 'communitarian tradition' were refusing to share platforms with politicians of another tendency who used the same cliché.

By then it seemed inevitable that a Scottish Parliament would be set up. The Constitutional Convention had drawn up the plans; the people were impatient. It was just a matter of waiting for the prevailing wind to change, for the long Conservative regime in London to fall. But how would the Parliament function? Could it function at all as a gain in democracy, if 'fredome' meant no more to Scotland's politicians than 'no surrender'?

17

What is it we want really?
For what end and how?
If it is something feasible, obtainable,
Let us dream it now,
And pray for a possible land
Not of sleep-walkers, not of angry puppets,
But where both heart and brain can understand
The movements of our fellows;
Where life is a choice of instruments and none
Is debarred his natural music . . .

Louis MacNeice, 'Autumn Journal'

I am sitting in the public gallery to watch the Scottish Parliament at work below. An old friend sits down beside me. After a moment, we lean over and silently shake hands – not in greeting, but in mutual congratulation.

Below us on the floor, some dull debate about injury compensation is going on. We did it! This is the child we helped to birth, but over which we have no claim or control whatever. It is sometimes just what we intended, and sometimes far worse, and occasionally far better.

The Scots who designed the Parliament and its arrangements and procedures planned it as unlike Westminster as they dared. The members, the MSPs, sit in a hemicycle and not in opposing ranks. They address each other by name, often by Christian name; they vote with electronic buttons rather than trooping through lobbies as MPs in the House of Commons do.

They work normal hours, to allow MSPs to be with their families in the evenings, and 37 per cent of the MSPs are women, the highest proportion in any European parliament with the exception of Sweden and Denmark. And they cooperate across party lines, as they are meant to. On my first day in the gallery, I watched with happy disbelief as Labour MSPs applauded a good point made by an SNP speaker.

They do most of their work in powerful subject committees, chaired by members of all parties, which prepare legislation and hear witnesses. They are elected by a form of proportional representation, so that no party has a monopoly of power, and the result is something distinctly 'un-British': Scotland is governed by a Labour–Liberal Democrat coalition. The terms of trade are reversed. A decision not to 'soil your hands' with other parties has become a decision never to hold office.

The devolution settlement of 1998 left Westminster with control over foreign and defence policy, the constitution, immigration, trade and macro-economics, and broadcasting. The rest of government became Scotland's responsibility, paid for out of a block grant from London which can – in theory – be supplemented by any Scottish government which dares to add three pence to the rate of income tax. Housing, education, the Health Service, farming and fisheries, most transport matters, culture and sport, the fabric of Scots law, all passed to Edinburgh. It was a huge transfer of power. Many full-blown federations give their component states less discretion.

But the first four-year Parliament had a rough ride. The much-loved First Minister, Donald Dewar, died suddenly in October 2000 and was replaced by Henry McLeish, a man of good intentions but limited experience. In the summer of 2001, McLeish lost control of the mess he had made of handling his Westminster constituency expenses and was forced to resign. McLeish's successor, Jack McConnell, was a man who had made a career as an astute and efficient Labour Party apparatchik. His first act was to fire almost the entire McLeish

Cabinet and replace it with men and women whose qualifications were loyalty to McConnell rather than any proven ability in government.

A succession of storms tried the foundations of the young Parliament and Executive. Some were petty and, after initial panic, were well handled by the steadying force of the Committees which had to cope with them. In late 1999, in the first months, there were scandals over influence-peddling by a public relations firm, and over special advisers (spin doctors) who tried to introduce the infamous Westminster practice of 'briefing against' their masters' rivals by unattributable leaks to journalists.

The governing coalition survived two threats of collapse in its initial year. The first crisis came over the insistence of the Liberal Democrats in the coalition that university tuition fees must be abolished. The second exploded around a bill to abolish the hated old 'warrant sales' practice, which had allowed Sheriff's Officers to invade the homes of poor debtors and seize their property for sale. In the warrant sales affair, Liberal Democrat ministers unwisely persuaded their coalition colleagues to block the bill, but the government was overwhelmed by an all-party backbench rebellion. To general rejoicing, the Parliament had won its first victory over the Executive. As the Labour left-winger John McAllion said, 'It is for days like this that I came into Scottish politics . . . it was the first big test of the sovereignty of the Scottish Parliament, and it has passed it resoundingly.'

All through its first four-year period, the Parliament was tormented by the 'Holyrood scandal'. The costs of the spectacular new Parliament building at Holyrood, designed by the Catalan architect Enric Miralles, escalated continuously and monstrously until by early 2002 they were approaching seven times the original estimate. There were a few excuses: changes of contractors, the sudden death of Miralles, alterations to the original design or problems with materials. But the Parliament had no real answer to the charge that it had totally failed to control the financing of its own great capital project. The new building was to have been ready by late 2001, and then by the end of 2002. But by the middle of that year, there was still no certainty that it would open its doors in time to welcome the new MSPs after the Parliament's second elections in 2003.

By far the most serious crisis was the unexpected eruption over 'Clause 2a'. The occasion for it was an absurdity. Back in 1986, the Thatcher government, courting the 'moral majority', had inserted into English and Scottish local government bills a clause prohibiting the promotion of homosexuality in schools or public libraries. This was pure gesture politics. Nobody was ever prosecuted for breaching the ban, and no Scottish local authority school had ever contemplated the teaching of gay rights. To repeal the clause, in the first months of the Scottish Parliament, seemed no more than a routine detail of political hygiene.

But, without warning, a frantic campaign to 'Keep the Clause' emerged and within a few months dominated the whole political scene. It rested on an 'unholy alliance' without precedent in Scottish history: Cardinal Tom Winning, the boldly political head of the Catholic Church in Scotland, made common cause with ultra-moral Presbyterians, and the campaign was paid for by the bus-line millionaire Brian Souter, a born-again evangelical Christian. They were backed by the tabloid *Daily Record*, usually a reliable supporter of the Labour Party, which now proclaimed: 'Cardinal Warns of Gay Threat to School Pupils'. In May 2000, Souter financed the distribution of an unofficial 'Keep the Clause' ballot paper to every household in Scotland. Homophobic attacks on gays in Scotland increased sharply.

The Parliament and Executive were appalled. Nothing had prepared them for this outburst, and some MSPs lost their nerve. Labour members from the West of Scotland, especially, hesitated to defy the old electoral alliance between Labour and the Catholic working class. Although most Scots boycotted Souter's referendum, the 34 per cent who returned a ballot paper voted six to one for retaining the clause. In the end, the Parliament rediscovered its courage and repealed the clause by a large majority, but the Clause camp were appeased with a new set of teaching guidelines emphasizing the importance of regular marriage.

The agitation died down, but real damage had been done. In the first place, the Parliament had been temporarily put in the position of seeming to ignore the feelings of the Scottish people. More profoundly, confidence in the 'new, modern Scotland' created by devolution was shaken. It was too easy for the Executive to blame the affair on 'cheque-book politics' and bloodthirsty editors. The true lesson of the episode was that 'Scotland was not yet rid of Scotland'. Dark intolerances inherited from the past still kept their grip on many Scottish imaginations, and the hopeful portrait of a small, enlightened European nation with much to teach the world fell off the wall. 'Modernity', it turned out, was not a consensus to build on. It was still an argument to be fought for and won.

The *Daily Record*'s ferocity over Clause 2a was only the ugliest chapter in a long story. The Scottish press had spent years enthusiastically agitating for a parliament. But with the final arrival of self-government the media suddenly switched into a new mode of aggressive, scalp-hunting hostility. The first *Scotsman* article declaring that the Parliament was a wretched disappointment which had failed to live up to the nation's hopes appeared within weeks of the first elections in 1999, even before the formal opening by the Queen. It was the first shot in an endless open season. The tabloids concentrated on revelations about the humdrum sexual and financial mishaps of MSPs. Broadsheets complained that the Parliament was wasting time and money on irrelevant issues of political correctness, such as the banning of hunting with dogs (in contrast to

England, fox-hunting was the sport of a tiny minority mostly confined to a few areas of the Lowlands). The real achievements – abolishing university tuition fees, providing free home care for the elderly, a radical land reform giving tenant communities a right to purchase the estates they lived on – were given only grudging coverage.

All this noisy harassing missed two points: the facts of public opinion, and the inner dynamics of the Parliament. Polls taken over the first three years showed significant changes. The small minority who thought the Parliament was doing a valuable job increased; the equally small minority who considered the MSPs a waste of time and money grew smaller. In between, the main block of those who waited to be convinced remained more or less stable. A second group of polls showed a steady and steep curve of disillusion among Scots who had expected that the Parliament would give a new and effective voice to 'ordinary people'. Given a little projection, these results suggested that the Parliament might win approval for what it was doing, but that it was not expected to produce any striking innovations in democracy.

On that point, public opinion is probably wrong. Surprisingly, the underlying drive of this new Parliament is not primarily towards making new laws, or abolishing poverty, or moving on from devolution to independence. It is about something far more ambitious: crossing the gap between power and people, in times when the old model of party politics and representative government is losing credibility throughout the Western world.

Equally unexpected, the source of this drive is not the Scottish Executive (the government) or the elected members. It is the staff of the Parliament itself. The engineers of change are the clerks of the committees, the 'participation services' who put out information, and the little-known men and women who run the parliamentary 'Corporate Body'.

In most legislatures, these people are no more than servitors.

Seen but not heard, they discreetly ease the task of the law-givers. But in Edinburgh, they are a formidable elite corps with a proud collective identity. They are not civil servants, although many used to work in the old Scottish Office, and they are free from the intrigues and constraints of a large state bureaucracy. They answer only to the Presiding Officer (speaker), Sir David Steel, and to the Corporate Body which manages the buildings, finances, staffing and services of the Parliament.

Strictly speaking, the responsibility for opening up the Parliament's structures to far wider public participation belongs to the MSPs, working through their committees. In practice, though, almost all the new ideas and the pressure to adopt them come from the parliamentary staff. They have their own radical vision of what the Parliament of Scotland should become, and in their routine contacts with MSPs, they identify those who have the capacity to grasp this vision and work towards it. Over the last couple of years, they have made many converts.

In the end, this is about the St Andrew's Fault. For that parliamentary *corps d'élite*, there is a dream and a fear. The dream is to throw bridges across that historic gap, the chasm which separates those who are accustomed to be heard and those taught by centuries of uprooting that their lot is to survive change, not to plan it. The fear is that, if the Fault cannot be closed, the Scottish Parliament will fail.

The House of Commons has authority because it has been there so long and because nobody can imagine Britain – or at least England – without it. But this is not an option for the new House in Edinburgh. This is an experiment, still unsteady and fragile. Unless it roots itself rapidly and deeply in its people, it may not survive.

This enlisting of the people is being approached in two ways; by the use of technology and by a change of heart among the MSPs and the ministers of the Scottish Executive. The

change of heart, still in its early stages, is the recognition that
'consultation is not enough'. Again and again, I heard in
Edinburgh the despairing phrase 'the usual suspects'. Ministers
in the Dewar and McLeish Cabinets learned that 'great
debates' on new legislation were essentially pantomimes, the
same old repertory company of organized lobbies and interest
groups parading the same well-worn views. One ex-minister
told me that she had been reduced to sending out her own private emissaries to tour the country and collect opinions. 'The
civil servants' idea of consultation is to put up the same old
faces every time. Their philosophy is predictability; if it
worked smoothly before, then repeat it.'

By the summer of 2001, anxiety about this failure to connect
had grown acute. The Parliament had to move forward from
devolution to democracy; how could the advance from 'consultation' to 'participation' be managed? The parliamentary
committees declared that they would leave Edinburgh more
often, and hold their sessions in cities, towns, even on islands,
outside the Central Belt. The Procedures Committee began a
long series of hearings – three of them off-centre in Paisley,
Galashiels and Ullapool – to assess progress towards the
Parliament's guiding principles, which included accessibility.
These were worthy moves, but unlikely on their own to break
significant holes in the barrier of Scottish public reticence.

The other prong of this effort to 'reach the people' is more
imaginative. This is a new and determined turn towards the
use of electronic media for communication between Parliament
and individual citizens. The MSPs are already well-armed with
e-mail and computer services to deal with constituency business, while both the Parliament and the Executive have
produced websites (the Parliament's site a model of interactive
clarity). But now the move into 'e-democracy' has shifted into
much higher gear.

By the second Scottish elections, in the summer of 2003, a
battery of assorted ICTs (information and communication

technologies) will be operating. An 'e-petitioning' facility already gives direct on-line access to the Public Petitions Committee. Webcasting transmits live 'streamed' pictures and sound from plenary and committee sessions to any personal computer with access to the Internet. This has been followed by 'forum' features on the bulletin-board model, inviting the public to give their opinions and suggestions on individual 'Members' Business' bills. Public libraries in each constituency have been provided with a flow of parliamentary documents and reports on paper. In theory, if not always in practice, these 'Partner Libraries' also offer the citizen a dedicated computer on which he or she can watch the Parliament at work, send it a petition, read up its past debates, study its documents and offer opinions on its bills before they are passed.

Fatuous claims are made for 'e-democracy' and its capacity to transform politics. To puncture them is easy enough. It is not as if the telematics innovators went around identifying holes in democracy and then devising equipment to plug them. Quite the opposite: as the German 'e-government' expert Klaus Lenk has said, the cyber-brains invent a new electronic solution and then design a social or political problem to fit it. In any case, such claims are part of the general inflation of expectations put out by software manufacturers. Much the same happened when the telephone came in. A century ago, the grand sales pitch was that telephones were a public news medium which would revolutionize government, diplomacy and commerce. In fact, they turned out to be an overwhelmingly local channel for private chatter.

The same mistake is being made today. The Internet can of course be used for high public purposes. Most people, however, use e-mail as a form of telephone, reminding daughters to turn the gas off or announcing that they are back from holiday. On the Net, anybody can read the world news, study for a geology degree, access Thomas Hobbes's *Leviathan* or post suggestions for the treatment of chronic pain on the Scottish Parliament website. But the total of 'serious' users will always be dwarfed by those who scan for factoids to crib in school essays, for pornography or for chat-rooms about surviving divorce and car theft.

Allowing for that pinch of humility, the Scottish Parliament's turn to 'new media' has been spectacular. Other legislatures have gone further in particular ways; the Bundestag in Berlin has a bigger e-petitions operation, while American Congressmen have more elaborate office software. No parliament, however, has such a combined panoply of on-line media as Edinburgh. Even the Parliament staff find it hard to realize that the Scottish Parliament has become the cutting-edge of new democratic communications, the most interactive parliament in the world.

The three branches of this sort of communication are 'e-government', 'e-community' and 'e-democracy'. The first is authority-led and essentially one-way: the citizen receives official information, including (if he or she is lucky) an answer to an on-line question. The second is mostly non-political. An 'e-community' is no more than a group of participants on a given site who keep up a virtual relationship. The group may be a religious congregation, a local recipe-swapping club or a few kids talking music releases. The 'e-community' may be the extension of a political party or – even more important – a 'physical' community, a village or town district which uses the Internet to keep in touch with itself over a host of private or public concerns.

But the third branch, 'e-democracy', is what the Scots reformers are after. At its far horizon, this means opening the process of law-making to public participation – not just through elected representatives, and not through the filter of 'usual suspect' interest groups, but by the direct intervention of individuals who have something to say. This is still a long way off. Citizens in Scotland can join MSPs in debate on a restricted number of parliamentary bills, but not yet at the crucial stage before the bill is finally drafted. There are plans to change that, step by step, until 'the punters' can participate in making any law at any stage. Meanwhile the 'digital divide' between those with access to the Internet and the rest is being swiftly narrowed. By 2005, the Executive intends to have all households in Scotland on-line.

On that horizon, frontiers define the limits of what is possible. A small example: the real digital divide in Scotland is not between those with money to buy the kit and those without. It runs between those who can read and write, and the tens of thousands who are functionally illiterate but who until now have busked their way through life without admitting it. And there is a taller fence out there. The far horizon marks the point where representative democracy ends and 'direct democracy' begins: a different, revolutionary constitution which the Scots show no signs of wanting.

A sensible man wrote that 'most people are not interested in most policy issues, but it is equally true that all are interested in some'. A condition of round-the-clock democracy in which an on-line nation spends its days in permanent plebiscite is unattainable in a modern state, and any attempt to attain it would lead straight to nervous breakdown and tyranny. The Scots are a long way from that condition, to put it mildly. The Parliament's astonishing output of information, webcasting and invitations to participate lands at their feet, and for the most part it stays there. There are encouraging signs that some of the 'forum' sites discussing new bills are now attracting those whom normal politics do not reach. On the whole, though, the uptake is slight. The beautifully planned website is not greatly visited; those who follow webcast debates are often scarcely more numerous than those sitting in the public gallery; the paper reports and proceedings sent to the 'Partner Libraries' too frequently stay unread on the shelves.

The Parliament's missionaries are not deterred. They see growing signs of interest in some of their programs, and they are sure that the final spurt to complete Scotland's 'digital inclusion' will give the citizenry more confidence in speaking to 'their' Parliament. They are probably right. The product is there, and it is cheap, and in spite of the prevailing cynicism about politicians and parties, it will eventually be taken up.

But at present, when people use this technology, they do so overwhelmingly for local issues. They research parliamentary debates or e-mail their MSPs in order to pursue unresolved grievances against local government. One librarian told me how her council had tried to close down their own Partner Library scheme. 'There's punters using our Library to get stuff for to sue the Council with; you cannae let them dae that!'

In this region, the St Andrew's Fault is a fracture of the imagination. Rationally, everyone knows that Holyrood makes laws for all Scotland. And yet this fact remains somehow unreal to most Scots. Three hundred years of living as a nation without a parliament or government of its own diverted Scotland's attention from the empty centre to the local reality. The 'town house' with its provost and bailies, the county council, the district or regional council were the places where political decisions were made which affected daily lives. This is why so many people use the Scottish Parliament as no more than a 'higher instance', an appeal court against decisions by the City of Glasgow, or Argyll & Bute Council. The idea of using the Parliament in order to make a fresh law for all – a simple idea to an outsider – is slow to spread.

Will devolution lead inexorably to independence? For the moment, this question has lost its urgency. Scots are more interested in whether devolution can lead to democracy. They want to know whether this new Parliament and its Executive can move Scotland towards 'a possible land . . . where life is a choice of instruments and none is debarred his natural music'.

This means reaching towards qualities of social justice, equality and sheer modernity which the United Kingdom as a whole has not achieved. In discussions about 'opening the Parliament to the people', and 'interactive government', I met nobody who suggested that these good aims could only be fulfilled in an independent Scotland. And yet I think that independence will probably come about.

There are pragmatic political reasons to think so, but also considerations from history. At the practical level, it is unlikely that the British political structure can absorb the tensions between – say – a right-wing Tory government in London and a Labour–Liberal coalition in Edinburgh. Confrontation would probably centre on finance for Scottish social programmes: the block grant. In those circumstances, it is not hard to imagine a 'velvet divorce' on the Czech/Slovak model. Slovakia's independence was not achieved by Slovak patriotic fervour. Instead it was dumped on the table by the Czechs, who grew tired of negotiating endless Slovak demands and walked away. As births of nations go, it was undignified.

But there are three deeper reasons to suspect that Scotland may not long remain in the United Kingdom. All are to do with the revival of traditions or – more precisely – with the selective rediscovery of elements in Scotland's past which are now being adapted to serve Scotland's future. One of these elements is Scotland's sense of European identity, as a small North Sea nation which needs to encounter the world directly rather than through the priorities of 'Great Britain'. A second is Scottish constitutional doctrine, now slowly re-emerging. This tradition, manifest in the Declaration of Arbroath and in the seventeenth-century Covenants, relies on the notion of a supreme law which is above monarchs and parliaments; here too, Scotland is gravitating towards a constitutional view of public life and popular sovereignty which is European rather than British. Sooner rather than later, the Scots will press for entrenched guarantees against political interference which the Westminster system cannot offer.

Finally, there is the particular, apparently indelible colouring of Scottish society. All generalizations are subjective. So I am speaking personally when I suggest that the Scots are communitarian rather than individualist, democratic in their obsession with equality, patriarchal rather than spontaneous in their respect for authority, spartan in their insistence that solidarity matters more than free self-expression. Not all of these are admirable or 'modern' qualities. But they are all being invoked as the Scots move beyond riddles of national identity towards establishing institutions which they recognize as their own. This, too, points towards a completion of self-government which lies outside the limits of the Union.

No continuity – not even 'fredome' – is stronger than these webs of mutual support. Scotland has survived and still exists as a chain of small collective loyalties: 'Society People' singing in the hills or clansmen enlisting with their chieftain, colonists on the Vistula or private partnerships in Bengal, crofting townships in Assynt or mining villages in Fife.

When Scotland's last deep coal mine at Longannet flooded and closed down for ever in March 2002, a man called George came home from the pit to find his telephone ringing. 'Dinnae worry, big man, we'll see you're no stuck for work.' This is a nation at home in hard, stony times. It will find its own way in the world.

Bibliography

Aiten, William, *A History of the Rencounter at Drumclog . . . and Reflections on Political Subjects*, W. M. Borthwick, Hamilton, 1821

Anderson, Benedict, *Imagined Communities: Reflections on the Origin and Spread of Nationalism*, Verso, 1983

Aneirin, *The Gododdin, The Triumph Tree: Scotland's Earliest Poetry: AD 550–1350*, ed. T. O. Clancy, Canongate, 1998

Armit, Ian, *Celtic Scotland*, Batsford, 1997

Ash, Marinell, *The Strange Death of Scottish History*, Ramsay Head Press, 1980

Barclay, Gordon, *Farmers, Temples and Tombs*, Canongate/Historic Scotland, 1998

Begg, Alan, *Deserted Settlements of Kilmartin Parish*, Argyll & Bute Council, 1999

Blackie, John Stuart, *The Scottish Highlanders and the Land Laws*, Chapman & Hall, 1885

Boyd, John Morton, *Fraser Darling's Islands*, Edinburgh University Press, 1986

Breeze, D., and Munro, G., *The Stone of Destiny, Symbol of Nationhood*, Historic Scotland, 1997

Broun, Dauvit, 'When Did Scotland Become Scotland?', *History Today*, Vol. 46, No. 10, October 1996

Burnet, Gilbert, *History of My Own Times*, Oxford University Press, 1897

Butter, Rachel, *Kilmartin: An Introduction and Guide*, Kilmartin House Trust, 1999

Cage, R. A., ed., *The Scots Abroad: Labour, Capital, Enterprise, 1750–1914*, Croom Helm, 1985

Calder, Angus, *Revolving Culture: Notes from the Scottish Republic*, I. B. Tauris, 1994

Calder, Jenni, ed., *The Enterprising Scots*, Royal Museum of Edinburgh, 1986

Campbell, Ewan, *Saints and Sea-Kings: The First Kingdom of the Scots*, Canongate/Historic Scotland, 1999

Campbell, Marion, *Argyll: the Enduring Heartland*, Kilmartin House, 2001

Campbell, Thorbjörn, *Standing Witnesses: An Illustrated Guide to the Scottish Covenanters*, Saltire Society, 1996

Canny, Nicholas, *Making Ireland British: 1580–1650*, Oxford University Press, 2001

Cockburn, Henry, *Memorials of His Time*, Adam and Charles Black, 1846

Cummins, W. A., *The Age of the Picts*, Sutton Publishing, 1996

Daiches, D., Jones, P., and Jones, J., eds, *A Hotbed of Genius: The Scottish Enlightenment 1730–1790*, Edinburgh University Press, 1986

Darling, Frank Fraser, *Island Years*, Bell, 1941

— *The Story of Scotland*, Collins, 1942

— *Island Farm*, Bell, 1944

— *Natural History in the Highlands & Islands*, Collins, 1947

— *West Highland Survey*, Oxford University Press, 1955

Davis, Michael, *Poltalloch and the Transformation of Mid-Argyll, 1750–1960*, Argyll & Bute Council, 1999

Devine, Tom, *The Scottish Nation: 1700–2000*, Allen Lane, 1999
— *Clanship to Crofters' War: The Social Transformation of the Scottish Highlands*, Manchester University Press, 1994
Devine, Tom, ed., *Scotland's Shame: Bigotry and Sectarianism in Modern Scotland*, Mainstream, 2000
Ferguson, William, *The Identity of the Scottish Nation*, Edinburgh University Press, 1998
Fletcher, Andrew, of Saltoun, *Political Works*, ed. John Robertson, Cambridge University Press, 1997
Fordun, John of, *Scotichronicon*, ed. F. Skene, Edmonston & Douglas, 1872
Foster, Sally, *Picts, Gaels & Scots*, Batsford/Historic Scotland, 1996
Fraser, Alexander, 'North Knapdale in the 17th and 18th Centuries', *Oban Times*, 1964
Fry, Michael, *The Scottish Empire*, Tuckwell, 2001
Geikie, Archibald, *Scottish Reminiscences*, Maclehose, 1904
Grant, Elizabeth, *The Highland Lady in Ireland*, Canongate, 1991
Hague, Euan, 'The Emigrant Experience: The Scottish Diaspora', *Scottish Affairs*, No. 31, Spring 2000
— 'National Tartan Day: Rewriting History in the United States', *Scottish Affairs*, No. 38, Winter 2002
Haldane, Elizabeth, *The Scotland of Our Fathers*, Maclehose, 1933
Hamilton, Iain, *The Taking of the Stone*, Moffat, 1991
Harvie, C., and Jones, P., *The Road to Home Rule*, Polygon, 2000
Haskell, Francis, *Rediscoveries in Art: Some Aspects of Taste, Fashion & Collecting in England and France*, Phaidon, 1976
Henderson, Isabel, *The Picts*, Thames and Hudson, 1967
Howie of Lochgoin, John, *Biographia Scoticana or a Brief Historical Account of the most eminent Scots Worthies . . .*, Edinburgh, 1775
Hume Brown, P., *A History of Scotland for Schools*, Part II, Oliver & Boyd, 1907
Hunter, James, *The Claim of Crofting*, Mainstream, 1991
— *A Dance Called America*, Mainstream, 1994

Hutton, James, *Theory of the Earth*, Royal Society of Edinburgh, 1798 (full edition)

Kay, Billy, *Scots: The Mither Tongue*, Mainstream, 1986

Keay, John and Julia, eds, *The Collins Encyclopaedia of Scotland*, HarperCollins, 2000

Kirkton, James, *The Secret & True History of the Church of Scotland*, John Ballantyne, 1817

Lane, Alan, and Campbell, Ewan, *Dunadd: An Early Dalriadic Capital*, Oxbow, 2000

Leonard, Tom, 'Unrelated Incidents', *Intimate Voices: Selected Work*, Vintage, 1985

Lithgow, William, *A Total Discourse of the Rare Adventures and Painfull Peregrinations of Long 19 Years* (1632), Maclehose, 1906

MacCaig, Norman, 'The Patriot' and 'A Man in Assynt', *Collected Poems*, Chatto & Windus, 1985

McCrone, David, *Understanding Scotland: The Sociology of a Stateless Nation*, Routledge, 1992

MacDiarmid, Hugh, 'On a Raised Beach' and 'The Highlanders are Not a Sensitive People', *Complete Poems 1920–1976*, Martin, Brian & O'Keefe, 1978

MacDonald, Angus and Patricia, *Above Edinburgh and South-East Scotland*, Mainstream, 1989

MacDougall, Carl, *Painting the Forth Bridge: A Search for Scottish Identity*, Aurum Press, 2001

Mackenzie, Alexander, *A History of the Highland Clearances*, Alexander Maclaren, 1883

Maclean, Alasdair, *Night Falls on Ardnamurchan*, Penguin Books, 1986

McLeod, Mona K., *Leaving Scotland*, National Museums of Scotland, 1996

— *Agents of Change: Scots in Poland, 1800–1918*, Tuckwell, 2000

MacNeice, Louis, *Autumn Journal*, Faber & Faber, 1939

MacPhail, I. M. M., *A History of Scotland for Schools*, Vol. I, Edward Arnold, 1954

Marr, Andrew, *The Battle for Scotland*, Penguin Books, 1992

Marshall, H. E., *Scotland's Story*, Nelson, 1907

Meikle, H. W., *The Story of Scotland for Junior Classes*, Oliver & Boyd, 1936

Miller, Hugh, *Edinburgh & Its Neighbourhood, Geological and Historical*, Adam and Charles Black, 1864

Mitchell, Ian, *Isles of the West*, Canongate, 1999

Mitchison, R., ed., *Why Scottish History Matters*, Saltire Society, 1997

Muir, Edwin, 'Scotland 1941', *The New Penguin Book of Scottish Verse*, ed. R. Crawford and M. Imlah, Allen Lane/Penguin Books, 2000

Murray, J. I. W., *Scotland through the Ages: to 1603*, McDougall, 1951

Paterson, Lindsay, *The Autonomy of Modern Scotland*, Edinburgh University Press, 1994

Ransford, Tessa, 'Incantation 2000', *Poetry Scotland*, No. 18, August 2001

Ray, Celeste, 'Comment on "The Confederate Tartan"', *Scottish Affairs*, No. 35, Spring 2001

Richards, Eric, 'Australia and the Scottish Connection', in R. A. Cage, ed., *The Scots Abroad*, Croom Helm, 1985

Ritchie, A., and Breeze, D., *Invaders of Scotland*, HMSO (Edinburgh), 1991

Ross, Mairi, 'Emerging Trends in Rock-Art Research: Hunter-Gatherer Culture, Land and Landscape', *Antiquity*, Vol. 75, No. 289, September 2001

Scott, Walter, 'The Lay of the Last Minstrel', *The New Penguin Book of Scottish Verse*, ed. R. Crawford and M. Imlah, Allen Lane/Penguin Books, 2000

— *Waverley*, Penguin Books, 1985

Sebesta, E., 'The Confederate Mermoral Tartan', *Scottish Affairs*, No. 31, Spring 2000

Seeley, Sir John, *The Expansion of England*, Macmillan, 1895

Seliga, S., and Koczy, L., 'Scotland and Poland: A Chapter of

Forgotten History', in W. Tomaszewski, ed., *The University of Edinburgh and Poland*, Aberdeen University Press, 1968

Sellar, Patrick, in R. J. Adam, ed., *Sutherland Estate Management, 1811–16*, Scottish History Society, 1972

Slade, H. Gordon, 'Craigston and Meldrum Estates, Carriacou, 1769–1841, *Proceedings of the Society of Antiquaries of Scotland*, No. 114, 1984

Smith, Iain Crichton, 'The Clearances', *Collected Poems*, Carcanet, 1992

Smith, John, 'Allt Beithe: The Desertion of a Settlement', *The Kist: Magazine of the Natural History and Antiquarian Society of Mid-Argyll*, No. 36, Autumn 1988

Smout, T. C., and Wood, S., eds, *Scottish Voices, 1745–1960*, Collins, 1990

Tolan-Smith, C., 'The Caves of Mid-Argyll', *Society of Antiquaries of Scotland*, Monographs No. 20, 2000

Watson, Don, *Caledonia Australis: Scottish Highlanders on the Frontiers of Australia*, Collins (Sydney), 1984

Whyte, Ian and Kathleen, *The Changing Scottish Landscape: 1500–1800*, Routledge, 1991

Williams, Gwyn A., *When Was Wales? A History of the Welsh*, Black Raven, 1985

Index

Permissions Acknowledgements

Hugh MacDiarmid's work appears in *Complete Poems*, Vols. 1 and 2, Carcanet Press, 1993 and 1994, and the extracts used here from 'On a Raised Beach', 'Why I Became a Scots Nationalist' and 'The Highlanders are Not a Sensitive People' are reprinted by kind permission of the publishers. The extract from Francis Haskell, *Rediscoveries in Art: Some Aspects of Taste, Fashion & Collecting in England and France*, Phaidon Press, 1976, is reprinted by kind permission of the publisher. The extract from *The Gododdin* by Aneirin is taken from the anthology *The Triumph Tree*, edited by Thomas Owen Clancy and first published in Great Britain as a Canongate Classic in 1998 by Canongate Books Ltd, Edinburgh, and is reprinted by kind permission of the publisher. 'Incantation 2000' by Tessa Ransford appears by kind permission of the poet. The extract from *Argyll: The Enduring Heartland* by Marion Campbell is reprinted by kind permission of the House of Lochar, Scottish Publishers, Isle of Colonsay, Argyll PA61 7YR. The extracts from 'The Patriot' and 'A Man in Assynt' are from *Norman MacCaig: Collected Poems*, Chatto & Windus, 1985, and are reprinted by kind permission of The Random House Group Ltd. 'Letter From America', words and music by Charles Reid and Craig Reid © 1987 Zoo Music Ltd, Warner/Chappell Music Ltd, London W6 8BS. Reproduced by permission of International Music Publications Ltd. All rights reserved. 'Unrelated Incidents' by Tom Leonard appears by kind permission of the poet. The extract from 'The Clearances' comes from *Ian Crichton Smith: Collected Poems*, Carcanet Press Limited, 1992 and is reprinted by kind permission of the publisher. The extract from Frank Fraser Darling, *Natural History in the Highlands and Islands*, appears by kind permission of HarperCollins Publishers Ltd; copyright © 1947 by Frank Fraser Darling. The extract from 'Scotland 1941' is taken from *Collected Poems* by Edwin Muir and is reprinted by kind permission of Oxford University Press, Inc., copyright © 1960 by Willa Muir. The extract from 'Autumn Journal' is taken from *Collected Poems* by Louis MacNeice and is reprinted by kind permission of Faber and Faber.